IMMIGRATION IN THE 21ST CENTURY: POLITICAL, SOCIAL AND ECONOMIC ISSUES

IMMIGRATION

SCREENINGS, DETENTION AND BORDER SECURITY

IMMIGRATION IN THE 21ST CENTURY: POLITICAL, SOCIAL AND ECONOMIC ISSUES

Additional books and e-books in this series can be found on Nova's website under the Series tab.

IMMIGRATION IN THE 21ST CENTURY: POLITICAL, SOCIAL AND ECONOMIC ISSUES

IMMIGRATION

SCREENINGS, DETENTION AND BORDER SECURITY

KLONIMIR JOVIĆ
EDITOR

snova
New York

Library of Congress Cataloging-in-Publication Data

ISBN: 978-1-53618-183-8

Published by Nova Science Publishers, Inc. † New York

CONTENTS

Preface		**vii**
Chapter 1	Immigration: Actions Needed to Strengthen USCIS's Oversight and Data Quality of Credible and Reasonable Fear Screenings *United States Government Accountability Office*	**1**
Chapter 2	Immigration Detention: Care of Pregnant Women in DHS Facilities *United States Government Accountability Office*	**125**
Chapter 3	Immigration: Recent Apprehension Trends at the U.S. Southwest Border *Audrey Singer and William A. Kandel*	**231**
Chapter 4	Border Security: U.S. Customs and Border Protection's Management of a Temporary Facility in Texas Raised Concerns about Resources Used *United States Government Accountability Office*	**259**
Index		**281**

PREFACE

Individuals apprehended by the Department of Homeland Security and placed into expedited immigration proceedings are to be removed from the country without a hearing in immigration court unless they express an intention to apply for asylum, or a fear of persecution, torture, or return to their country. Chapter 1 examines (1) USCIS and EOIR data on fear screenings, (2) USCIS policies and procedures for overseeing fear screenings, and (3) USCIS and EOIR processes for workload management.

Customs and Border Protection (CBP) temporarily holds individuals in its facilities and processes them for further action, such as release or transfer to ICE. ICE manages the nation's immigration detention system. ICE utilizes various facility types to detain individuals, such as those owned and operated by ICE and contract facilities. Chapter 2 examines (1) what available data indicate about pregnant women detained or held in DHS facilities, (2) DHS policies and standards that address the care of pregnant women, and (3) what is known about the care provided to pregnant women in DHS facilities.

Unauthorized migration across the U.S. Southwest border poses considerable challenges to federal agencies that apprehend and process unauthorized migrants (aliens) due to changing characteristics and motivations of migrants in the past few years as reported in chapter 3.

Department of Homeland Security's (DHS) U.S. Customs and Border Protection (CBP) experienced a significant increase in the number of individuals apprehended at or between U.S. ports of entry along the southwest border. To help address this issue, in May 2019, CBP determined it needed a temporary soft-sided facility for processing and holding single adults in the El Paso Border Patrol sector as discussed in chapter 4.

Chapter 1 - Individuals apprehended by DHS and placed into expedited immigration proceedings are to be removed from the country without a hearing in immigration court unless they express an intention to apply for asylum, or a fear of persecution, torture, or return to their country. Those with such "fear claims" are referred to USCIS for a credible fear screening. Individuals who have certain criminal convictions or who have a reinstated order of removal and claim fear are referred for a reasonable fear screening. Those with negative outcomes can request a review by EOIR's immigration judges. GAO was asked to review USCIS's and EOIR's processes for fear screenings. This chapter examines (1) USCIS and EOIR data on fear screenings, (2) USCIS policies and procedures for overseeing fear screenings, and (3) USCIS and EOIR processes for workload management. GAO analyzed USCIS and EOIR data from fiscal years 2014 through mid-2019; interviewed relevant headquarters and field officials; and observed fear screenings in California, Texas, and Virginia, where most screenings occur.

Chapter 2 - In December 2017, the Department of Homeland Security (DHS) updated its policy on pregnant women, removing language that stated that pregnant women would generally not be detained except in extraordinary circumstances or as mandated by law. Within DHS, CBP temporarily holds individuals in its facilities and processes them for further action, such as release or transfer to ICE. ICE manages the nation's immigration detention system. ICE utilizes various facility types to detain individuals, such as those owned and operated by ICE and contract facilities. GAO was asked to review issues related to the care of pregnant women in DHS facilities. This chapter examines (1) what available data indicate about pregnant women detained or held in DHS facilities, (2) DHS policies and standards that address the care of pregnant women, and (3) what is known about the care provided to pregnant women in DHS facilities. GAO analyzed available DHS data and documents from calendar years 2015 through 2019, including detention data, inspection reports and data, and complaints; reviewed policies related to the care of pregnant women; and interviewed agency officials and three national non-governmental organizations. GAO also interviewed a non- generalizable sample of 14 pregnant women detained or released by DHS and five non-governmental organizations in four field locations that had the greatest number of detentions of pregnant women, among other things.

Chapter 3 - Unauthorized migration across the U.S. Southwest border poses considerable challenges to federal agencies that apprehend and process unauthorized migrants (aliens) due to changing characteristics and motivations of migrants in the past few years. Unauthorized migration flows are reflected by the number of migrants apprehended by the Department of Homeland Security's (DHS's) Customs and Border Protection (CBP). In FY2000, total annual apprehensions at the border were at an all-time high of 1.64 million, before gradually declining to 303,916 in FY2017, a 45-year low. Apprehensions then increased to 396,579 in FY2018 and 851,508 in FY2019, the highest level since FY2007. More notably, the character of unauthorized migrants has changed during the past decade. Historically, unauthorized migrant flows involved predominantly single adult Mexicans, traveling without families, whose primary motivation was U.S. employment. As recently as FY2011, Mexican nationals made up 86% of all apprehensions, and relatively few requested asylum. In FY2019, however, "Northern Triangle" migrants from El Salvador, Guatemala, and Honduras comprised 81% of all apprehensions that year. Economic migrants exclusively seeking employment no longer dominate the unauthorized migrant flow, which is now driven to a greater extent by asylum seekers and those escaping violence and domestic insecurity, or those with motivations involving a mixture of protection and economic opportunity. CBP classifies apprehended unauthorized migrants into single adults, family units (at least one parent/guardian and at least one child), and unaccompanied alien children (UAC). In 2012, single adults made up 90% of apprehended migrants at the Southwest border. In FY2019, however, persons in family units and UAC together accounted for 65% of all apprehended migrants that year. In FY2019, CBP apprehended a record 473,682 persons in family units, exceeding all apprehensions of family unit members from FY2012-FY2018 combined. Mothers headed almost half of all family units apprehended in FY2019. In addition, apprehended persons in family units shifted from mostly Mexican nationals (80%) in FY2012 to mostly Salvadoran, Guatemalan, and Honduran nationals (91%) in FY2019. Similar changes occurred in the origin countries of unaccompanied alien children, whose total apprehensions also reached a record (76,020) in FY2019. The changing character of the migrant flow has led to logistical and resource challenges for federal agencies, particularly CBP. These include a general capacity shortfall in CBP holding facilities, the lack of appropriate facilities to detain families in Immigration Customs and Enforcement (ICE) detention centers, the reassignment of some CBP personnel who monitor the border to process and respond to migrants in holding facilities, and rapidly expanding immigration court backlogs that delay expeditious proceedings. The changing underlying motivations and border migration strategies of recent migrants also makes apprehension data less useful than in the past for measuring border enforcement. Because many unauthorized migrants now actively seek out U.S. Border Patrol agents in order to request asylum, increases or decreases in apprehension numbers may not reflect the effectiveness of border enforcement strategies. In response, the Trump Administration has changed existing policies for apprehended migrants, including implementing the Migrant Protection Protocols (MPP), also known as the "remain in Mexico" immigration policy, which allow DHS to return migrants seeking U.S. admission to the contiguous country from which they arrived on land, pending removal proceedings. Options for Congress could include legislative responses to the series of policies that the Administration has developed to address the changing flow of migrants at the Southwest border. Some proposals may consider changes to the appropriations of agencies charged with processing unauthorized migrants to reshape the system from one that was designed to apprehend and return single unauthorized adults from Mexico with no claims for protection, to one that can more quickly adjudicate those seeking humanitarian protection. Other options may include greater supervision of unauthorized migrants who are released into the United States, and mandating the collection and publication of more-detailed and timely data from CBP to more completely assess the flow of unauthorized migrants, including those in the MPP program, and their impact on border enforcement and the immigration court system.

Chapter 4 - This is an edited, reformatted and augmented version of the United States Government Accountability Office Publication No. GAO-20-231R, dated March 11, 2020.

In: Immigration
Editor: Klonimir Jović

ISBN: 978-1-53618-183-8

Chapter 1

IMMIGRATION: ACTIONS NEEDED TO STRENGTHEN USCIS'S OVERSIGHT AND DATA QUALITY OF CREDIBLE AND REASONABLE FEAR SCREENINGS*

United States Government Accountability Office

ABBREVIATIONS

Border Patrol	U.S. Border Patrol
CBP	U.S. Customs and Border Protection
DHS	Department of Homeland Security
DOJ	Department of Justice
EOIR	Executive Office for Immigration Review
FDNS	Fraud Detection and National Security Directorate
ICE	U.S. Immigration and Customs Enforcement

* This is an edited, reformatted and augmented version of United States Government Accountability Office; Report to Congressional Addressees; Accessible Version, Publication No. GAO-20-250, dated February 2020.

OFO	Office of Field Operations
RAIO	Refugee, Asylum, and International Operations Directorate
USCIS	U.S. Citizenship and Immigration Services
VTC	Video teleconferencing

WHY GAO DID THIS STUDY

Individuals apprehended by DHS and placed into expedited immigration proceedings are to be removed from the country without a hearing in immigration court unless they express an intention to apply for asylum, or a fear of persecution, torture, or return to their country. Those with such "fear claims" are referred to USCIS for a credible fear screening. Individuals who have certain criminal convictions or who have a reinstated order of removal and claim fear are referred for a reasonable fear screening. Those with negative outcomes can request a review by EOIR's immigration judges. GAO was asked to review USCIS's and EOIR's processes for fear screenings.

This chapter examines (1) USCIS and EOIR data on fear screenings, (2) USCIS policies and procedures for overseeing fear screenings, and (3) USCIS and EOIR processes for workload management. GAO analyzed USCIS and EOIR data from fiscal years 2014 through mid-2019; interviewed relevant headquarters and field officials; and observed fear screenings in California, Texas, and Virginia, where most screenings occur.

WHAT GAO RECOMMENDS

GAO is making four recommendations, including that USCIS provide additional pre-departure training to USCIS asylum officers before they begin screening families, systematically record case outcomes of family members, and collect and analyze information on case delays. DHS concurred with GAO's recommendations.

What GAO Found

Data from the Department of Homeland Security's (DHS) U.S. Citizenship and Immigration Services (USCIS) and Department of Justice's Executive Office for Immigration Review (EOIR) indicate that their credible and reasonable fear caseloads generally increased from fiscal year 2014 through fiscal year 2018.

- USCIS's caseloads nearly doubled during this timeframe—from about 56,000 to almost 109,000 referrals for credible and reasonable fear screenings. Further, the credible fear caseload was larger in the first two quarters of fiscal year 2019 alone than in each of fiscal years 2014 and 2015. Referrals to USCIS for reasonable fear screenings also increased from fiscal years 2014 through 2018. USCIS asylum officers made positive determinations in 71 percent of all credible and reasonable fear screenings between fiscal years 2014 and the first two quarters of fiscal year 2019. The outcomes of the remaining screenings were generally split evenly (14 percent each) between negative determinations or administrative closures (such as if the applicant was unable to communicate).
- EOIR's caseload for immigration judge reviews of USCIS's negative credible and reasonable fear determinations also increased between fiscal year 2014 and fiscal year 2018. EOIR's immigration judges reviewed about 55,000 cases from fiscal year 2014 through the third quarter of 2019 (the most recent data available), and judges upheld USCIS's negative determinations in about three-quarters of all reviews.

USCIS has developed various policies and procedures for overseeing credible and reasonable fear screenings in accordance with the regulations governing those screenings, such as interview requirements and mandatory supervisory review. USCIS provides basic training for new asylum officers and other training at individual asylum offices that includes credible and reasonable fear. The training at asylum offices includes on-the-job training for officers newly-assigned to credible and reasonable fear cases and ongoing weekly training for incumbent officers—some of which includes credible and reasonable fear. However, USCIS asylum offices do not all provide additional pre-departure training before officers begin screening families in person at DHS's family residential centers. Asylum Division officials told GAO that additional training for asylum officers before they begin screening such cases is important—in particular, credible fear screenings at these facilities represent about one- third of USCIS's caseload. Almost all USCIS asylum offices send officers to the family residential centers, including those offices with small fear caseloads at the local level. Some asylum offices provide pre-departure training to officers being sent to screen families, but such training is inconsistent across offices. By comparison, officials from the Chicago and New York offices stated they do not provide formal pre -departure training, but rather direct or recommend that officers review Asylum Division guidance and procedures on family processing independently before they travel. Officials from two other offices stated they rely on the training asylum officers may receive throughout the year related to credible and reasonable fear, which can vary. Providing pre-departure training, in addition to USCIS's basic training for new asylum officers, would help USCIS ensure that officers from all asylum offices are conducting efficient and effective fear screenings of families.

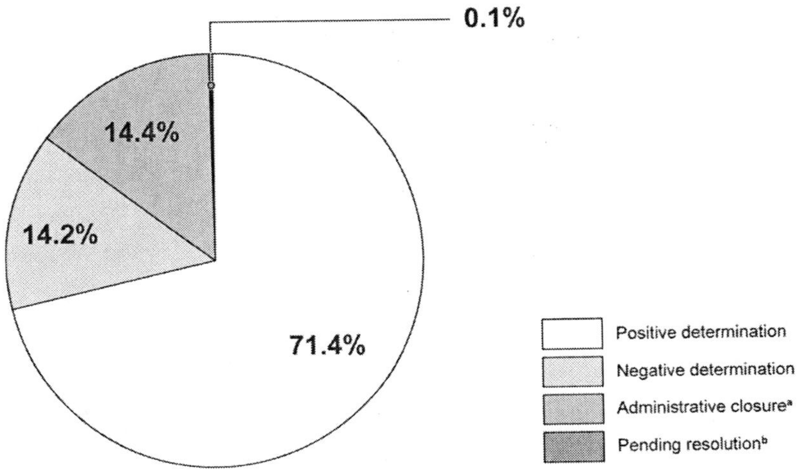

Source: GAO analysis of USCIS data. | GAO-20-250.

[a]According to USCIS, administrative closures occur when the asylum officer conducting the screening closes the case without a determination for reasons such as death, presence in state or federal custody, inability to communicate, or other reasons.

[b]USCIS cases occurred from October 1, 2013 through March 30, 2019 and their status was as of July 22, 2019. Cases that remained in progress as of July 22, 2019 were "pending resolution."

Outcomes of U.S. Citizenship and Immigration Services (USCIS) Credible and Reasonable Fear Screenings, Fiscal Years 2014 through the First Two Quarters of Fiscal Year 2019.

Further, consistent with regulation, USCIS policy is to include any dependents on a principal applicant's credible fear determination if the principal applicant receives a positive determination, resulting in the principal and any dependents being placed into full removal proceedings with an opportunity to apply for various forms of relief or protection, including asylum. For example, a parent as a principal applicant may receive a negative determination, but his or her child may receive a separate positive determination. In the interest of family unity, USCIS may use discretion to place both the parent and child into full removal proceedings rather than the parent being expeditiously ordered removed in accordance with the expedited removal process. However, USCIS's case management system does not allow officers to record whether an individual receives a determination on his or her case as a principal applicant, dependent, or in the interest of family unity. Without complete data on all such outcomes, USCIS is not well-positioned to report on the scope of either the agency's policy for family members who are treated as dependents, pursuant to regulation, or USCIS's use of discretion in the interest of family unity.

USCIS and EOIR have processes for managing their respective credible and reasonable fear workloads. For example, USCIS uses national- and local-level staffing models to inform staffing allocation decisions. USCIS also sets and monitors timeliness goals for completing credible and reasonable fear cases. Although USCIS monitors overall processing times, it does not collect comprehensive data on some types of case delays, which officers told us can occur on a regular basis. Asylum officers whom GAO interviewed stated that certain delays could affect the number of credible or reasonable fear cases they can complete each day. Collecting and analyzing additional information on case delays would better position USCIS to mitigate the reasons for the delays and improve efficiency. EOIR has developed processes for immigration courts and judges to help manage its workload that include performance measures with timeliness goals for credible and reasonable fear reviews. EOIR data indicate that about 30 percent of credible and reasonable fear reviews are not completed within the required timeframes. EOIR officials said they plan to implement an automated tool in early 2020 to monitor court performance, including the credible and reasonable fear performance goals. Because implementation of the automated tool is planned for early 2020, it is too soon to know if EOIR will use the tool to monitor adherence to the required credible and reasonable fear review time frames or if it will help EOIR understand reasons for case delays.

February 19, 2020
Congressional Addressees

The Department of Homeland Security's (DHS) U.S. Customs and Border Protection (CBP) has reported a significant increase in recent years in apprehensions of noncitizen adults and family units[1] who claim an intention to apply for asylum, a fear of persecution or torture, or a fear of return to their country.[2] CBP may place apprehended adults and family units into full or expedited removal proceedings before an immigration court, consistent with the Immigration and Nationality Act.[3] In full removal proceedings, they may apply for various forms of relief or protection, including asylum. U.S. immigration law provides that noncitizens physically present within the United States, whether or not at a designated port of entry, may be granted asylum if they are found to be unable or unwilling to return to their home country because of past persecution, or a well-founded fear of future persecution on account of their race, religion, nationality, membership in a particular social group, or political opinion (referred to as "protected grounds").[4] If they are precluded

---

[1] CBP's October 2015 *National Standards on Transport, Escort, Detention, and Search* defines a "family unit" to include one or more non-U.S. citizen juvenile(s) accompanied by their parent(s) or legal guardian(s). Therefore, in this chapter, we generally use the term "noncitizen" to refer to individuals who would meet the definition of "alien." The Immigration and Nationality Act defines the term "alien" as "any person not a citizen or national of the United States." See 8 U.S.C. § 1101(a)(3). In addition, for the purposes of this chapter, we use the term "parent" to refer to "noncitizen parent(s) or legal guardian(s)."

[2] Within CBP, the U.S. Border Patrol (Border Patrol) apprehends individuals at U.S. borders between ports of entry, and the Office of Field Operations (OFO) encounters individuals that arrive at ports of entry. According to CBP officials, OFO encounters noncitizens (instead of apprehending) them because, at ports of entry, individuals do not enter the United States until OFO officers have processed them. For the purposes of this chapter, we use the term "apprehend" to describe both Border Patrol and OFO's first interactions with noncitizens at the border. In addition, while OFO typically refers to its officers as "Customs and Border Protection officers," we use the term "OFO officers" in this chapter for clarity.

[3] See 8 U.S.C. §§ 1225(b), 1229a; see also 8 C.F.R. § 235.3(b)(4) .With some exceptions, including unaccompanied alien children (UAC), noncitizens present in the United States without being admitted or paroled who are encountered by an immigration officer within 100 air miles of any U.S. international land border, and who have not established to the satisfaction of an immigration officer that they have been physically present in the United States continuously for 14 days may be placed into expedited removal. See 69 Fed. Reg. 48,877, 48,880 (Aug. 11, 2004); see also 6 U.S.C. § 279(g)(2) (defining "unaccompanied alien child"). DHS published a notice designating additional noncitizens as eligible for expedited removal on July 23, 2019, including eliminating the 100 air miles requirement and expanding the 14-day time frame to two years. See 84 Fed. Reg. 35,409 (July 23, 2019). This rulemaking was enjoined by the district court for the District of Columbia on September 27, 2019 and as of November 2019, litigation was ongoing. Make the Road New York v. McAleenan, No. 19-2369 (D. D.C. Sept. 27, 2019) (order granting preliminary injunction).

[4] The laws governing asylum protection were first established in statute with the passage of the Refugee Act of 1980, Pub. L. No. 96-212, tit. II, § 201, 94 Stat. 102, 102-06 (1980)

from obtaining asylum based on, for example, past convictions of certain crimes, but their life or freedom would be threatened based on the protected grounds or they would potentially be tortured if removed, they may also seek withholding of removal.[5]

If noncitizens are placed into expedited removal proceedings instead of full removal proceedings, they are to be ordered removed from the United States without further hearing before an immigration judge unless they indicate either (1) an intention to apply for asylum or (2) a fear of persecution or torture, or a fear of return to their country (referred to throughout this chapter as making a "fear claim"). In such cases, they are referred to DHS's U.S. Citizenship and Immigration Services (USCIS) for a credible fear screening by an asylum officer. If they have been issued a final administrative removal order after conviction for an aggravated felony or have a prior order of removal that is reinstated, and express a fear of return, they are referred to an asylum officer for a reasonable fear screening.[6] USCIS data indicate that its credible fear caseload nearly

---

(codified at 8 U.S.C. §§ 1101(a)(42), 1157-1159). The legal standard for a refugee and asylee are generally the same, but noncitizens must apply for refugee status from outside the United States and for asylum status from within the United States.

[5] See 8 U.S.C. § 1231(b)(3); 8 C.F.R. §§ 208.13(c) (establishing a number of grounds for mandatory denial of asylum, including, among others, conviction of certain crimes, being reasonably regarded as a danger to the security of the United States, and the third country asylum bar), 208.16 (codifying both withholding of removal under the Immigration and Nationality Act and the Convention against Torture). For the purposes of this chapter, we refer to withholding of removal under the Immigration and Nationality Act and withholding of removal under the Convention against Torture collectively as "withholding of removal." If an individual is found to be entitled to protection under the Convention against Torture, but is subject to a provision for mandatory denial of withholding of removal, such as a prior conviction of a particularly serious crime, the individual may be granted deferral of removal. This type of protection can be terminated at any time, resulting in the individual's removal from the United States, based on new evidence or diplomatic assurances provided by the Department of State. See 8 C.F.R. § 208.17.

[6] See 8 C.F.R. §, 208.31. Noncitizens convicted of crimes that meet the definition of an "aggravated felony" in the Immigration and Nationality Act or whose prior removal order is reinstated may be placed into streamlined removal proceedings where they cannot apply for asylum. However, if they express a fear of persecution or torture, they are to be screened for "reasonable fear," which is a screening for withholding or deferral of removal, more limited forms of humanitarian protection. An "asylum officer" is defined as an immigration officer who has had professional training in country conditions, asylum law, and interview techniques comparable to that provided to full-time adjudicators of asylum applications and is supervised by an officer who has had such training and has had substantial experience adjudicating asylum applications. See 8 U.S.C. § 1225(b)(1)(E). We use this term to refer to any officer conducing credible and reasonable fear screenings.

doubled from fiscal years 2015 to 2016 (approximately 48,000 to 91,000 cases) and generally remained at that level through fiscal year 2018. Further, USCIS reported that it received more than 105,000 credible fear cases in fiscal year 2019.

Through these screenings, USCIS makes a determination about whether these individuals have a credible or reasonable fear of persecution or torture if returned to their country and the likelihood they can establish in a hearing before an immigration judge that these threats exist. If USCIS determines that the individual has a credible fear of persecution or torture, he or she will be placed into full immigration proceedings. If the individual receives a negative determination, he or she can request a review of that determination by an immigration judge within the Department of Justice's (DOJ) Executive Office for Immigration Review (EOIR).

We were asked to review DHS's and DOJ's processes for screening noncitizens who arrive at the southwest border expressing an intention to apply for asylum, a fear of persecution or torture, or a fear of return to their country, and the resources needed to carry out these screenings within applicable time frames.[7] This chapter discusses (1) what USCIS and EOIR data show about the credible fear and reasonable fear processes, (2) the extent to which USCIS has policies and procedures for overseeing credible fear and reasonable fear screenings, and (3) the extent to which USCIS and EOIR have processes for managing their respective credible fear and reasonable fear-related workloads.

For these objectives, we interviewed DHS and DOJ officials. Specifically, we interviewed officials from CBP's Border Patrol and Office of Field Operations (OFO); ICE's Enforcement and Removal Operations; USCIS's Asylum Division; and EOIR. We conducted site visits at Border Patrol stations and OFO ports of entry in Arizona, California, and Texas; ICE single adult and family residential centers in California and Texas; and USCIS asylum offices in Texas and Virginia, from September 2018 to April 2019. During these site visits, we interviewed Border Patrol, OFO, ICE, USCIS, and EOIR officials and observed credible and reasonable fear

---

[7] See Pub. L. No. 116-26, tit. V, § 506, 133 Stat. 1018, 1027 (2019).

interviews, among other activities. To select these locations, we reviewed USCIS data on credible and reasonable fear cases in fiscal year 2018, and identified specific locations that received the vast majority of cases during that year. We also considered the geographical proximity of multiple CBP and ICE facilities to maximize observations. Our observations during site visits are not generalizable to all Border Patrol, OFO, ICE, USCIS, or EOIR operations, but provided us the opportunity to learn more about policies and procedures for credible and reasonable fear.

To address the first objective, we reviewed record-level data from USCIS and EOIR. For USCIS, we reviewed record-level data from USCIS's automated case management system to identify the number, characteristics, and outcomes of credible and reasonable fear cases between fiscal year 2014 through the second quarter of fiscal year 2019 (the most current data available from USCIS at the time of our review) . For EOIR, we reviewed data on immigration judge reviews of credible and reasonable fear cases posted on its public website. We also requested data from EOIR on credible and reasonable fear reviews for those individuals detained in ICE's family residential centers. Further, we reviewed EOIR data on credible and reasonable fear reviews from fiscal year 2014 through the third quarter of 2019 (the most current data available from EOIR at the time of our review). To assess the reliability of USCIS and EOIR data, we completed a number of data reliability steps, including (1) performing electronic testing for obvious errors in accuracy and completeness, such as running logic tests; (2) reviewing information about the data and systems that produced them, such as relevant training materials for USCIS officers who use agency data systems; and (3) discussing data entry issues and data limitations with USCIS and EOIR officials. We determined the data were sufficiently reliable to describe the number, outcomes, and characteristics of credible and reasonable fear cases.

To address the second objective, we reviewed USCIS policy documents, training materials, and other guidance documents, such as procedures manuals for credible and reasonable fear. In particular, we reviewed USCIS Asylum Division quarterly training reports for fiscal year 2018 to analyze the weekly training activities in each asylum office for each week of the reporting quarter. We also reviewed asylum officer training materials, reports from the Asylum Division's periodic quality assurance reviews of credible and reasonable fear cases at individual asylum offices conducted between November 2017 and May 2018, and USCIS guidance on processing families in credible and reasonable fear cases. In addition, we conducted interviews with USCIS headquarters and asylum office officials, and we observed asylum officers screening credible and reasonable fear cases. We compared USCIS policies and procedures to *Standards for Internal Control in the Federal Government* related to developing competent individuals qualified to carry out assigned responsibilities, ongoing monitoring activities and evaluation of results, and obtaining high quality data.[8]

To address the third objective, we reviewed USCIS and EOIR documents and data and conducted interviews with USCIS and EOIR officials, to evaluate the extent to which USCIS and EOIR have processes for managing their respective credible and reasonable fear -related workloads. For USCIS, we reviewed policy documents, training materials, and other guidance documents related to USCIS's staffing allocation model for the credible and reasonable fear workload. In addition, we analyzed record-level USCIS data to calculate processing times and case delays for credible and reasonable fear cases from fiscal year 2014 through the second quarter of fiscal year 2019. We also reviewed USCIS's publicly-reported data on credible fear processing times during this time period. We compared USCIS policies and procedures to *Standards for Internal Control in the Federal Government* related to obtaining data on a timely basis for management to use for effective monitoring and processing data into high quality information.[9] For EOIR, we reviewed required time frames for EOIR's review of USCIS's credible and reasonable fear determinations; data that EOIR has publicly reported about its workload and case adjudications; and policy documents, such as EOIR's 2018 memorandum on case priorities. In addition, we analyzed

---

[8] GAO, *Standards for Internal Control in the Federal Government*, GAO-14-704G (Washington, D.C.: September 2014).

[9] GAO-14-704G.

summary data on EOIR's credible and reasonable fear review processing times for fiscal year 2014 through the third quarter of fiscal year 2019 (the most current data available at the time of our review) and compared EOIR's processing times with required time frames. To assess the reliability of the data, we reviewed documentation on USCIS's and EOIR's data systems, interviewed knowledgeable officials, and conducted electronic testing of USCIS's record-level data for obvious errors. We determined that the USCIS and EOIR data we reviewed on credible and reasonable fear workloads and processing times were sufficiently reliable to describe credible and reasonable fear processing times and case delays. For more information about our scope and methodology, see appendix I.

We conducted this performance audit from November 2018 to February 2020 in accordance with generally accepted government auditing standards. Those standards require that we plan and perform the audit to obtain sufficient, appropriate evidence to provide a reasonable basis for our findings and conclusions based on our audit objectives. We believe that the evidence obtained provides a reasonable basis for our findings and conclusions based on our audit objectives.

BACKGROUND

Within CBP, Border Patrol is responsible for securing U.S. borders and apprehending individuals arriving at the border between ports of entry. Also within CBP, OFO is responsible for inspecting travelers and cargo seeking to enter the United States through ports of entry and encounters or apprehends individuals determined to be inadmissible to the country. Upon apprehension of individuals at or between ports of entry, Border Patrol agents and OFO officers generally decide whether to (1) place apprehended adults and family units into expedited removal proceedings, or (2) initiate full immigration proceedings, according to CBP officials. If agents or officers place individuals into expedited removal proceedings, CBP will transfer them to DHS's U.S. Immigration and Customs Enforcement (ICE) for longer-term detention (see appendix II for more information on eligibility, screening standards, and possible screening outcomes for credible and reasonable fear cases).[10] Noncitizen adults and family units may make a fear claim in CBP custody at any point after apprehension, and during the pendency of their expedited removal proceedings in ICE custody (see appendix III for data on apprehensions of noncitizens placed into expedited removal who claimed fear of returning to their country, along with other characteristics of their cases).

ICE is generally responsible for referring any fear claims to USCIS for a fear screening after individuals enter detention. If USCIS makes a negative determination and the determination is either not reviewed by an immigration judge, because the noncitizen has declined immigration judge review, or, if reviewed, is upheld by a reviewing immigration judge, ICE is then responsible for removing the person from the country.[11]

Within USCIS, the Refugee, Asylum, and International Operations Directorate (RAIO) is to provide, among other things, services for people who are fleeing oppression, persecution, or torture or facing urgent humanitarian situations. RAIO is made up of two divisions: the Asylum Division and the International and Refugee Affairs Division. USCIS's Asylum Division is responsible for, among other responsibilities, adjudicating affirmative asylum applications—that is, claims made at the initiative of the individual who files an application for asylum with USCIS—and screening credible and reasonable fear cases. As of March 2019, USCIS had 546 asylum officers on board and eligible to screen credible and reasonable fear cases (out of 745 authorized positions).[12]

---

[10] Generally, individuals placed into expedited removal proceedings are required to be detained until removal or, if applicable, until receiving a final determination of credible fear. See 8 U.S.C. § 1225(b)(1)(B)(iii)(IV). ICE manages the U.S. immigration detention system, which detains noncitizens, including families, whose immigration cases are pending or who have been ordered removed from the country. Since June 2014, ICE has operated four family residential centers in Texas, Pennsylvania, and New Mexico for family units who may be subject to removal while they await the resolution of their immigration cases or who have been ordered removed from the United States As of October 2019, ICE maintains three family residential centers—in Dilley and Karnes, Texas, and Leesport, Pennsylvania—with a cumulative capacity of 3,326 beds. The facility in New Mexico ceased operating as a family residential center in November 2014.

[11] See generally 8 U.S.C. §§ 1228, 1231(a)(5); 8 C.F.R. §§ 208.30-208.31.

[12] USCIS reported it executed a plan in fiscal year 2019 to hire 500 staff for the Asylum Division by the end of December 2019. According to USCIS, this includes new asylum officer,

Asylum officers screen cases at the Asylum Prescreening Center in Arlington, Virginia, and eight asylum offices nationwide.[13] USCIS established the Asylum Pre-Screening Center in fiscal year 2016 to provide additional support for the credible and reasonable fear caseload. As of April 2019, the Asylum Pre-Screening Center and the Arlington asylum office together had jurisdiction over 27 ICE detention centers across the United States.

EOIR is responsible for conducting immigration court proceedings, appellate reviews, and administrative hearings to fairly, expeditiously, and uniformly administer and interpret U.S. immigration laws and regulations. As of September 30, 2019, 442 immigration judges presided over EOIR's 63 immigration courts nationwide. In addition to removal proceedings, immigration judges also conduct certain other types of hearings, such as the review of negative credible fear determinations. Table 1 provides additional information about DHS's and DOJ's roles in the credible and reasonable fear processes.

In July 2019, USCIS made several changes to its credible fear screening processes in response to an interim final rule implementing a new mandatory bar to asylum, known as the "third country transit bar."[14]

---

supervisory asylum officer, and mission operations staff positions to fill staffing needs in all Asylum Offices. The Asylum Division reported it achieved its goals for selecting individuals to fill these positions, 304 of whom had entered onto duty as of September 30, 2019.

[13] The Asylum Pre-Screening Center is co-located with the asylum office in Arlington, Virginia. According to USCIS officials, asylum officers from the Arlington asylum office may also be assigned to screen credible and reasonable fear cases that are under the jurisdiction of the Asylum Pre -Screening Center. In addition to its eight asylum offices, USCIS maintains two asylum sub-offices in Metairie, Louisiana and Boston, Massachusetts.

[14] The regulations governing the credible fear process were amended by an interim final rule published on July 16, 2019, which became effective on the date of publication. See 84 Fed. Reg. 33,829 (July 16, 2019) (codified as amended at 8 C.F.R. §§ 208.13, 208.30). However, in a lawsuit filed to challenge, a district court granted a nationwide preliminary injunction, preventing DHS from taking any action to implement the rule. See East Bay Sanctuary Covenant v. Barr, No. 19-04073 (N. D. Cal. July 24, 2019) (order granting preliminary injunction). This injunction was then briefly limited to the jurisdiction of the court of appeals for the Ninth Circuit before it was ultimately appealed to the Supreme Court of the United States, which allowed the interim final rule to go into effect nationwide on September 11, 2019, pending further proceedings. See Barr v. East Bay Sanctuary Covenant, No. 19-A230 (U.S. September 11, 2019) (opinion staying nationwide injunction). As of February 2020, this litigation was ongoing.

Table 1. Department of Homeland Security (DHS) and Department of Justice (DOJ) Roles and Responsibilities in the Credible and Reasonable Fear Processes

Agency	Role
DHS's U.S. Customs and Border Protection's (CBP) U.S. Border Patrol (Border Patrol) and Office of Field Operations (OFO)	Among other things, OFO officers conduct immigration and customs inspections at ports of entry and Border Patrol agents secure the U.S. border between ports of entry. Among other processing activities, CBP's Border Patrol agents and OFO officers run background checks on immigration and criminal history, and use this and other information to inform processing decisions. For example, among other things, Border Patrol agents and OFO officers determine whether to place an individual in expedited removal.[a] Border Patrol agents and OFO officers are to interview apprehended noncitizens to obtain the specifics of their cases and record that information on DHS's Form I-213, *Record of Deportable/Inadmissible Alien.*[b] After placing an individual into expedited removal proceedings, Border Patrol agents and OFO officers are to record any fear claims in the individual's alien file (or "A-file") and their agencies' respective automated data systems.
DHS's U.S. Immigration and Customs Enforcement (ICE)	ICE, among other things, receives referrals from Border Patrol and OFO for aliens whom CBP has deemed inadmissible and placed in expedited removal. ICE officers are to review the A-files prepared by Border Patrol agents or OFO officers and have the authority to accept or deny a referral for detention from CBP based on detention space availability. Upon acceptance, ICE officers determine whether to detain, release, or remove individuals based on a variety of factors, including statutory requirements, medical considerations, and the availability of space at one of its single adult detention centers or family residential centers. ICE officers collect and record information on individuals in ICE's automated data systems. ICE is responsible for referring individuals, as appropriate, to U.S. Citizenship and Immigration Services (USCIS) for a credible fear or reasonable fear screening. Pending the outcome of the credible or reasonable fear screening, ICE will refer individuals determined to have a credible fear to EOIR for full removal proceedings before an immigration judge.

Table 1. (Continued)

Agency	Role
DHS's U.S. Immigration and Customs Enforcement (ICE)	For those found not to have a credible fear, ICE will process them for removal from the country. ICE will also decide whether to continue detaining or to release individuals who are awaiting full removal proceedings. Individuals who are transferred from expedited removal proceedings to full removal proceedings after establishing a credible fear of persecution or torture are generally ineligible for release on bond and must be detained until removal proceedings conclude, unless granted parole by ICE.[c]
DHS's U.S. Citizenship and Immigration Services (USCIS)	In screening noncitizens for credible or reasonable fear,[d] an asylum officer's tasks include, but are not limited, to, reviewing various forms from the referring officer to ensure that USCIS has jurisdiction to conduct the credible or reasonable fear interview; performing background checks; interviewing the individual to obtain more details on his or her fear claim, overall credibility, and the nature of any relationships with family members with whom they were apprehended; and determining whether there are any dependents who could potentially be included in the individual's fear determination.[e] USCIS officers are to conduct the interview in a non-adversarial manner, separate and apart from the general public.
	A USCIS asylum officer is to determine if the individual has any bars to asylum or withholding of removal that will be pertinent if the individual is referred to immigration court for full removal proceedings.[f] For cases in which the USCIS asylum officer concludes a credible fear screening with a positive determination, USCIS is to issue a Notice to Appear, thereby placing the individual into full removal proceedings before an EOIR immigration judge. Similarly, for reasonable fear cases where the asylum officer makes a positive determination, USCIS issues a Notice of Referral to an immigration judge for removal proceedings to consider the applicants' eligibility for withholding of removal or deferral of removal.[g] For cases in which the USCIS asylum officer concludes a credible or reasonable fear screening with a negative determination, USCIS is to refer the individual to ICE for removal from the United States, unless the noncitizen requests a review of the negative determination by an immigration judge. If this review is requested, USCIS will issue a Notice of Referral to the immigration judge.

Agency	Role
DOJ's Executive Office for Immigration Review (EOIR)	Within EOIR, immigration judges preside over removal proceedings for respondents detained by ICE or released pending the outcome of their proceedings, to determine their removability and eligibility for any relief being sought. In addition to removal proceedings, immigration judges conduct certain other types of hearings, such as to review negative credible or reasonable fear determinations at the noncitizen's request. After receiving a referral for such a review, EOIR must generally complete reviews of negative determinations of credible fear by USCIS within seven days and negative determinations of reasonable fear cases within 10 days.

Source: GAO analysis of statutes and DHS and DOJ documents. | GAO-20-250.

[a]Generally, noncitizens placed into expedited removal proceedings are required to be detained for the duration of their credible fear screening or, if found not to have a credible fear, until removal. See 8 U.S.C. § 1225(b)(1)(B)(iii)(IV). As a result, Border Patrol and OFO officials stated that Border Patrol agents and OFO officers must determine whether ICE has space in its detention facilities before placing individuals into expedited removal proceedings. If agents and officers place noncitizens into full immigration removal proceedings, they typically issue individuals a Notice to Appear before immigration court, where they may seek various forms of immigration relief such as asylum.

[b]The Immigration and Nationality Act defines the term "alien" as "any person not a citizen or national of the United States." See 8 U.S.C. § 1101(a)(3). We use the term "noncitizen" to refer to individuals who would meet the definition of "alien."

[c]See 8 U.S.C. § 1225(b)(1)(B)(ii); 8 C.F.R. § 235.3(b)(2)(iii). See also Matter of M-S-, 27 I & N Dec. 509 (A.G. 2019); Jennings v. Rodriguez, 138 S. Ct. 830, 844–45 (2018) (recognizing that the expedited removal statute generally mandates detention throughout the completion of removal proceedings unless the alien is paroled).

[d]See generally 8 U.S.C. § 1225(b)(1)(B)(iii); 8 C.F.R. §§ 208.30-208.31, 1208.30-1208.31. In addition to conducting credible and reasonable fear screenings, USCIS is also responsible for adjudicating affirmative asylum applications—that is, claims made at the initiative of the individual who files an application for asylum with USCIS.

[e]See 8 C.F.R. § 208.2(c)(2).

[f]In June 2019, Border Patrol agents on assignment to USCIS began conducting credible fear interviews and, in September 2019, began conducting credible fear interviews at the family residential center in Dilley, Texas. Border Patrol agents conducting credible fear interviews are to receive credible fear training from USCIS before conducting interviews and are to be supervised by a supervisory asylum officer with substantial experience adjudicating asylum applications in order to satisfy the statutory definition of an asylum officer. See 8 U.S.C. § 1225(b)(1)(E).

[g]U.S. immigration law provides that noncitizens physically present within the United States, whether or not at a designated port of arrival, may be granted asylum if they are found to be unable or unwilling to return to their home country because of past persecution, or a well-founded fear of future persecution based on their race, religion, nationality, membership in a particular social group, or political opinion (referred to as "protected grounds"). Additionally, if they are precluded from asylum based on, for example, past convictions of serious crimes, but their life or freedom would be threatened based on the protected grounds or would be tortured if removed, they may also seek withholding of removal. See 8 U.S.C. §§ 1101(a)(42), 1157-1159; See 8 U.S.C. § 1231(b)(3); 8 C.F.R. § 208.16 (codifying both withholding of removal under the Immigration and Nationality Act and the Convention against Torture). For the purposes of this chapter, we refer to withholding of removal under the Immigration and Nationality Act and withholding of removal under the Convention against Torture collectively as "withholding of removal."

Under the interim final rule, noncitizens who enter, attempt to enter, or arrive in the United States across the southern land border on or after July 16, 2019, after transiting through at least one country outside their country of citizenship, nationality, or last lawful habitual residence en route to the United States, must be found ineligible for asylum unless they demonstrate that they fall under an exception to the third country transit bar.[15]

USCIS's and EOIR's Credible and Reasonable Fear Caseloads Generally Increased from Fiscal Years 2014 through 2018, and a Majority of USCIS Screening Outcomes Were Positive

USCIS's Credible and Reasonable Fear Caseload Nearly Doubled from Fiscal Years 2014 through 2018

As shown in Table 2, USCIS's credible and reasonable fear caseloads nearly doubled from fiscal year 2014 (over 56,000 referrals to USCIS) to fiscal year 2018 (almost 109,000 referrals)—the most recent full year of USCIS data available at the time of our analysis. From fiscal year 2014 through the first two quarters of fiscal year 2019, referrals to USCIS for credible fear screenings comprised about 89 percent of all credible and reasonable fear referrals. The number of referrals for credible fear screenings in the first two quarters of fiscal year 2019 alone was larger

---

[15] See 8 C.F.R. § 208.13(c)(4). These exceptions are: (1) if the noncitizen demonstrates that he or she applied for protection from persecution or torture in at least one country outside the noncitizen's country of citizenship, nationality, or last lawful habitual residence through which the noncitizen transited en route to the United States, and received a final judgment denying protection in such country; (2) the noncitizen demonstrates the he or she meets the definition of "victim of a severe form of trafficking in persons (as defined in 8 C.F.R. § 214.11 to generally mean either commercial sex trafficking or involuntary servitude or slavery); or (3) the countries through which the noncitizen transited in route to the United States were not, at the time of transit, parties to international refugee and humanitarian protection agreements.

than the total number of referrals in each of fiscal years 2014 and 2015. Referrals for reasonable fear screenings also increased from fiscal years 2014 to 2018, and comprised between 9 and 15 percent of all referrals during that time period. Appendix III contains additional information on the characteristics of credible and reasonable fear applicants from fiscal year 2014 through March 2019.

Table 2. Credible and reasonable fear referrals to U.S. Citizenship and Immigration Services (USCIS), fiscal years 2014 through the first two quarters of fiscal year 2019

Fiscal year	**Total number of credible fear** referrals	**Percent of total** referrals	**Total number of reasonable fear** referrals	**Percent of total** referrals	**Total credible fear and reasonable** fear referrals
2014	47,754	85	8,602	15	56,356
2015	48,089	86	8,000	14	56,089
2016	91,598	91	9,274	9	100,872
2017	77,698	89	9,792	11	87,490
2018	98,083	90	10,697	10	108,780
2019 (first two quarters)	50,091	89	6,121	11	56,212
Total	413,313	89	52,486	11	465,799

Source: GAO analysis of USCIS data. | GAO-20-250.

Notes: With some exceptions, including unaccompanied alien children, apprehended individuals may be placed into administrative removal proceedings before an immigration judge or, if the individual is an arriving alien or encountered within 14 days and 100 miles of entry and is inadmissible based on fraud or misrepresentation, may be placed into expedited removal. Individuals placed into expedited removal are to be ordered removed from the United States without further hearing unless the individual indicates either an intention to apply for asylum or a fear of persecution or torture, or a fear of return, in which case they are to be referred to USCIS for credible fear of persecution screening, as appropriate. See 8 U.S.C. § 1225(b); 8 C.F.R. § 208.30. Noncitizens issued a final administrative order of removal after conviction for crimes that meet the definition of an "aggravated felony" in the Immigration and Nationality Act or whose prior removal order is reinstated may be placed into streamlined removal proceedings where they cannot apply for asylum. However, if they express a fear of return, they are to be screened for "reasonable fear," which is a screening for withholding or deferral of removal, more limited forms of humanitarian protection. See 8 C.F.R. §§ 208.31, 208.16.

A Majority of Credible and Reasonable Fear Referrals to USCIS from Fiscal Year 2014 through the First Two Quarters of Fiscal Year 2019 Resulted in Positive Determinations

As shown in Figure 1, USCIS asylum officers made positive determinations in about 71 percent of all credible and reasonable fear screenings between fiscal years 2014 and the first two quarters of fiscal year 2019. The remaining credible and reasonable fear screenings were almost evenly divided between negative determinations and administrative closures (approximately 14 percent each) with a small remainder of screenings pending resolution (0.1 percent).[16] Individually, from fiscal year 2014 through the first 2 quarters of fiscal year 2019, USCIS asylum officers made positive determinations in nearly 77 percent of all credible fear screenings; officers made positive determinations in about 30 percent of reasonable fear screenings.

Regarding credible fear screenings specifically, the percentage of positive determinations ranged from about 73 to 80 percent of total credible fear cases completed each year from fiscal year 2014 through the first two quarters of fiscal year 2019 (see Figure 2).

Regarding reasonable fear screenings, as shown in Figure 3, outcomes for reasonable fear cases from fiscal year 2014 through the first two quarters of fiscal year 2019 were generally split evenly each year among positive determinations (from 28 to 32 percent), negative determinations (from 29 to 35 percent), and administrative closures (from 35 to 42 percent).[17]

---

[16] According to USCIS officials, administrative closures occur when the asylum officer conducting the screening closes the case without a determination for reasons such as death, presence of the applicant in state or federal custody, inability of the applicant to communicate, dissolved cases due to withdrawals of fear claims, or other reasons.

[17] Since 2014, administrative closures decreased by about 7 percentage points, while positive and negative determinations increased by about 2 and 5 percentage points, respectively.

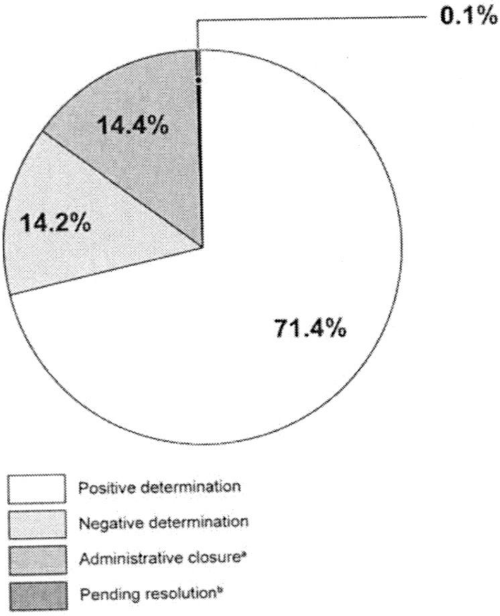

Source: GAO analysis of USCIS data. | GAO-20-250.

Notes: USCIS cases included in our analysis were referred to USCIS from October 1, 2013 through March 30, 2019 and the status of cases was as of July 22, 2019.

With some exceptions, including unaccompanied alien children, apprehended individuals may be placed into administrative removal proceedings before an immigration judge or, if the individual is an arriving alien or encountered within 14 days and 100 miles of entry and is inadmissible based on fraud or misrepresentation, may be placed into expedited removal. Individuals placed into expedited removal are to be ordered removed from the United States without further hearing unless the individual indicates either an intention to apply for asylum or a fear of persecution or torture, or a fear of return, in which case they are to be referred to USCIS for credible fear of persecution screening, as appropriate. See 8 U.S.C. § 1225(b); 8 C.F.R. § 208.30. Noncitizens issued a final administrative order of removal after conviction for crimes that meet the definition of an "aggravated felony" in the Immigration and Nationality Act or whose prior removal order is reinstated may be placed into streamlined removal proceedings where they cannot apply for asylum. However, if they express a fear of return, they are to be screened for "reasonable fear," which is a screening for withholding or deferral of removal, more limited forms of humanitarian protection. See 8 C.F.R. §§ 208.31, 208.16.

Total percentages do not equal 100 percent due to rounding.

[a]According to USCIS officials, administrative closures occur when the asylum officer conducting the screening closes the case without a determination for reasons such as death, presence of the applicant in state or federal custody, inability of the applicant to communicate, dissolved cases due to withdrawals of fear claims, or other reasons.

[b]We considered cases that remained in progress as of July 22, 2019 to be "pending resolution."

Figure 1. Outcomes of U.S. Citizenship and Immigration Services (USCIS) Credible and Reasonable Fear Screenings, Fiscal Years 2014 through the First Two Quarters of Fiscal Year 2019.

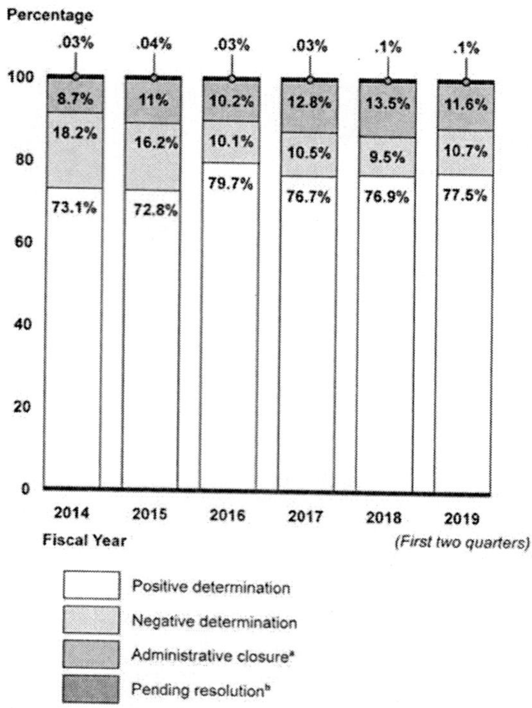

Source: GAO analysis of USCIS data. | GAO-20-250.

Notes: USCIS cases included in our analysis were referred to USCIS from October 1, 2013 through March 30, 2019 and the status of cases was as of July 22, 2019.

With some exceptions, including unaccompanied alien children, apprehended individuals may be placed into administrative removal proceedings before an immigration judge or, if the individual is an arriving alien or encountered within 14 days and 100 miles of entry and is inadmissible based on fraud or misrepresentation, may be placed into expedited removal. Individuals placed into expedited removal are to be ordered removed from the United States without further hearing unless the individual indicates either an intention to apply for asylum or a fear of persecution or torture, or a fear of return, in which case they are to be referred to USCIS for credible fear of persecution screening. See 8 U.S.C. § 1225(b); 8 C.F.R. § 208.30.

Total percentages do not equal 100 percent due to rounding.

[a]We considered cases that remained in progress as of July 22, 2019 to be "pending resolution." For fiscal year 2014 through the first 2 quarters of fiscal year 2019, these cases were still in progress and accounted for 0.1 percent or less of total credible fear cases.

[b]According to USCIS officials, administrative closures occur when the asylum officer conducting the screening closes the case without a determination for reasons such as death, presence of the applicant in state or federal custody, inability of the applicant to communicate, dissolved cases due to withdrawals of fear claims, or other reasons.

Figure 2. Outcomes of U.S. Citizenship and Immigration Services (USCIS) Credible Fear Screenings, Fiscal Years 2014 through the First Two Quarters of 2019.

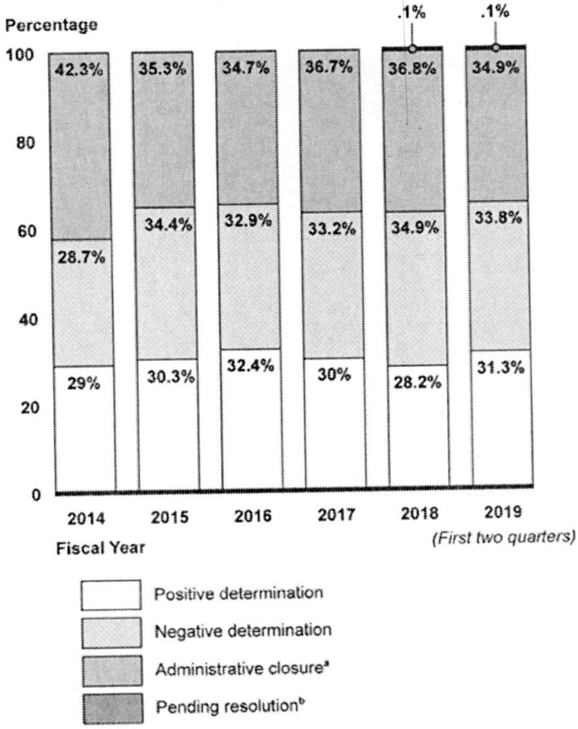

Source: GAO analysis of USCIS data. | GAO-20-250.

Notes: USCIS cases included in our analysis were referred to USCIS from October 1, 2013 through March 30, 2019 and the status of cases was as of July 22, 2019.

Noncitizens issued a final administrative removal order after conviction for crimes that meet the definition of an "aggravated felony" in the Immigration and Nationality Act or whose prior removal order is reinstated may be placed into streamlined removal proceedings where they cannot apply for asylum. However, if they express a fear of persecution or torture, they are to be screened for "reasonable fear," which is a screening for withholding or deferral of removal, more limited forms of humanitarian protection. See 8 C.F.R. §§ 208.31, 208.16.

Total percentages do not equal 100 percent due to rounding.

[a]We considered cases that remained in progress as of July 22, 2019 to be "pending resolution." For fiscal year 2014 through the first 2 quarters of fiscal year 2019, these cases are still in progress and accounted for 0.1 percent or less of total credible fear cases.

[b]According to USCIS officials, administrative closures occur when the asylum officer conducting the screening closes the case without a determination for reasons such as death, presence of the applicant in state or federal custody, inability of the applicant to communicate, dissolved cases due to withdrawals of fear claims, or other reasons.

Figure 3. Outcomes of U.S. Citizenship and Immigration Services (USCIS) Reasonable Fear Screenings, Fiscal Years 2014 through the First Two Quarters of 2019.

EOIR Reviewed over 50,000 USCIS Credible Fear Decisions from Fiscal Year 2014 through the First Three Quarters of Fiscal Year 2019; Immigration Judges Upheld Most Decisions

EOIR's credible and reasonable fear workload increased by about 16 percent—from about 8,100 reviews to about 9,400 reviews each year—between fiscal year 2014 and fiscal year 2018. According to EOIR data, from fiscal year 2014 through the third quarter of 2019 (the most recent data available at the time of our analysis), EOIR's immigration judges, at the noncitizens' requests, reviewed about 55,000 cases in which USCIS asylum officers made a negative credible or reasonable fear determination (see Figure 4).[18] Approximately 10 percent of these reviews were for individuals detained at the Karnes, Dilley, or Berks family residential centers.[19]

As shown in Figure 4, immigration judges upheld USCIS's negative credible and reasonable fear determinations in 77 percent of all reviews judges conducted from fiscal year 2014 through the third quarter of fiscal year 2019. During this time period, immigration judges vacated (or overturned) 22 percent of USCIS's negative determinations—meaning, judges found that those individuals had a credible or reasonable fear, as appropriate. As a result, individuals found to have a credible fear were to be placed in full removal proceedings and individuals found to have a reasonable fear were to be placed into more limited removal proceedings to consider the applicants' eligibility for withholding of removal or deferral of removal. Immigration judges upheld 45 percent of USCIS's negative determinations and vacated 54 percent of USCIS's negative determinations for individuals in ICE's Dilley, Karnes, or Berks family residential centers.

---

[18] We obtained aggregate EOIR data from fiscal year 2014 through June 2019—the most recent, complete data available at the time of our review. The most recent, full year for which data were available at the time of our analysis was fiscal year 2018.

[19] We excluded reviews that took place at the Artesia Family Residential Center from this analysis, as Artesia was operational for only 6 months, from June through November 2014. According to USCIS data, credible and reasonable fear screenings at Artesia represent less than 1 percent of all screenings at ICE's family residential centers from fiscal years 2014 through March 2019.

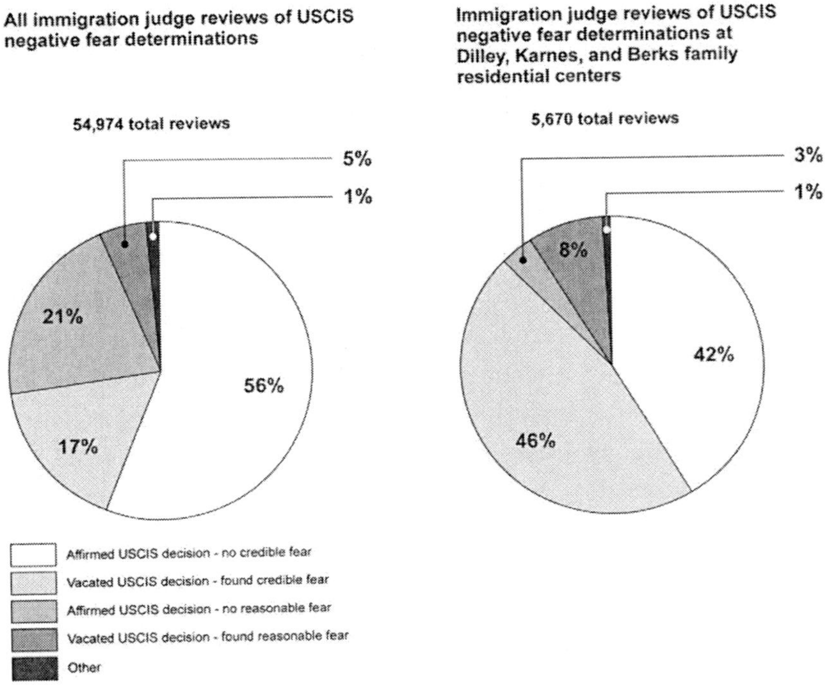

Source: GAO analysis of EOIR data. | GAO-20-250.

Note: Procedures for review of negative credible and reasonable fear findings by an immigration judge are governed by 8 C.F.R. §§ 1208.30-1208.31. According to EOIR, "other" includes administrative closures.

Figure 4. Numbers and Outcomes of Executive Office for Immigration Review (EOIR) Immigration Judge Reviews of Negative U.S. Citizenship and Immigration Services Fear (USCIS) Determinations, Fiscal Year 2014 through June 2019.

In addition, EOIR publicly reports data on the outcomes of removal cases across immigration courts that originated with a positive credible fear determination.[20] EOIR reported that, from fiscal years 2014 through March 2019, immigration judges completed about 135,000 cases that began with a positive credible fear determination.[21] Individuals in about 75,800 of the completed removal cases filed applications for asylum (56 percent). In

---

[20] As previously stated, an individual who receives a positive credible fear determination is placed into full removal proceedings where he or she can apply for multiple forms of relief or protection before an immigration judge, including asylum.

[21] As of April 2019, EOIR reported that there were 214,855 pending removal cases that originated with a positive credible fear claim.

about 59,200 of the completed removal cases (44 percent), individuals did not file an asylum application. However, as previously described, individuals who have received positive credible fear determinations may apply for other forms of relief or protection besides asylum, such as withholding of removal, and those applications are not represented in the statistics on EOIR's website.

Further, EOIR officials told us that, for data reporting purposes, each member of a family who receives a Notice to Appear before an immigration judge is counted as one EOIR removal case and each removal case may or may not include an asylum application. However, for a number of immigration applications before the court, including asylum and the related screening for credible fear, a spouse or child (defined as an unmarried natural or legally adopted child under 21 years of age) may be included as a dependent on a principal's application and derive lawful immigration status from the principal applicant if the application is granted.[22] As previously discussed, individuals detained in family residential centers—including individuals who could be eligible dependents for credible fear screening and asylum application purposes—comprise a substantial proportion of those who receive positive credible fear determinations. As such, according to EOIR officials, each family member would not be expected to file a separate asylum application. For example, a mother and her two children whose removal cases originated with a positive credible fear screening would comprise three removal cases in EOIR's publically reported data, but it is likely that only the mother's case would include an application for asylum, with her children as dependents on that application. For those removal cases in which the noncitizen applied for asylum, immigration judges granted asylum in about 19,300 cases (25 percent of the 75,800 completed removal cases with an asylum application).[23]

---

[22] See 8 U.S.C. § 1101(b)(1); see also 8 C.F.R. § 208.30(b).

[23] According to EOIR officials, spouses or children included as dependents on a spouse or parent's asylum application are included in the total number of asylum grants.

USCIS Has Policies and Procedures for Overseeing Credible and Reasonable Fear Screenings, but Gaps in Training, Quality Assurance, and Family Processing Exist

USCIS Has Policies and Procedures for Managing and Overseeing the Credible and Reasonable Fear Screening Process, Including Requiring Supervisory Review of All Cases

USCIS has developed various policies and procedures related to managing and overseeing credible and reasonable fear cases in accordance with the regulations governing credible and reasonable fear screenings, including setting requirements for interview procedures, background and security checks, and supervisory review.[24] In particular, USCIS has a *Credible Fear Procedures Manual* and a *Reasonable Fear Procedures Manual* that outline the procedures officers are to follow in screening these cases.

Interview Procedures

As of July 2019, an asylum office is to wait a minimum of one full calendar day from the applicant's arrival at an ICE detention facility before conducting a credible fear interview; an asylum office is to wait 48 hours after an initial orientation on the reasonable fear process before a reasonable fear interview, according to USCIS policy.[25] However, both credible and reasonable fear interviews generally occur at least 48 hours after the applicant's arrival at a detention facility, according to USCIS officials.[26] Asylum officers may conduct credible and reasonable fear

---

[24] See 8 C.F.R. §§ 208.30-208.31.

[25] Prior to July 2019, USCIS policy was to wait at least 48 hours from the applicant's arrival at an ICE detention facility to conduct the credible fear interview. USCIS policy for reasonable fear interviews has not changed, according to officials.

[26] At the time of our February 2019 site visit to ICE's family residential centers in Dilley and Karnes, Texas, Houston asylum office policy was to wait 72 hours between an orientation on the credible or reasonable fear process, and the interview. The orientation consisted of a

interviews either in-person or on the phone. Asylum officers are to arrange the assistance of an interpreter, generally connected over the phone, if the applicant is unable to proceed effectively in English pursuant to regulation.[27] Asylum officers are to verify and document that applicants have received and understood information regarding the credible or reasonable fear process before they begin asking substantive questions during the interview about the applicant's claim.

According to USCIS documents and officials, during the interview, asylum officers are to elicit all information relevant to a credible or reasonable fear claim, and regulation requires they conduct interviews in a non-adversarial manner. For example, asylum officers are to ask applicants questions to determine whether they can establish a credible or reasonable fear of persecution based on their race, religion, nationality, membership in a particular social group, or political opinion. In addition, asylum officers are to ask applicants questions to determine whether they can establish a credible or reasonable fear of torture if returned to their home country.[28] During our observations of in-person and telephone interviews, we observed asylum officers asking questions to ensure they fully explored any aspect of the claim related to a protected ground that could result in a positive determination. For example, we observed asylum officers asking

---

short video describing the credible or reasonable fear process, followed by additional explanations in-person from an asylum officer. At that time, asylum officers would also answer any questions applicants had about the process, according to USCIS officials. As of November 2019, USCIS officials stated they continued to show the short video describing the credible or reasonable fear process at the family residential center in Dilley; USCIS was no longer conducting the in-person orientations at the family residential center in Dilley.

[27] See 8 C.F.R. § 208.30(d)(5). According to Asylum Division policy, an asylum officer fluent in the applicant's language can conduct an interview in a language other than English if their language ability has been certified by the Department of State.

[28] As part of the analysis to determine whether the applicant is likely to be persecuted based on a protected ground or tortured, if an applicant says they were harmed or threatened, asylum officers are to ask questions related to government involvement. In general, persecution does not include the actions of private citizens unless the government is complicit in those acts or is unwilling or unable to take steps to prevent them. Individuals and asylum officers are also to assess whether an applicant could have safely relocated within their country of origin unless the persecutor is the government or is government -sponsored. See generally 8 C.F.R. §§ 208.13-208.31; see also, e.g., Halim v. Holder, 755 F.3d 506, 513 (7th Cir. 2014). We observed asylum officers asking questions about the level of government involvement, such as whether the applicant saw the individual who harmed them interacting with the police, and what exactly they saw or experienced that made them think the individual was connected with the police.

applicants separate questions about each protected ground, even if the applicant had not previously expressed they were harmed because of their political beliefs or race.

USCIS policy notes the applicant's credibility is dependent on various factors such as comparing information provided during the interview with that previously provided in the applicant's sworn statement to Border Patrol or OFO when initially apprehended. If asylum officers identify an issue with the applicant's credibility, they are to inform the applicant of the concerns and ask the applicant for his or her perspectives. During our site visits, we observed asylum officers questioning applicants on inconsistencies, in a non-adversarial manner, between information provided during the interview as compared to the applicant's sworn statements to Border Patrol agents upon apprehension. At the end of the interview, asylum officers are to provide a verbal summary of the material facts of the applicant's claim, and provide an opportunity for the applicant to make any corrections or additions. We observed asylum officers providing such summaries in all but one of the interviews that we observed in full.[29]

According to USCIS policy, asylum officers are to record key information about the applicant's claim, as well as specific details of the determination, on required forms that serve as the official record of the credible or reasonable fear screening.[30] In addition, asylum officers use a "checklist" to record more detailed legal analysis related to the applicant's claim. Asylum officers also generally type notes during interviews in a question and answer format, capturing each question and follow-up question they ask, and each response the applicant provides. We observed asylum officers documenting interviews in this way during all of the interviews where we observed the asylum officer in person.[31]

---

[29] Of the 20 interviews we observed in full, 19 included a verbal summary at the end. The remaining interview did not include a verbal summary at the end.

[30] For credible fear cases, the official record of the screening is USCIS Form I-870, *Record of Determination/Credible Fear Worksheet*. For reasonable fear cases, the official record is USCIS Form I-899, *Record of Determination/Reasonable Fear Worksheet.*

[31] We observed the asylum officer in person for 17 interviews.

Background and Security Checks

USCIS policy requires asylum officers to ensure certain background and security checks are conducted. If security checks or information discovered during the interview raises concerns related to fraud, public safety, or national security, asylum officers are to refer the case to USCIS's Fraud Detection and National Security Directorate (FDNS) for assistance.[32] FDNS officials told us the short time frames in the credible and reasonable fear process, among other factors, make direct involvement in individual cases less likely than in other caseloads at USCIS, such as affirmative asylum cases.[33] As such, the scope and extent of FDNS investigations into credible and reasonable fear cases is limited relative to other USCIS caseloads. FDNS data indicate that asylum officers referred approximately 1,400 total credible and reasonable fear cases to FDNS between fiscal years 2017 and 2018.[34] Of those, 13 cases resulted in a formal finding, called a *Statement of Finding*.[35] FDNS officials told us referrals from asylum officers on credible and reasonable fear cases typically result in FDNS conducting research related to an applicant's criminal history or travel patterns. FDNS may refer this information, in turn, to ICE to

---

[32] FDNS is responsible for leading USCIS's efforts to detect immigration benefit fraud and help detect national security issues and public safety concerns. FDNS's roles and responsibilities related to the credible and reasonable fear process include performing enhanced security checks and vetting of cases referred for assistance; conducting investigations in cases of suspected fraud or national security concerns, as appropriate; prescreening files in order to identify fraud trends and national security concerns prior to interviews; and, providing training to asylum office staff on local trends in fraud, national security, and public safety. For more information about FDNS's roles and responsibilities in the affirmative asylum process, see GAO, *Asylum: Additional Actions needed to Assess and Address Fraud Risks*, GAO-16-50 (Washington, D.C.: Dec. 2, 2015).

[33] Affirmative asylum applications involve claims filed with USCIS at the initiative of the noncitizen. An affirmative asylum applicant may be in the United States lawfully or unlawfully, and must file for asylum directly with USCIS within 1 year of his or her most recent arrival in the country unless he or she can demonstrate changed or extraordinary circumstances.

[34] FDNS made improvements to its data system in fiscal year 2016, including the ability to track the types of cases referred for review. Data for fiscal years 2017-2018 was the most recent, complete year data available at the time of our review.

[35] According to officials, FDNS prepares a *Statement of Findings* in the credible and reasonable fear context when FDNS immigration officers find information related to egregious public safety concerns, national security, or fraud that rises to the level of a finding. When this occurs, FDNS officers document a summary of the finding and relay the information to ICE, as appropriate.

reference in the applicant's removal proceedings, as appropriate. In contrast, according to FDNS officials, a fraud referral in the affirmative asylum context may result in a more formal finding of fraud in a *Statement of Finding*.

Supervisory Review

USCIS oversight of credible and reasonable fear cases includes a required supervisory review of each case after an asylum officer makes a positive or negative determination.[36] USCIS officials said supervisors are to review cases for legal sufficiency and accuracy, including a review of the screening checklist and the asylum officer's supporting interview notes. According to officials, supervisors are to communicate the results of their review to the asylum officer informally (e.g., via email or in-person discussion) for small issues, such as an administrative error, or through a formal write-up for larger issues, such as if the asylum officer's legal analysis was insufficient and requires a second interview with the applicant.[37]

USCIS Provides Initial Training on Credible and Reasonable Fear to New Asylum Officers and Asylum

Offices Are Required to Provide Ongoing on-the-Job Training

USCIS oversight of credible and reasonable fear cases includes basic training for new asylum officers and ongoing training for incumbent

[36] A supervisory asylum officer reviews each credible fear case pursuant to 8 CFR § 208.30(e)(7) and each reasonable fear case pursuant to USCIS policy.

[37] As a result of his or her review, a supervisor may take one of the following actions: (1) concur with the determination, with no adjustments needed; (2) concur with the determination, but ask the asylum officer to make adjustments to the analysis, or correct any inaccuracies; (3) non-concur with the determination, and discuss the evidence and legal analysis with the asylum officer. If the supervisor and asylum officer cannot come to an agreement on the determination, a second line supervisor makes the determination. In addition, a supervisor may request that the asylum officer re-interview the applicant to gain additional information needed for the legal sufficiency of the determination. A re-interview may result in the same determination, or may change the determination.

officers at asylum offices; these trainings include information specific to credible fear and reasonable fear screenings. As of the time of our review, the initial training program for asylum officers is comprised of two main components:

- Distance Training. New asylum officers participate in 3 weeks of self-paced RAIO Directorate and Asylum Division distance training in their respective asylum offices. During distance training, asylum officers are expected to participate in webinars, read the training materials and complete exercises and quizzes in preparation for residential training. The Asylum Division distance training includes course readings on credible and reasonable fear, and observations of credible and reasonable fear interviews.
- Residential Basic Training. Asylum officers participate in a 6-week residential basic training program, which includes 3 weeks of training in issue areas common across USCIS's Refugees, Asylum, and International Operations Directorate, as well as three weeks of Asylum Division-specific training. In the first 3-week session, courses include classroom instruction, practical exercises, and interviewing exercises on a variety of topics and skills relevant to multiple areas of USCIS's work, such as on affirmative asylum and refugee adjudications. The legal topics and skills covered in this initial training include eligibility for asylum, an applicant's nexus to protected grounds, and eliciting testimony, among others. The second 3-week session focuses on division-specific policy, procedure, and law related to asylum adjudications and screenings. For example, the 3-week session includes training on the affirmative asylum process, and multiple mock affirmative asylum interviews, among others, as well as 2 days of training specific to credible and reasonable fear cases. These 2 days include practical exercises; one mock credible fear interview exercise; and formal presentations on interviewing skills and security checks in a credible fear context, forms required for credible and reasonable fear, and on the Convention against Torture. At the end of the 6-

week residential training course, new asylum officers must pass final exams with a score of at least 70 percent. We reviewed a version of the exam and found that it included questions specific to credible and reasonable fear screenings.[38]

Asylum Division officials said the 9 combined weeks of distance and residential basic training constitute the minimum amount of formal training required for asylum officers to effectively screen credible and reasonable fear cases. However, Asylum Division officials said it is important for individual asylum offices to provide additional, on-the-job training to new officers assigned to screen credible and reasonable fear cases, specifically. Asylum officers screen credible and reasonable fear cases under shorter time frames and with less corroborating documentation compared to affirmative asylum cases. As such, Asylum Division officials told us that officers accustomed to adjudicating affirmative asylum cases may need to adjust to the shorter time frames required in credible and reasonable fear cases.[39] For example, some asylum offices have developed formal presentations on local policies and procedures, or provide officers with an opportunity to observe other officers conducting credible or reasonable fear interviews and gradually increase the number of cases they screen per day. Given their caseloads, the Houston and Arlington asylum offices provide 3 and 4 weeks of additional credible and reasonable fear training for new asylum officers, respectively. By comparison, the San Francisco and Newark asylum offices provide 1 week of training on credible and reasonable fear procedures for new asylum officers and Los Angeles provides 2 days of such training, according to officials.

For incumbent asylum officers, USCIS policy requires asylum offices to allocate four hours per week for formal or informal training. The

---

[38] For example, some questions included example credible or reasonable fear fact patterns. Questions also tested asylum officers on the legal standards for these screenings and how to elicit testimony in a credible fear interview, among other topics.

[39] In addition, credible and reasonable fear cases may require an asylum officer to assess the likelihood that an individual will receive protection from removal, such as withholding of removal under the Convention against Torture, a type of protection that can be granted by an immigration judge, but is not generally adjudicated by an asylum officer handling affirmative asylum cases.

training can range from classroom instruction by a training officer, to individual study time that asylum officers can use to review case law, research country conditions affecting asylum applicants, or read new USCIS procedures and guidance. Individual asylum offices design their weekly training programs based on the types of cases their office generally receives, according to Asylum Division officials. The Asylum Division requires training officers to track the date and topic of each weekly training session and report that information to Asylum Division headquarters on a quarterly basis. Our analysis of fiscal year 2018 quarterly training reports for all asylum offices and sub-offices indicates that offices with larger credible and reasonable fear caseloads generally provided more weekly trainings on these topics. For example, Houston and Arlington conducted seven or more weekly training sessions on credible and reasonable fear screenings in fiscal year 2018. By comparison, two offices with smaller credible and reasonable fear caseloads—Newark and New York—conducted one or fewer weekly sessions on credible and reasonable fear (see app. III for credible and reasonable fear workload data by asylum office).[40]

In addition to this training program for asylum officers, USCIS trains officers from outside the Asylum Division to screen credible and reasonable fear cases, including refugee officers and others.[41] Refugee

---

[40] USCIS elicits and evaluates feedback on training needs from asylum officers and supervisors every two years through a training needs assessment. The 2018 Asylum Division Training Needs Assessment surveyed approximately 755 asylum officers, supervisory asylum officers, training officers, and refugee officers on detail to the Asylum Division. USCIS received responses from 616 individuals. The assessment includes multiple questions specific to training needs for credible and reasonable fear. For the 2018 Asylum Division training needs assessment, the majority of responding officers said two to seven weekly training sessions each year should be spent on credible and reasonable fear topics.

[41] In addition to refugee officers, former refugee or asylum officers now working with USCIS's Field Office Directorate, Service Center Operations, and Fraud Detection and National Security Directorate conduct credible and reasonable fear screenings for USCIS. Refugee officers on detail to the Asylum Division, particularly those assigned to the Houston or Arlington asylum office, screen credible fear cases at the family residential centers. For example, in fiscal year 2018, 105 refugee officers screened cases at the family residential centers, according to USCIS. In addition, beginning in June 2019, Border Patrol agents on assignment to USCIS began screening credible fear cases only, including credible fear cases at the family residential center in Dilley, Texas. Border Patrol agents screening credible fear cases are to receive credible fear training from USCIS before conducting interviews and be supervised by a supervisory asylum officer who has substantial experience adjudicating

officers receive some of the same basic training as asylum officers, as they participate in the same RAIO distance training and RAIO Directorate residential training. Refugee officers do not participate in Asylum Division distance training or residential training. As a result, USCIS provides refugee officers with 3 days of training on screening credible fear cases before they can begin screening cases. We reviewed training materials for the refugee officer training, and found the sessions are similar to Asylum Division residential training sessions on credible fear screening.

In addition, some materials provide information and guidance on the differences between adjudicating refugee cases and screening credible fear cases. Officials said refugee officers generally screen credible fear cases, including at the family residential centers, only if they are detailed to the Houston and Arlington asylum offices. Both Houston and Arlington provide refugee officers detailed to their offices with 1-2 weeks of additional training on credible fear screening, similar to the procedural training they provide to new asylum officers. At both offices, trainings include formal presentations or exercises on legal concepts and procedures specific to credible fear, credible fear interview observations, and a gradual increase in the number of cases refugee officers screen each day.

Pre-departure Training for USCIS Asylum Officers Screening Family Units at ICE Family Residential Centers Is Inconsistent Across Asylum Offices

Although all new asylum officers receive basic training on the credible and reasonable fear screening process and may also receive on-the-job training in their home offices, not all offices provide additional pre - departure training to asylum officers before they begin screening cases for family units at ICE family residential centers. Credible fear screenings at ICE's family residential centers, in particular, represent a significant percentage—about 34 percent—of all credible fear cases asylum officers

asylum applications in order to satisfy the statutory definition of an asylum officer. See 8 U.S.C. § 1225(b)(1)(E).

screened from fiscal year 2014 though the second quarter of fiscal year 2019. As discussed previously, asylum offices with relatively small credible and reasonable fear local caseloads generally provide less on-the-job training throughout the year on credible and reasonable fear. However, almost all asylum offices send officers to the family residential centers in Texas for in-person interviews, including those offices with small credible and reasonable fear caseloads at the local level. Asylum Division officials said they require asylum offices to send a specific number of asylum officers—a number in proportion to the size of the office—with the largest offices sending the most officers to the family residential centers each year. For example, in fiscal year 2018, Newark, Los Angeles, Houston, and Chicago sent the most officers to the family residential centers, as shown in Figure 5 below.

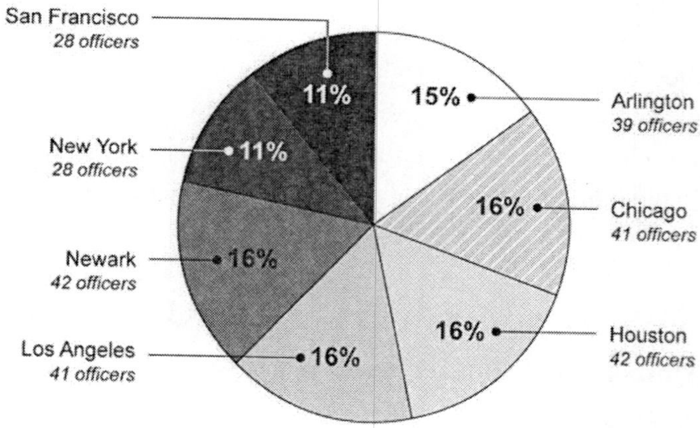

Source: GAO analysis of USCIS data. | GAO-20-250.

Notes: According to USCIS officials, the Miami asylum office did not send asylum officers to the family residential centers in order to focus on reducing its affirmative asylum backlog during fiscal year 2018. However, officials said the Miami asylum office did send officers in previous years.

Total percentages do not equal 100 percent due to rounding.

Figure 5. Number of U.S. Citizenship and Immigration Services (USCIS) Asylum Officers Screening Families in U.S. Immigration and Customs Enforcement Family Residential Centers in Fiscal Year 2018, by Asylum Office.

At least two asylum offices provide pre-departure training to asylum officers being sent to ICE's family residential centers. To support officers who are more accustomed to adjudicating affirmative asylum cases, the Los Angeles asylum office provides pre-departure training for officers before they travel to the family residential centers. In Los Angeles, officers observe credible and reasonable fear interviews and gradually increase to a full caseload of credible or reasonable fear cases at their home office, according to officials. In San Francisco, officers receive pre-departure training highlighting procedures unique to the family residential centers or to processing family units in credible and reasonable fear. Specifically, San Francisco pre-departure training includes a formal presentation on family residential center procedures, including discussion of challenges officers may experience, according to officials. By comparison, officials from the Chicago and New York offices told us they do not provide formal pre-departure training but rather direct or recommend that officers review Asylum Division guidance and procedures on family processing independently before they travel. Officials from two other offices told us they rely on the training asylum officers may receive throughout the year related to credible and reasonable fear, which can vary, as previously discussed.

Asylum officers also noted inconsistent pre-departure training prior to their temporary duty during our February 2019 visits to two Texas family residential centers in Dilley and Karnes. For example, some asylum officers we interviewed said they screened credible and reasonable fear cases at their home office in preparation for their assignment. Others said they reviewed procedures independently on family processing in credible and reasonable fear cases. Officers from one asylum office said they relied primarily on an email from USCIS support staff located at the family residential centers to learn about screening family cases.

Asylum officers are to review the procedures on family processing in credible and reasonable fear before they arrive at the family residential centers, according to officials. However, there is no minimum amount of pre-departure training, or required content for such training, that all asylum offices are to provide before officers begin screening family units. Asylum

Division officials acknowledged that training on screening of family units for credible and reasonable fear varies by asylum office and noted that offices have been given discretion to determine what, if any, pre-departure training to provide on screening family units. Arlington and Houston asylum office officials stated that inconsistent asylum officer training on credible and reasonable fear cases negatively impacts efficiency at the family residential centers. Specifically, these officials noted that asylum officers who typically adjudicate affirmative asylum applications benefit from training on key differences between credible fear, reasonable fear, and affirmative asylum. For example, officials said more training could reduce administrative errors in applicants' paperwork, and changes needed during supervisory review, both of which occur more often for officers with less experience and training, according to officials. Further, officials said asylum officers less experienced in credible and reasonable fear may not be able to handle a full caseload at the family residential centers when they first arrive. As a result, Houston officials said they may spend the first week of a 2-week assignment providing additional support to inexperienced officers as they gradually increase to a full caseload.

Standards for Internal Control in the Federal Government states management should demonstrate a commitment to recruit, develop, and retain competent individuals. The standards also note that competence is the qualification to carry out assigned responsibilities, and requires relevant knowledge, skills, and abilities, which are gained largely from professional experience, training, and certifications. As previously noted, Asylum Division officials told us additional training for asylum officers before they begin screening cases at the family residential centers is important. Officials also said their intention is to balance such training against the need for rapid deployment, in some cases. Although additional training may not be feasible before every deployment, providing asylum officers additional pre-departure training before they begin screening credible and reasonable fear cases for family units would better prepare officers and help ensure efficient and effective case processing at ICE's family residential centers.

USCIS Conducts Various Quality Assurance Reviews of Credible and Reasonable Fear Cases, but Does Not Document Results in a Consistent Manner

USCIS relies primarily on two quality assurance reviews for assessing quality of credible and reasonable fear cases, but does not document the results of one of these reviews in a consistent manner.[42]

Annual, Asylum Division-Wide Reviews

The Asylum Division conducts division-wide quality assurance reviews on a random sampling of credible fear, reasonable fear, or affirmative asylum cases selected proportionally from asylum offices nationwide. To do so, the Asylum Division works in collaboration with the RAIO Directorate. The reviews occur each year, and rotate between a sampling of credible fear cases, reasonable fear cases, and affirmative asylum cases.[43]

For credible and reasonable fear reviews, USCIS randomly selects a specified number of cases after supervisory review, but before officers serve determinations to the applicant.[44] Reviewers use a checklist to identify and track quality issues arising in each reviewed case, such as accurate data entry, appropriate legal analysis, asylum officer notes that reflect a skilled interview, and others. The review process for each case

---

[42] USCIS also conducts weekly reviews of credible and reasonable fear cases that assess a small number of cases. Officials said the weekly reviews provide limited information on the overall quality of credible fear and reasonable fear cases. The officials added that, due to the limited information provided, they are considering discontinuing these weekly reviews in the future. They noted that, at various points throughout the year, they temporarily suspended weekly reviews of reasonable fear cases to focus Asylum Division resources on other priorities, such as credible fear cases.

[43] USCIS conducted a pilot Asylum Division-wide review of credible fear cases in 2015, and a pilot for reasonable fear cases in 2016. Subsequently, USCIS conducted full Asylum Division- wide reviews of credible fear cases in 2016 and 2018, and of reasonable fear cases in 2017.

[44] USCIS works with a statistician to develop the sampling methodology used for the Asylum Division-wide reviews. For example, for the 2018 review of credible fear cases, USCIS considered the overall number of credible fear cases from October 1, 2017 through June 17, 2018, and used a standard approach to calculate a sample size for the given population. Asylum offices were then to select credible fear cases for review using specified parameters.

includes two lines of review. If the two reviewers come to different conclusions, they discuss any differences in their reviews and reach consensus about how to score the case. USCIS records the results of these reviews in a document that lays out the numbers and percentages of errors in areas covered in the review checklist. For example, for the 2018 review of credible fear cases, the document states asylum officer notes did not reflect a skilled interview in an estimated 58 percent of cases.[45] For most of these cases, the reason for the error that reviewers noted was insufficient follow-up questions. USCIS officials said while the sample across asylum offices is generalizable with respect to the credible or reasonable fear caseloads nationwide, the samples taken from each asylum office are not large enough to draw conclusions about trends at individual asylum offices. Officials said they rely on periodic reviews to identify trends by asylum office.

Periodic, Asylum Office Reviews

In addition to the Asylum Division-wide quality assurance reviews, the Asylum Division began conducting periodic reviews at asylum offices in November 2017. As of November 2019, the Asylum Division had conducted periodic reviews of credible and reasonable fear cases or affirmative asylum adjudications at some asylum offices, as well as a review of credible and reasonable fear cases at the family residential centers. For periodic reviews, the Asylum Division selects cases over a period of several weeks. For example, based on the Asylum Division's draft standard operating procedures for the periodic reviews, an asylum office may send two to four credible and reasonable fear cases every day for several weeks to reach the required total number of cases. According to the draft standard operating procedures, Asylum Division reviewers are to use a reviewer checklist, modeled off the checklist used for the Asylum Division-wide reviews, as a starting point for what factors to review.

However, USCIS does not document the results of the periodic reviews in a consistent manner. We reviewed the reports resulting from six periodic

[45] Percentage estimates from the 2018 review of credible fear cases have margins of error at the 90 percent confidence level of plus or minus 4 percentage points or fewer.

reviews conducted at the Arlington, Chicago, Miami, and Houston asylum offices, the New Orleans sub-office, and the family residential centers.[46] We found that all reports included information on strengths and weaknesses, and some reports further organized analysis into additional categories. For example, some reports had analysis on details related to procedures, eliciting testimony, and issues related to fraud detection and national security. Other reports included analysis of specific trends in persecution cases and in Convention against Torture cases. Some reports also included analysis on legal sufficiency, applicant country of origin, determination outcomes, and others. According to the draft standard operating procedure, reviewers are to note trends, common errors, and collect samples to create a deliverable, such as a short report or other deliverables, for the asylum office at the end of the review. However, the Asylum Division has not provided guidance on what specific information is important to include in reports resulting from periodic reviews in order to track trends within an asylum office over time, or across asylum offices.

Standards for Internal Control in the Federal Government states management should establish and operate monitoring activities to oversee the internal control system and evaluate the results. Management should document the results of ongoing monitoring and separate evaluations to identify internal control issues, and should use this evaluation to determine the effectiveness of the internal control system. Asylum Division officials told us the primary purpose of the periodic reviews is to collect information about current, office-specific trends, and provide timely support in the form of training sessions and other guidance. Further, the Asylum Division historically has not used the periodic reviews to compare one office to another, though they have sometimes noted issues from these reviews requiring similar guidance across multiple offices. Documenting the results of periodic reviews in a consistent manner would help the

---

46 These six periodic reviews took place between November 2017 and May 2018 and represented all those periodic review reports available at the time of our review. As of November 2019, the Asylum Division had also conducted periodic reviews of credible and reasonable fear cases at the Newark and San Francisco asylum offices, the Boston sub-office, and a second review at the Houston asylum office, according to officials. In addition, Asylum Division officials told us they conducted periodic reviews of affirmative asylum adjudications at the remaining asylum offices.

Asylum Division identify trends and provide support across asylum offices.

The draft standard operating procedures for the periodic review provides general directions for reviewers to share information on trends to asylum office personnel, such as strengths, weaknesses, and other developing trends. However, the draft standard operating procedures do not specify requirements for documenting the results of these reviews. Asylum Division officials told us the periodic review standard operating procedures are in draft form, and that they may provide more specific guidance on aspects of the reviews in the future. However, officials also said they are not planning any changes or additions to the standard operating procedure as of September 2019. More specific guidance on requirements for documenting results would better position USCIS to track trends in a consistent manner for credible and reasonable fear reviews within and across asylum offices.

USCIS Does Not Systematically Record Case Outcomes When Screening Family Members for Credible Fear

By regulation, dependents, specifically a spouse or child, of a noncitizen (referred to as the "principal applicant") can be included in the applicant's credible fear determination if the dependent (1) arrived in the United States concurrently with the principal applicant, and (2) desires to be included in the principal applicant's determination.[47] However, any noncitizen may have his or her credible fear determination made separately, if he or she expresses such a desire.

USCIS policy is to include any dependents on a principal applicant's credible fear determination if the principal applicant receives a positive

---

[47] See 8 C.F.R. § 208.30(b). For a number of immigration applications, including asylum and the related screening for credible fear, a spouse or child (defined as an unmarried natural or legally adopted child under 21 years of age) may be included as dependents on a principal's application and derive lawful immigration status from the principal applicant if the application is granted. See 8 U.S.C. § 1101(b)(1).

determination, resulting in both the principal applicant and any dependents being issued a Notice to Appear for full removal proceedings.[48]

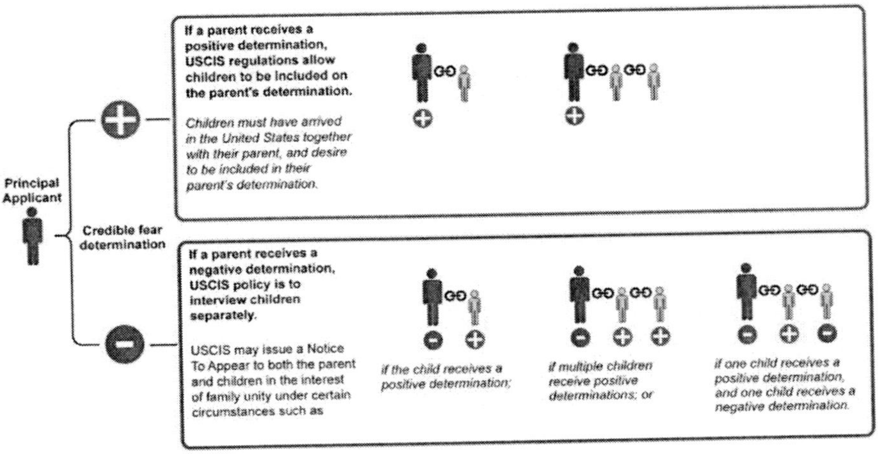

Source: 8C.F.R. § 208.30(b) and USCIS policy. | GAO-20-250.

Notes: For a number of immigration applications, including asylum and the related screening for credible fear, a spouse or child (defined as an unmarried natural or legally adopted child under 21 years of age) may be included as dependents on a principal's application and derive lawful immigration status from the principal applicant if the application is granted. See 8 U.S.C. § 1101(b)(1). Separately, the exercise of discretion to issue a Notice to Appear to both the parent and children in the interest of family unity is limited to children under the age of 18 because, according to the policy, family unity interests are more compelling when the child is a minor.

Figure 6. U.S. Citizenship and Immigration Services (USCIS) Credible Fear Processing for Parents and Children Detained Together in U.S. Immigration and Customs Enforcement Family Residential Centers.

For example, USCIS may process credible fear cases together for family units detained at ICE's family residential centers, including children as dependents on a parent's case, or issuing a Notice To Appear for the parent and children in the interest of family unity (see Figure 6). We observed asylum officers at the family residential centers asking principal

---

[48] For cases in which the asylum officer concludes the screening with a positive determination, USCIS is to issue a Notice to Appear before an immigration court, thereby placing the individual into full removal proceedings before an EOIR immigration judge.

applicants whether they were apprehended with any family members. If yes, asylum officers asked for the names and dates of birth of those family members, and recorded the information in their typed notes. For parents who received a positive determination, we observed asylum officers including the child on the parent's case as a dependent.

Further, if a parent receives a negative credible fear determination, and his or her child receives a positive credible fear determination, USCIS may issue a Notice to Appear to the child as a positive credible fear determination and to the parent in the interest of family unity. In that case, because a parent could not be a "dependent" of a child under the regulation, USCIS policy is to use its discretion to issue a Notice to Appear to both the child receiving a positive determination and the parent he or she arrived with, in the interest of family unity, even though the parent initially received a negative determination. Issuing the parent and child a Notice to Appear places them into full removal proceedings where they can apply for multiple forms of relief or protection before an immigration judge, including asylum, rather than being expeditiously ordered removed in accordance with the expedited removal process. The exercise of this discretion to issue a Notice to Appear to both the child receiving a positive determination and the parent he or she arrived with in the interest of family unity is limited to cases in which the children are under the age of 18 because, according to the policy, family unity interests are more compelling when the child is a minor.

USCIS data indicate that asylum officers screened more than 141,000 credible fear cases at ICE's four family residential centers between fiscal years 2014 and the first two quarters of 2019 (see Table 3).[49] In addition, USCIS data indicate that positive credible fear determination rates are higher at the family residential centers—87 percent compared with the nationwide rate of 77 percent from fiscal year 2014 through the second quarter of fiscal year 2019 (see app. III for data on reasonable fear cases screened at ICE's family residential centers).

---

[49] ICE detained families at the family residential centers (Artesia Family Residential Center, Berks County Residential Center, Karnes County Residential Center, and the South Texas Family Residential Center) for varying periods between fiscal year 2014 and fiscal year 2019.

Table 3. Credible fear referrals to U.S. Citizenship and Immigration Services (USCIS) from U.S. Immigration and Customs Enforcement's (ICE) family residential centers, and related positive outcomes, fiscal years 2014 through the first two quarters of 2019

Fiscal year	Total credible fear referrals to USCIS	Total credible fear referrals from ICE's family residential centers	Percentage of credible fear referrals from ICE's family residential centers	Total and percentage of positive determinations for all credible fear referrals	Total and percentage of positive determination from ICE's family residential centers only
2014	47,754	1,549	3	34,901 (73)	1,021 (66)
2015	48,089	9,933	21	34,996 (73)	8,818 (89)
2016	91,598	41,254	45	72,989 (80)	36,697 (89)
2017	77,698	31,574	41	59,581 (77)	27,762 (88)
2018	98,083	44,062	45	75,473 (77)	37,180 (84)
2019 (first two quarters)	50,091	12,796	26	38,844 (78)	10,697 (84)
Total	413,313	141,168	34	316,784 (77)	122,175 (87)

Source: GAO analysis of USCIS data. | GAO-20-250.

Notes: With some exceptions, including unaccompanied alien children, apprehended individuals may be placed into administrative removal proceedings before an immigration judge or, if the individual is an arriving alien or encountered within 14 days and 100 miles of entry and is inadmissible based on fraud or misrepresentation, may be placed into expedited removal. Individuals placed into expedited removal are to be ordered removed from the United States without further hearing unless the individual indicates either an intention to apply for asylum or a fear of persecution or torture, or a fear of return, in which case they are to be referred to USCIS for credible fear of persecution screening, as appropriate. See 8 U.S.C. § 1225(b); 8 C.F.R. § 208.30.

Asylum officers are to record individual case outcomes for all family members in USCIS's automated case management system. However, Asylum Division officials said their system does not allow asylum officers to record whether an individual receives a credible fear determination as a principal applicant, dependent, or in the interest of family unity. Instead, asylum officers are to record positive determinations in the USCIS case management system for both (1) dependents on the basis of the principal applicant's positive case, and (2) parents with negative determinations, on the basis of their child's positive case. USCIS does record more specific information related to outcomes for family units in the family members' individual hardcopy alien files, but this information is not readily available in an automated manner.[50]

USCIS's case management system allows asylum officers to record family relationships—that is, officials stated that asylum officers are to record who is a principal applicant, and who is a spouse, child, parent, or sibling of the principal applicant. According to USCIS officials, asylum officers are to record a parent who receives a positive credible fear determination as the principal applicant, and record any children as a child. Further, asylum officers are to link known family members' cases in the system, but adding a description of the family relationship is up to asylum officers' discretion. However, the system does not allow officers to record whether an applicant's determination stems from his or her own case, or from a family member's case. As a result, USCIS does not maintain automated data in a readily accessible manner on outcomes for family members in a manner that indicates whether (1) an eligible family member received a positive determination as a dependent on a principal applicant's positive case or (2) whether a parent was issued a Notice to Appear based on his or her child's positive determination, after the parent received a negative determination.

Standards for Internal Control in the Federal Government states that management should process obtained data into quality information that supports the internal control system. Quality information is appropriate, current, complete, accurate, accessible, and provided on a timely basis. Although USCIS data indicate that positive credible fear determination rates are higher at the family residential centers compared to rates of positive credible fear determinations across all detention facilities, USCIS

---

[50] If a principal applicant receives a positive determination, asylum officers are to record biographic information for all their dependents, and to record whether dependents entered the United States concurrently with the principal applicant, on the principal applicant's USCIS Form I-870, *Record of Determination/Credible Fear Worksheet.* If a parent receives a negative determination, asylum officers are to interview the child. If the child receives a positive credible fear determination, asylum officers are also to include a note in the comment section on the child's Form I-870 that the parent was present for the interview. Asylum officers are also to include a note in the comment section of the child's Form I-870 that the parent received a negative determination, but that USCIS was using its discretion to place the parent into full removal proceedings in the interest of family unity.

officials stated the higher rates result from the ability to (1) include children under 18 on a parent's positive credible fear determination, and (2) record all family members as positive in the system when USCIS uses its discretion in the interest of family unity. USCIS officials told us that systematically recording all outcomes of credible fear screenings for family members in a more complete manner would require changes to their case management system; according to Asylum Division officials, they are continually exploring options to improve the system's capabilities. Without complete data in its case management system on all outcomes of credible fear screenings at family residential centers, USCIS is not well-positioned to report on the scope of either the agency's policy for family members who are treated as dependents, pursuant to regulation, or USCIS's use of discretion in the interest of family unity.

USCIS and EOIR Have Processes for Managing Credible and Reasonable Fear Workloads, but USCIS Does Not Have Complete Data on Case Delays

USCIS Makes Staffing Allocation Decisions Based on National and Local Staffing Models

USCIS manages its credible and reasonable fear workloads using national- and local-level staffing models to inform staffing allocation decisions. Specifically, USCIS has an agency-wide staffing model to allocate staff to different workload categories, including credible and reasonable fear workloads, for each upcoming fiscal year.[51]

---

[51] According to USCIS, the Asylum Division's authorized staffing level increased from 605 permanent, full-time federal employees in fiscal year 2012 to 1,712 in fiscal year 2019. USCIS reported that the increase in hiring, particularly in fiscal year 2019, was necessary to meet the increase in the credible fear and affirmative asylum workloads.

Asylum Division headquarters officials stated they collaborate with USCIS's Office of Performance and Quality,[52] USCIS administrative offices, and local asylum offices to develop the national staffing model. Headquarters officials said the national staffing model is intended to allocate staff for each workload category for the upcoming fiscal year. They begin working on the staffing model in June for any given year in anticipation of resource decisions the agency will make before a new fiscal year begins, usually in September or October. According to officials, the national staffing model for credible and reasonable fear is based on historical case receipt and workload data, historical staffing data and future staffing workload forecasting data, bi-weekly reports on staffing and workload data, and observations from asylum offices submitted to headquarters, among other things.

The Asylum Division also maintains staffing models that guide local staffing deployment, according to headquarters officials. Asylum offices make local staffing allocation decisions in collaboration with the Asylum Division at headquarters. Headquarters officials stated they consider several factors in allocating staff specifically for the credible and reasonable fear workloads for local asylum offices. Such factors include workload projections, available facilities and planned facilities projects, and existing workforce and vacancy levels (Table 4 shows the number of asylum officers authorized and on board for each asylum office in March 2019). In addition, headquarters officials said they work with local asylum offices to review the number of credible and reasonable fear case receipts and current staffing allocations by asylum office on a daily basis. Headquarters officials stated they change staffing allocation as necessary to address changes in credible or reasonable fear case receipts.

---

[52] Asylum Division officials noted USCIS's Office of Performance and Quality is responsible for establishing national annual staffing recommendations and manages the statistical models that forecast future workload volume, which support their recommendations.

Table 4. Number of U.S. Citizenship and Immigration Services (USCIS) asylum officers authorized and on board, as of March 2019

Asylum Office	Total number of asylum officers authorized	Total number of asylum officers onboard	Percent of asylum officers onboard
Arlington Pre-Screening Center and Arlington[a]	133	96	72
Chicago	70	61	87
Houston and New Orleans Sub Office[a]	138	91	66
Los Angeles	97	78	80
Miami	70	56	80
Newark and Boston Sub Office[a]	91	70	77
New York	65	42	65
San Francisco	81	52	64
Total	745	546	73

Source: GAO analysis of USCIS data. | GAO-20-250.

[a]The number of asylum officers are combined for asylum offices and their respective sub offices.

In the Houston and Arlington asylum offices, in particular, officials stated they review headquarters data on workload projections to assign personnel to the credible and reasonable fear workloads for their offices. For example, officials in the Houston office said they look at the projected credible and reasonable fear workload to determine the number of officers they may need. Houston office officials said they assign officers based on officer availability, considering factors such as leave or training schedules. Similarly, a senior official responsible for staffing in the Arlington office said they look at the projected numbers of credible and reasonable fear cases, as well as the location of the cases, to determine the target number of officers assigned to a specific workload. Once they set targets for the number of officers needed, a senior official responsible for staffing in the Arlington office said they assign personnel based on a number of factors, including officer preferences, seniority, and locations with the greatest need.

Although USCIS uses national and local staffing models for determining staffing needs and allocating staff at and across field offices, senior Asylum Division officials stated that predicting future workload for credible fear cases is challenging. Moreover, headquarters officials told us that USCIS's credible fear workload projections have been off by as much as 50 percent when comparing projected and actual credible fear workload volume in recent years.[53] For example, the USCIS projections for credible fear cases in fiscal year 2015 were 78,485, but actual case receipts totaled 48,052.[54] More recently in fiscal year 2018, USCIS projected 70,000 credible fear case receipts, but actual case receipts totaled 99,035. Headquarters officials stated that a variety of external factors—unpredictable changes in country conditions, and CBP and ICE decisions to either place individuals in expedited removal or issue Notices to Appear before an immigration judge—make it difficult to project this workload. Furthermore, headquarters officials stated the volume of credible fear cases can fluctuate on a weekly basis, while reasonable fear projections have been fairly accurate, since the number of reasonable fear cases has remained relatively stable in recent years.

To manage its workload of credible and reasonable fear cases, USCIS relies on a flexible workforce to respond to fluctuations in cases, in addition to asylum officers who generally screen credible and reasonable fear cases. For example, USCIS pulls asylum officers from affirmative asylum adjudications and uses overtime hours to handle surges in credible and reasonable fear case receipts, according to officials. Senior Asylum Division officials stated they do not receive staffing increases to account for lost or stopped work in other workload categories, such as affirmative asylum, that result from surges in credible fear case receipts. They stated surges in credible and reasonable fear case receipts may require immediate staff redeployment from the affirmative asylum workload. As a result, asylum offices have sometimes canceled planned affirmative asylum interviews and have prioritized credible and reasonable fear screenings over affirmative asylum cases, which have significantly contributed to the current backlog in pending affirmative asylum cases, according to

[53] USCIS established a Volume Projection Committee composed of subject matter experts from various directorates to collaborate and project the workload for all operational forms for USCIS. The Office of Chief Financial Officer and the Office of Performance and Quality co-chair the committee, and Asylum Division officials stated they collaborated with the two offices to project the credible fear workload.

[54] Actual case receipt numbers are from USCIS's publicly-reported data on credible fear case receipts.

headquarters officials. As previously discussed, asylum offices across the country also send officers on details to ICE's family residential centers to conduct credible and reasonable fear screenings.[55]

In addition, the Asylum Division headquarters tracks the number of asylum officers assigned to the credible and reasonable fear workload, among other workload categories such as affirmative asylum, through biweekly reports received from local asylum offices. Headquarters officials told us they use the reports to respond to specific requests for information about Asylum Division staffing allocation. For example, Congress may request information on the number of USCIS personnel working on credible fear cases for a particular time period, according to headquarters officials, so they maintain these reports to fulfill such requests.

Specifically, with regard to the biweekly reports, asylum offices record the number of asylum officers assigned to credible and reasonable fear cases for each day in the 2-week pay period.[56] The resulting biweekly reports are spreadsheets with 15 tabs, one tab for each day in a pay period and one tab summarizing the pay period, with 26 separate spreadsheets for each year per asylum office. Headquarters officials stated the biweekly reports are manually compiled and may contain errors, but the biweekly reports have historically provided the overall number of personnel performing credible and reasonable fear work for any particular date or pay period. As of October 2019, headquarters officials said they are developing automated software that will track information similar to that collected in the biweekly reports, which will allow more systematic analysis of the staffing data that the current biweekly reports contain.

---

[55] Further, USCIS has historically assigned detailees from outside the Asylum Division to conduct credible fear screenings, including refugee officers and former asylum or refugee officers now working with USCIS's Field Office Directorate, Service Center Operations Directorate, and FDNS.

[56] These reports also include asylum and refugee officers who may be temporarily assigned to the asylum office (from other asylum offices or USCIS headquarters) to conduct credible and reasonable fear screenings, among other categories of work.

USCIS Monitors Credible and Reasonable Fear Processing Times to Help Manage Its Workload

USCIS sets and monitors timeliness goals for completing credible and reasonable fear cases.

Monitoring Timeliness Goals for Credible Fear Cases

USCIS monitors credible fear processing times by setting timeliness goals for completing credible fear cases and those goals have changed over time. USCIS regulation does not require that credible fear cases be completed in a specific time frame; however, Asylum Division headquarters officials said they have used timeliness goals to help monitor their credible fear workload. In addition, case delays may occur for credible fear cases (discussed further below). Specifically, from fiscal year 2009 through the first quarter of fiscal year 2018, USCIS used a 14-day goal to monitor credible fear case processing times.[57] In other words, USCIS monitored the extent to which officers completed credible fear cases within 14 calendar days of USCIS receiving referral documents from ICE and created an electronic file for the case in their case management system.[58] According to our analysis, USCIS completed at least 81 percent of credible fear cases in 14 or fewer days for each fiscal year from 2014 to 2017—the last full fiscal year under the 14-day goal (see Table 5).[59]

---

[57] According to Asylum Division headquarters officials, credible fear processing times are measured in calendar days and reasonable fear processing times are measured in court days. According to USCIS officials, court days are equivalent to business days.

[58] According to USCIS documents, the clock automatically starts for credible fear cases when USCIS receives a referral for individuals in expedited removal proceedings. ICE is responsible for referring any fear claims to USCIS for a fear screening after individuals enter detention. For nondetained individuals, the clock starts for credible fear cases when a USCIS asylum office conducts the interview for a fear screening.

[59] In calculating credible fear case processing times, we used the difference between beginning and end dates for credible fear cases. We considered the case processing time to begin when a credible fear case was referred to an asylum office. According to USCIS documents, the date an asylum office receives a referral automatically starts the clock for case processing. We considered the case processing time to end when a credible fear case either received a fear determination or an administrative closure. Specifically, for credible fear cases that received a fear determination, we used the date when an applicant was served a decision from USCIS. Administrative closures occur when the USCIS asylum officer conducting the screening closes the case without a determination for reasons such as death of the

Table 5. U.S. Citizenship and Immigration Services (USCIS) credible fear case processing times, fiscal years 2014 through 2017

Fiscal year	Total number and percentage of credible fear cases processed in 14 days or less	Total number and percentage of credible fear cases processed in over 14 days	Total number of credible fear cases
2014	43,310 (91)	4,435 (9)	47,745
2015	39,862 (83)	8,219 (17)	48,081
2016	74,415 (81)	17,168 (19)	91,583
2017	63,187 (81)	14,491 (19)	77,678
Total	220,774 (83)	44,313 (17)	265,087

Source: GAO analysis of USCIS data. | GAO-20-250.

Notes: For the purposes of our analysis of USCIS data, we calculated the number of days for credible fear case processing times in calendar days, which includes weekends and federal holidays. In calculating case processing times, we used the difference between beginning and end dates for credible fear cases. We considered the case processing time to begin when a credible fear case was referred to an asylum office. According to USCIS documents, the date an asylum office receives a referral automatically starts the clock for case processing. For nondetained individuals, the clock starts for credible fear cases when a USCIS asylum office conducts the interview for a fear screening. According to USCIS documents, a nondetained individual's interview date is used as the starting clock date. We used the starting clock date for detained and nondetained individuals provided by USCIS for our analysis. We considered the case processing time to end when a credible fear case either received a fear determination or an administrative closure. We included credible fear cases that either received a fear determination or an administrative closure for detained and nondetained individuals. Specifically, for credible fear cases that received a fear determination, we used the date when an individual was served a decision from USCIS. Administrative closures occur when the USCIS asylum officer conducting the screening closes the case without a determination for reasons such as death of the individual, inability of the individual to communicate, dissolved cases due to withdrawals of fear claims, or other reasons, according to officials. Additionally, the case processing clock automatically stops for cases that receive an administrative closure, according to USCIS documents.

In February 2018, USCIS lowered its credible fear processing time goal to 10 days.[60] USCIS completed 68 percent of credible fear cases in 10 or fewer days between February and September 2018.[61]

---

individual, inability of the individual to communicate, dissolved cases due to withdrawals of fear claims, or other reasons, according to officials. Additionally, the case processing clock automatically stops for cases that receive an administrative closure, according to USCIS documents.

60 USCIS reports data on credible fear processing time by fiscal year. The processing time goal listed on its public website changed in the second quarter of fiscal year 2018.

Monitoring Timeliness Requirements for Reasonable Fear Cases

USCIS monitors reasonable fear processing times by setting a 10-day goal. Pursuant to regulation, asylum officers are to conduct reasonable fear interviews and make a determination within 10 days of receiving a referral from CBP or ICE with an indication that the individual has made a fear claim, absent exceptional circumstances.[62] Additionally, a 2015 settlement agreement in the *Alfaro-Garcia v. Johnson* case ("Alfaro-Garcia" Settlement Agreement) requires USCIS to achieve an average national reasonable fear determination period of no more than 10 court days (i.e., business days), calculated on a monthly basis, for cases in which individuals are detained by DHS.[63] For reasonable fear cases subject to this settlement agreement that take longer than 20 court days to complete, asylum offices are to notify the Chief of the Asylum Division in writing and provide an explanation for the delay. Further, USCIS must provide class counsel in the Alfaro-Garcia case a notice and remedial plan of action for cases that exceed 20 days that are subject to that settlement agreement.

Consistent with USCIS policy and the Alfaro-Garcia settlement agreement,[64] officers may pause the clock for reasonable fear cases— and thus case processing times—in the following limited circumstances:

---

[61] We report on USCIS credible fear processing times in 10 or fewer days between February and September 2018 because USCIS started using the 10-day goal in February 2018. We ended our analysis in September 2018 to complete the remaining months in fiscal year 2018. Our analysis of USCIS data further showed that from fiscal year 2014 through March 2019, USCIS completed 89 percent of all credible fear cases in 20 or fewer calendar days.

[62] See 8 C.F.R. § 208.31(b).

[63] See Alfaro Garcia v. Johnson, No. 14-1775 (N.D. Cal. Oct. 27, 2015) (settlement agreement and release) (*Settlement Agreement*). An average of 10 court days is achieved, according to the agreement, if the average is less than 10.5 court days. Cases subject to this agreement may also be tolled for exceptional circumstances, consistent with 8 C.F.R. § 208.31(b). Exceptional circumstances do not include unusual but reasonably foreseeable circumstances, shall be determined on an individualized basis, and shall be of limited duration. The agreement applies to eligible individuals referred to as "class members" who: (1) are subject to a reinstated order of removal or administrative order of removal; (2) have expressed, or in the future expresses, a fear of returning to their country of removal; (3) are detained in the custody of DHS; and (4) have not received, or do not receive, an initial reasonable fear determination by USCIS under 8 C.F.R. § 208.31 within 10 days of referral to USCIS. The agreement specifies that reasonable fear processing times are calculated in court days. According to USCIS officials, court days are equivalent to business days.

[64] *Settlement Agreement* at 5, No. 14-1775 (N.D. Cal. Oct. 27, 2015). The settlement agreement refers to pausing the clock as "tolling" the reasonable fear determination period.

Table 6. U.S. Citizenship and Immigration Services (USCIS) reasonable fear case processing times for nondetained and detained cases without clock pauses, fiscal years 2014 through the first two quarters of fiscal year 2019

Fiscal year	Total number and percentage of reasonable fear cases processed in 10 days or less	Total number and percentage of reasonable fear cases processed in 1 1-20 days	Total number and percentage of reasonable fear cases processed over 20 days	Total number of reasonable fear cases
2014	2,119 (25)	975 (11)	5,508 (64)	8,602
2015	3,856 (50)	1,559 (20)	2,298 (30)	7,713
2016	6,912 (92)	579 (8)	33 (0.44)	7,524
2017	7,574 (95)	379 (5)	26 (0.33)	7,979
2018	7,991 (91)	741 (8)	4 (0.05)	8,736
2019 (first two quarters)	4,624 (92)	418 (8)	0 (0)	5,042
Total	33,076 (73)	4,651 (10)	7,869 (17)	45,596

Source: GAO analysis of USCIS data. | GAO-20-250.

Notes: A 2015 settlement agreement in the Alfaro Garcia v. Johnson case ("Alfaro-Garcia Settlement Agreement") requires USCIS to achieve an average national reasonable fear determination period of no more than 10 court days, calculated on a monthly basis, for reasonable fear cases in which individuals are detained by the Department of Homeland Security and to report these averages to class counsel. See Alfaro Garcia v. Johnson, No. 14-1775 (N.D. Cal. Oct. 27, 2015) (settlement agreement and release). For the purposes of our analysis of USCIS data of nondetained and detained reasonable fear cases, we calculated the number of days for reasonable fear case processing times in court days, where we excluded weekends and federal holidays. In calculating case processing times, we used the difference between beginning and end dates for reasonable fear cases. According to USCIS documents, the date an asylum office receives a proper referral starts the clock for case processing for detained reasonable fear cases. For nondetained individuals, the clock starts for reasonable fear cases when a USCIS asylum office conducts the interview for a reasonable fear screening. According to USCIS documents, a nondetained individual's interview date is used as the starting clock date. We used the starting clock date for detained and nondetained individuals provided by USCIS for our analysis. We considered the case processing time to end when a reasonable fear case had a determination that was served, or for a case that was administratively closed. We included reasonable fear cases that either received a fear determination or an administrative closure for both detained and nondetained individuals. Specifically, for reasonable fear cases that received a fear determination, we used the date when the individual was served a determination from DHS. Administrative closures occur when the USCIS asylum officer conducting the screening closes the case without a determination for reasons such as death of the individual, inability of the individual to communicate, dissolved cases due to withdrawals of fear claims, or other reasons, according to officials. Additionally, the case processing clock automatically stops when cases are administratively closed, according to USCIS procedures. We excluded approximately 13 percent of reasonable fear cases that had at least one pause in case processing time from our analysis. Percentages do not equal 100 percent due to rounding.

- the applicant or the applicant's representative requests to defer the reasonable fear interview;
- the applicant refuses to participate in the reasonable fear interview or accept service of a reasonable fear determination; or
- exceptional circumstances.

USCIS pauses processing times for detained reasonable fear cases by recording the dates when the case was paused and when processing resumed, once the basis for pausing the clock no longer exists. Asylum Division headquarters officials said pauses in reasonable fear case processing times are separate from case delay reasons, but case delays may occur for reasonable fear cases. In our case processing time analysis of USCIS data, we excluded approximately 13 percent of reasonable fear cases that had at least one pause in case processing time from our analysis because, in conducting our analysis, we could not systematically confirm the appropriate order of dates for those cases. As shown in Table 6, our review of USCIS data for cases that did not include pauses found that USCIS completed at least 91 percent of reasonable fear cases within 10 or fewer court days from fiscal year 2016 to the second quarter of fiscal year 2019.

USCIS Does Not Have Complete Data on Reasons for Case Delays

Although the Asylum Division monitors overall processing times for credible and reasonable fear cases, it does not collect comprehensive data in its case management system on some types of case delays. For example, USCIS tracks whether cases are delayed for certain reasons related to the individual—such as if he or she has a medical condition that prevents the asylum officer from conducting the interview, if the individual requests that the interview be rescheduled, or if the individual is detained in a remote location. In addition, USCIS's system can track if cases are delayed for logistical or resource constraints. Specifically, asylum officers may select “lack of resources” as one case delay reason in the system. However, this field in the system does not allow officers to distinguish more specific types of delays—such as a lack of space in detention facilities for officers to screen fear cases, telephones not working properly, and other types of delays—which officers told us occur on a regular basis.[65]

Asylum officers we interviewed in the Arlington and Houston offices stated that logistical delays could affect the number of credible or reasonable fear cases they can complete each day. Specifically, some asylum officers said they have experienced delays up to 30 minutes waiting for phone lines to work properly at detention facilities. Moreover, supervisors we interviewed in the Arlington office stated telephone and interpreter delays could add 20 or 30 minutes per case, resulting in a cumulative delay that could affect an officer’s productivity for any given day. Moreover, supervisors in the Arlington office said it is challenging to identify the appropriate number of cases to assign to officers because the number depends on whether or not disruptions occur. Asylum officers in Arlington said they are expected to conduct a certain number of credible or reasonable fear screenings per day, but expectations for completing their assigned cases may be tempered by circumstances such as interpreter availability or if there are issues at the detention facility, including physical space shortfalls or difficulty in locating the individual at the facility.[66] Similarly, asylum officers in Houston said they are expected to complete a certain number of credible or reasonable fear cases per day, but supervisors understand that they may face logistical challenges such as interpreter or telephone issues.

In addition to system limitations in tracking case delay reasons, Asylum Division headquarters officials said their case management system

---

[65] Asylum Division headquarters officials stated they completed the transition to a new data system in February 2018. While the prior system tracked similar case delays, headquarters officials said some case delay reasons that migrated from the prior system to the new system may no longer be relevant due to modernization efforts and the current environment of conducting credible and reasonable fear determinations.

[66] As part of its hiring plan for fiscal year 2019, USCIS also reported that it is seeking to ameliorate a physical space shortfall for approximately 159 of the new employees within its facilities. According to USCIS, the Asylum Division has identified certain solutions to address the space shortfall, including expanded telework for qualifying workloads and space sharing.

does not have the capability to track how long case delays may last. Our analysis of USCIS data from fiscal year 2014 through the second quarter of fiscal year 2019 indicates that 21,528 credible fear cases and 6,724 reasonable fear cases[67] had delays. USCIS's system can calculate the number of days for each credible and reasonable fear case—in other words, the total processing time for each case—and the system can produce daily reports noting these overall processing times. However, officials in the Houston office told us they must investigate individual cases on an ad hoc basis to understand how long cases have been delayed during processing. Specifically, officials in the Houston office said they maintain weekly "late reports" using information from USCIS's case management system that show pending credible and reasonable fear cases with the longest processing times and that they must spend time researching cases on the report to determine the length of the delays.

Standards for Internal Control in the Federal Government state that management should obtain data on a timely basis so that they can be used for effective monitoring.[68] These standards also state that management should process the obtained data into quality information that supports the internal control system. As previously discussed, USCIS's case management system does not track specific logistical reasons for any delays in credible and reasonable fear cases, which affect the number of cases an officer can complete in a day. Furthermore, USCIS's system can calculate the number of processing days for each credible and reasonable fear case. However, the system cannot track how long a case delay lasts. Headquarters officials said they evaluate the usefulness of their system, and consider options for improvements or changes, on an ongoing basis.

---

[67] This figure includes all reasonable fear cases with case delays, including those cases with clock pauses pursuant to the Alfaro-Garcia Settlement Agreement that we did not include in the data analysis presented in table 6. As previously mentioned, officers may pause the clock for detained reasonable fear cases in certain limited circumstances as outlined in the Alfaro-Garcia settlement agreement, including if the applicant requests to defer the interview, refuses to participate in the interview or accept service of the decisions, or if exceptional circumstances apply. See *Settlement Agreement* at 5, No.14-7775 (N.D. Cal. Oct.27, 2015). The clock may be paused only for these reasons, but, according to Asylum Division headquarters officials, case delays, which do not pause the clock, may also occur for other reasons, such as delays for logistical or resource constraints.

[68] GAO-14-704G.

However, as of October 2019, they stated they did not have plans for significant changes to the system to track more specific case delay reasons. Collecting additional information in its automated case management system on case delays would provide USCIS with more readily available information and analyzing such data could help USCIS identify case delay reasons relevant in the current environment for officers conducting fear screenings and better position USCIS to mitigate the reasons for the delays and improve efficiency in case processing.

EOIR Has Processes to Manage the Credible and Reasonable Fear Review Workload and Is Developing a Tool to Monitor Adherence to Required Review Processing Times

EOIR has developed processes for immigration courts and judges to help manage its workload related to credible and reasonable fear reviews. As previously discussed, in the event of a negative outcome of their credible or reasonable fear screening, noncitizens can request a review of USCIS's negative determination by an immigration judge. The Immigration and Nationality Act, as amended, and regulation require that such reviews occur within certain time frames. Specifically,

- immigration judge reviews of negative credible fear determinations are to be conducted no later than 7 days after referral from USCIS, to the maximum extent practicable,[69] and
- immigration judge reviews of negative reasonable fear determinations are to be conducted within 10 days of referral, in the absence of exceptional circumstances.[70]

EOIR officials told us that increased resources, beginning in fiscal year 2015, and a faster process for hiring immigration judges have allowed

[69] See 8 U.S.C. § 1225(b)(1)(B)(iii)(III).
[70] See 8 C.F.R. § 208.31(g).

EOIR to increase the number of immigration judges. As of September 30, 2019, EOIR reported that it had 442 immigration judges on board, including 173 judges hired in fiscal year 2018 and fiscal year 2019. EOIR reports that the number of immigration judges has increased each year from fiscal year 2015 through fiscal year 2019. EOIR officials told us that they plan to hire an additional 100 judges in fiscal year 2020.[71] Additionally, EOIR officials told us that they prioritize credible and reasonable fear reviews and that these reviews can generally be accommodated within EOIR's existing resources—specifically, by finding efficiencies within judges' existing schedules to add credible or reasonable fear review hearings or by conducting hearings via video teleconferencing (VTC).[72] EOIR officials also said that credible and reasonable fear reviews for individuals in ICE's family residential centers comprise a small portion of EOIR's overall workload.

According to EOIR officials, each ICE detention facility is assigned to the jurisdiction of an immigration court, and the workload for credible and reasonable fear reviews is managed locally by the court to which each detention facility is assigned. ICE officers are to initiate the immigration judge's review by filing a request with the appropriate immigration court.[73] Some courts are co-located with ICE detention facilities in which the detainee requesting the credible or reasonable fear review is housed. EOIR officials said that reviews in those locations are typically heard in person

---

[71] In 2017, we reported that EOIR did not have efficient practices for hiring new immigration judges, which contributed to immigration judges being staffed below authorized levels. We recommended that the Director of EOIR assess the immigration judge hiring process to identify opportunities for efficiency; use the assessment results to develop a hiring strategy to target short- and long-term human capital needs; and implement any corrective actions related to the hiring process resulting from this assessment, among other things. In response, EOIR stated that it assessed the immigration judge hiring process and had actions under way to implement a hiring streamlining plan. As of November 2019, we are continuing to monitor EOIR's actions in response to our recommendation. See GAO, *Immigration Courts: Actions Needed to Reduce Case Backlog and Address Long-Standing Management and Operational Challenges*, GAO-17-438 (Washington, D.C.: June 1, 2017).

[72] EOIR officials estimated that judges spend about 30 to 45 minutes on each credible or reasonable fear review and that court staff require about 25 to 30 minutes to complete the paperwork associated with each review.

[73] Immigration judges are to receive the following documentation, among other things: the record of the USCIS negative credible fear determination, including the asylum officer's notes, as well as other materials upon which the determination was made. See 8 C.F.R. §§ 1208.30-1208.31.

by immigration judges assigned to that facility, and that the court finds room in the judge's regular calendar to hear credible and reasonable fear reviews.[74] For individuals in detention facilities without a co-located immigration court, including ICE family residential centers, immigration judges typically conduct credible and reasonable fear reviews via VTC.[75] Judges conducting credible or reasonable fear reviews via VTC may be located in any immigration court in the United States.[76] According to EOIR officials, the Assistant Chief Immigration Judge for each court is responsible for managing the court's workload, including seeking support from judges outside the court in circumstances where there are too many cases for the court's assigned judges. EOIR officials told us that the use of VTC technology—which is available in all courtrooms—provides flexibility to the courts in balancing workloads related to credible and reasonable fear reviews, among other workloads.

In addition, EOIR officials stated that judges' credible and reasonable fear workload is impacted, in particular, by immigration enforcement priorities and USCIS credible or reasonable fear determinations. For example, if DHS places more noncitizens into expedited removal proceedings who subsequently express fear or intent to apply for asylum, EOIR's related workload might increase. In addition, because immigration judges do not review USCIS's positive credible fear determinations, if USCIS's screenings result in more negative determinations, EOIR's caseload related to credible or reasonable fear reviews might increase.

As of January 2018, EOIR has performance measures that include timeliness goals for credible and reasonable fear reviews, and these

---

[74] EOIR officials said that for courts co-located with ICE detention facilities, DHS owns and manages all of the space in which the courts are located, including the courtrooms and any telephone or broadband infrastructure that EOIR uses.

[75] In locations other than ICE detention facilities, the judge conducts the credible or reasonable fear review from their regular courtroom via VTC connected to a hearing room in the ICE detention facility. Officials said that limited bandwidth or internet connection may limit the number of credible or reasonable fear reviews that can occur simultaneously, particularly for ICE detention facilities in rural locations.

[76] In recent years, EOIR has opened two courts that exclusively conduct proceedings via VTC. EOIR officials said that these courts provide capacity for surges in workload and coverage for judges on leave. These courts are located in Fort Worth, Texas (capacity for about 15 judges), and in Falls Church, Virginia (five judges).

timeliness goals align with the required credible and reasonable fear review time frames. However, EOIR data we reviewed indicate that about 30 percent of credible and reasonable fear reviews are not completed within the required time frames. Specifically, EOIR's memorandum on *Case Priorities and Immigration Court Performance Measures* states that 100 percent of credible fear reviews should be completed within seven days of an asylum officer's negative determination and that 100 percent of reasonable fear reviews should be completed within 10 days of the filing of a negative reasonable fear determination.[77] Further, according to EOIR officials, courts are to assign credible and reasonable fear reviews to a judge within 48 hours of receipt of the request from ICE, and immigration judges are to complete such reviews within 24 hours after they are assigned.

EOIR officials said their automated case management system maintains data on the date when courts receive a request from ICE for an immigration judge review, the date the review is assigned to a judge, and the date the review takes place.[78] EOIR headquarters officials told us that they monitor the extent to which judges are completing reviews within 24 hours after they are assigned using an automated immigration judge performance dashboard, which allows officials to review this performance measure for all judges combined, for individual courts, or for individual judges. Further, EOIR officials told us that if courts are scheduling credible and reasonable fear reviews within 48 hours after receipt and judges are completing reviews within 24 hours after they are assigned, they expect that EOIR should be meeting the required time frames (7 days after ICE's referral for credible fear reviews and 10 days after ICE's referral for reasonable fear review) for conducting credible and reasonable fear reviews.

---

[77] Department of Justice, Executive Office for Immigration Review, Office of the Director, *Case Priorities and Immigration Court Performance Measures*, Memorandum to The Office of the Chief Immigration Judge, All Immigration Judges, All Court Administrators, and All Immigration Court Staff (January 17, 2018).

[78] According to EOIR officials, the system also tracks some reasons for delays immigration judges may experience when completing reviews, such as incomplete DHS paperwork, an applicant under medical quarantine, and others.

EOIR data we reviewed indicate that, from fiscal year 2014 through June 2019, approximately 28 percent of credible fear and 36 percent of reasonable fear reviews exceeded the required time frames, as shown in Table 7 below.

As previously discussed, the Immigration and Nationality Act and regulation allow for some flexibility with regard to the required credible and reasonable fear review time frames. Specifically, credible fear reviews are to be completed within 7 days, to the maximum extent practicable, and reasonable fear reviews are to be completed within 10 days, absent exceptional circumstances. EOIR officials we spoke with said there are a variety of court, judge, or applicant-related reasons that reviews could exceed the required time frames. For example, case file documentation sent from USCIS to the court may be incomplete. Further, a detention facility may have a medical quarantine that restricts court proceedings for a certain period of time.

Table 7. Executive Office for Immigration Review (EOIR) credible and reasonable fear review time frames, fiscal years 2014 through third quarter 2019

Fiscal year	Credible fear reviews			Reasonable fear reviews		
	0-7 Days	More than 7 days	Percent More than 7 days	0-10 days	More than 10 days	Percent More than 10 days
2014	4,889	1,411	22	1,031	681	40
2015	5,000	1,618	24	1,516	1,052	41
2016	5,664	1,800	24	1,672	869	34
2017	4,150	2,347	36	1,568	877	36
2018	4,449	2,188	33	1,769	1,001	36
2019[a]	4,986	1,895	28	1,680	688	29
Total	29,138	11,259	28	9,236	5,168	36

Source: EOIR data. | GAO-20-250.

[a]Data include credible and reasonable fear reviews through the third quarter of fiscal year 2019.

EOIR headquarters officials told us that, as of October 2019, they review weekly reports that include the median processing times for completed credible and reasonable fear reviews. For example, according to one weekly report from October 2019, the median completion time for credible fear reviews was 7 days.[79] These reports also include information about the average and median number of days pending per case, for those credible and reasonable fear reviews that are not complete. For example, the weekly report we reviewed from October 2019 showed that EOIR had 553 pending credible fear reviews that week, with a median of 7 days pending and an average of 18 days pending. While these weekly reports allow EOIR headquarters officials to monitor some information about their credible and reasonable fear workload, they do not provide information to EOIR officials about the proportion of EOIR's credible and reasonable fear reviews that are completed within the required time frames, or whether any reviews are delayed for reasons within the limits set out in the law or regulation.

EOIR officials said they plan to implement an automated court operations dashboard in early 2020 which is to, among other things, monitor court performance against the performance goals EOIR established in January 2018, including the credible and reasonable fear performance goals. This automated dashboard is to be similar to the immigration judge performance dashboard, which EOIR implemented in early 2019. According to EOIR, the court operations dashboard is intended to operationalize EOIR's performance measures—including completion of 100 percent of credible fear reviews with 7 days and 100 percent of reasonable fear reviews within 10 days—by providing court staff with daily alerts and warning notices to help court administrators prioritize the scheduling of cases based on the performance measures. This prioritization, combined with EOIR's monitoring of judge performance to ensure that credible and reasonable fear reviews are completed within 24 hours after they are scheduled, should provide EOIR officials with sufficient information to monitor EOIR's adherence to the required credible and reasonable fear review time frames. Because implementation of the court operations dashboard is planned for early 2020, it is too soon to know if EOIR will use the dashboard to monitor adherence to the required credible and reasonable fear review time frames or if it will help

[79] This chapter showed the median processing time for credible fear reviews completed from October 1 through October 25, 2019, according to EOIR officials.

EOIR understand reasons for delays in those cases that take longer than 7 or 10 days.

CONCLUSION

The number of credible and reasonable fear cases has increased since fiscal year 2014, and USCIS policies and procedures require completion of those cases within short time frames. The Asylum Division provides training for credible and reasonable fear cases to new asylum officers in basic training, given the differences between these screenings and affirmative asylum adjudications. However, not all offices provide additional training on screening such cases at the family residential centers. Ensuring that all asylum offices provide such training, in addition to basic training for new officers, would better prepare them to screen those cases efficiently and effectively. In addition, USCIS relies on its periodic quality assurance reviews to assess the quality of credible and reasonable fear cases across asylum offices. Developing and implementing more specific guidance on requirements for documenting the results of its periodic quality assurance reviews would better position the agency to track trends for credible and reasonable fear reviews across asylum offices. USCIS data show that positive credible fear determination rates are higher at the family residential centers than they are nationwide, in part because USCIS's automated case management system does not track whether an individual receives a credible fear determination as a principal applicant, dependent, or in the interest of family unity. Without systematically recording credible fear determinations involving family members, USCIS may not have complete data on credible fear determination rates, and the agency may not be in a position to report on the scope of its policy for family members in the credible fear process.

Asylum officers have experienced logistical delays that can affect the number of credible and reasonable fear cases they complete each day. Although USCIS tracks some of these delays in its case management system, the system does not distinguish between specific reasons for logistical case delays, such as telephones nor working properly or lack of space at detention facilities for officers to screen cases. Furthermore, USCIS's system can calculate the number of processing days for each credible and reasonable fear case. However, the system cannot track how long case delays last. By collecting and analyzing additional information on case delays, including specific reasons for delays and how long they last, USCIS can identify relevant case delays for officers conducting fear screenings. Moreover, analyzing specific case delay information could help USCIS mitigate reasons for case delays and improve efficiency in case processing.

RECOMMENDATIONS FOR EXECUTIVE ACTION

We are making the following four recommendations to USCIS:

The Director of USCIS should ensure that, in addition to USCIS's basic asylum officer training, all asylum offices provide pre-departure training on the credible and reasonable fear processes before their officers begin screening cases at the family residential centers. (Recommendation 1)

The Director of USCIS should develop and implement more specific guidance on requirements for documenting results of Asylum Division periodic quality assurance reviews. (Recommendation 2)

The Director of USCIS should ensure asylum officers systematically record in USCIS's automated case management system if individuals receive credible fear determinations as principal applicants, dependents, or in the interest of family unity, pursuant to regulation or USCIS policy. (Recommendation 3)

The Director of USCIS should collect and analyze additional information on case delays, including specific reasons for delays and how long they last, that asylum officers may face when screening credible and reasonable fear cases. (Recommendation 4)

Agency Comments

We provided a draft of this chapter to DHS and DOJ for review and comment. DHS provided formal, written comments, which are reproduced in full in appendix IV. DHS also provided technical comments, which we incorporated as appropriate. DOJ told us they had no comments on the draft report. DHS concurred with our recommendations and described actions planned or underway to address them. For example, regarding our recommendation that all USCIS asylum offices provide officers with pre-departure training on credible and reasonable fear before they officers begin screening cases at family residential centers, DHS stated that USCIS plans to develop a standardized pre-departure training and provide this training to all asylum officers prior to their deployment to the family residential centers. In addition, regarding our recommendation that USCIS ensure that asylum officers record in their automated case management system if individuals receive credible fear determinations as principal applicants, dependents, or in the interest of family unity, DHS noted USCIS will explore ways to modify its case management system to ensure that asylum officers record such data and train officers on any subsequent system changes.

We are sending copies of this chapter to the appropriate congressional committees, the Acting Secretary of Homeland Security, the Attorney General, and other interested parties.

Rebecca S. Gambler
Director, Homeland Security and Justice

List of Addressees

The Honorable Ron Johnson
Chairman
Committee on Homeland Security and Governmental Affairs
United States Senate

The Honorable Shelley M. Capito
Chairman

The Honorable Jon Tester
Ranking Member
Subcommittee on Homeland Security
Committee on Appropriations
United States Senate

The Honorable Bennie G. Thompson
Chairman
Committee on Homeland Security
House of Representatives

The Honorable Lucille Roybal-Allard
Chairwoman

The Honorable Chuck Fleischmann
Ranking Member
Subcommittee on Homeland Security
Committee on Appropriations
House of Representatives

The Honorable Zoe Lofgren
Chairwoman
Subcommittee on Immigration and Citizenship
Committee on the Judiciary
House of Representatives

Appendix I: Objectives, Scope, and Methodology

We were asked to review processes for screening noncitizens[80] who arrive at the southwest border expressing an intention to apply for asylum, a fear of persecution or torture, or a fear of return to their country, and the resources needed to carry out these screenings within applicable time frames[81] by the Department of Homeland Security's (DHS) U.S. Citizenship and Immigration Services (USCIS) and Department of Justice's (DOJ) Executive Office for Immigration Review (EOIR). This chapter discusses (1) what USCIS and EOIR data show about the credible fear and reasonable fear processes, (2) the extent to which USCIS has policies and procedures for overseeing credible fear and reasonable fear screenings, and (3) the extent to which USCIS and EOIR have processes for managing their respective credible fear and reasonable fear-related workloads.

To address all three objectives, we interviewed USCIS headquarters personnel from the Refugee, Asylum, and International Operations Directorate (RAIO) and RAIO's Asylum Division who are responsible for managing USCIS's credible and reasonable fear screening processes. We also interviewed officials from USCIS's Fraud Detection and National Security Directorate (FDNS), which is responsible for leading USCIS's efforts to detect and deter immigration benefit fraud and help detect national security and public safety threats. We conducted site visits at two of USCIS's eight asylum offices—Houston, Texas and Arlington, Virginia—in April 2019.[82] We selected these asylum offices based on the relatively large size of their credible and reasonable fear caseloads in fiscal year 2018—the most recent, complete data available at the time of our review. During these visits, we conducted in-person, semi-structured

---

[80] The Immigration and Nationality Act defines the term "alien" as "any person not a citizen or national of the United States." 8 U.S.C. § 1101(a)(3). For the purposes of this chapter, we use the term "noncitizen" to refer to individuals who would meet the definition of "alien."

[81] See Pub. L. No. 116-26, tit. V, § 506, 133 Stat. 1018, 1027 (2019).

[82] The Arlington asylum office and the Arlington Pre-Screening Center are collocated. The Arlington Pre-Screening Center provides additional support for the credible and reasonable fear caseloads.

interviews with asylum officers, supervisory asylum officers, training officers, FDNS immigration officers, and asylum office management. During these interviews, we discussed topics related to data quality, supervisory review, training, quality assurance, family processing, and resource allocation. While the views expressed in these interviews do not represent those of all Houston and Arlington asylum office officials, they provide valuable insights from stakeholders who have experience with credible and reasonable fear policies and procedures. In addition, we collected written responses from the remaining six asylum offices on the same topics.

Further, we conducted site visits to U.S. Immigration and Customs Enforcement (ICE) adult detention centers and family residential centers. Specifically, we visited single adult detention facilities in San Diego, California (September 2018), and Port Isabel and Pearsall, Texas (October 2018 and February 2019, respectively). We selected these ICE single adult facilities based on their geographic proximity to various CBP field locations we visited (discussed below). In addition, in February 2019, we visited ICE's Enforcement and Removal Operations field office in San Antonio, Texas, as well as ICE's South Texas Family Residential Center in Dilley, Texas, and Karnes County Residential Center in Karnes, Texas. We selected these two ICE family residential centers for field visits because they accounted for more credible and reasonable fear referrals to USCIS than any other single adult detention facility or family residential center. We also selected them to examine unique aspects of ICE and USCIS processing of credible and reasonable fear claims made by members of family units.

During these visits to USCIS asylum offices and ICE detention facilities, we observed USCIS asylum officers conducting credible or reasonable fear screenings of single adults and family unit members either in person or via telephone. In total, we observed more than 20 credible and reasonable fear interviews across our site visits. Our observations are not generalizable to all USCIS asylum offices conducting credible and reasonable fear screenings, but provided us the opportunity to learn more about how USCIS personnel conduct interviews, make fear determinations, process these cases, and coordinate with ICE officials.

For additional context about how noncitizens are apprehended at the border, processed into expedited or full immigration removal proceedings, transferred to ICE, and ultimately referred to USCIS for credible and reasonable fear screenings, as appropriate, we interviewed headquarters personnel from DHS's U.S. Customs and Border Protection's (CBP) Office of Field Operations (OFO) and U.S. Border Patrol (Border Patrol) who are responsible for apprehending noncitizens at or between U.S. ports of entry. In addition, we conducted site visits at CBP facilities in California and Texas from September 2018 to October 2018. In California, we visited Border Patrol's San Diego sector headquarters and Imperial Beach station, and OFO's San Ysidro port of entry. In Texas, we visited CBP's Central Processing Center and McAllen Border Patrol station in McAllen, Texas; Border Patrol's Fort Brown, Weslaco, and Harlingen stations; and OFO's Hidalgo and Brownsville ports of entry. During these visits, we interviewed Border Patrol and OFO officials and observed how CBP personnel processed apprehended individuals and, as appropriate, documented whether those individuals expressed an intention to apply for asylum, a fear of persecution or torture, or a fear of return to their country. To select these locations, we assessed CBP data on Border Patrol and OFO apprehensions along the southwest border and targeted specific locations that saw the greatest increase in the number of apprehensions of individuals from fiscal year 2016 to 2017. As noted previously, we also considered the geographical proximity of multiple CBP and ICE facilities to maximize observations. Our observations during site visits are not generalizable to all Border Patrol and OFO operations along the southwest border, but provided us the opportunity to learn more about policies and procedures for processing noncitizens into removal proceedings and documenting any fear claims.

To address the first objective, we obtained and analyzed data and documentation from USCIS and EOIR. Regarding USCIS, we analyzed record-level data from USCIS's automated case management system from fiscal year 2014 through the second quarter of fiscal year 2019 (March

2019)—the most recent time period for which complete data were available at the time of our review.[83] We analyzed these data to identify the number, characteristics, and outcomes of credible and reasonable fear cases. According to USCIS officials, USCIS's system creates a unique number, or "case ID" for each case.[84] USCIS officials told us that a previous system used a different identifier for each case—the individual's Alien number (or "A-number") —and did not use a "case ID" field. USCIS transitioned from its previous system to its current system in February 2018 and, according to USCIS officials, cases originally opened prior to the transition to the new system may have been re-opened under the same "case ID" number in the new system. As part of our data reliability testing, we checked for unique "case ID" numbers by searching for duplicate values and determined the data did not have duplicate values for "case ID" numbers. For our analysis of USCIS data specifically for ICE detention facilities and family residential centers, we only included credible and reasonable fear cases for detained individuals. To assess the reliability of USCIS data, we completed a number of steps, including (1) performing electronic testing for obvious errors in accuracy and completeness, such as running logic tests; (2) reviewing existing information about the data and the systems that produced them, such as relevant training materials for USCIS officers who use the system; and (3) discussing data entry issues and data limitations with USCIS officials. We determined the data were sufficiently reliable to describe the number, outcomes, and characteristics of credible and reasonable fear cases.

Regarding EOIR, we reviewed data on immigration judge reviews of credible and reasonable fear cases posted on its public website. Specifically, we reviewed EOIR data on credible and reasonable fear reviews from fiscal year 2014 through June 2019—the most recent, complete data available at the time of our review. We also obtained and analyzed summary data from EOIR on credible and reasonable fear

---

[83] We used "cases" rather than "individuals" as the unit of analysis for the USCIS data we reported because an individual may have been screened for fear by USCIS multiple times during the time period covered by our data.

[84] According to USCIS officials, the "case ID" field is not a number used during the adjudication process, nor is the "case ID" reflected in an individual's file.

reviews for those individuals detained in ICE's family residential centers. We analyzed the data to determine the outcomes of all credible and reasonable fear reviews and compared the outcomes of all reviews with the outcomes of reviews at ICE's family residential centers. Finally, we reviewed EOIR data on the outcomes in immigration court for those completed removal cases that began with a positive credible or reasonable fear determination. In addition, we interviewed immigration judges and other court personnel serving both detained and nondetained dockets from EOIR's Otay Mesa Immigration Court and San Diego Immigration Court in California, and from EOIR's Harlingen Immigration Court in Texas. We also observed two immigration judge reviews of negative credible fear determinations. Our observations are not generalizable to all immigration judge reviews, but provided us the opportunity to learn more about EOIR's processes.

We interviewed EOIR officials about their data entry and management practices for credible and reasonable fear reviews. We determined that the data EOIR provided, much of which they report publicly on their website, are sufficiently reliable for analyzing the number and duration of credible and reasonable fear reviews that are received, completed, and pending.

To provide additional context on the numbers, characteristics, and outcomes of CBP apprehensions, we obtained and analyzed record-level data on all apprehensions by Border Patrol and OFO from fiscal year 2014 through the second quarter of fiscal year 2019. We also obtained and analyzed record-level data on ICE detentions from fiscal year 2014 through fiscal year 2018 (see app. III for the results of our analyses). To assess the reliability of Border Patrol, OFO, and ICE data, we completed a number of data reliability steps, including (1) performing electronic testing for obvious errors in accuracy and completeness, such as running logic tests; (2) reviewing existing information about the data and systems that produced them, such as relevant training materials for Border Patrol agents and OFO, and ICE officers who use agency data systems; and (3) discussing data entry issues and data limitations with Border Patrol, OFO, and ICE officials. We also received demonstrations on the data systems from Border Patrol, OFO, and ICE officials at headquarters and in the field. As described below, we determined that the data are sufficiently reliable for providing information on the numbers, characteristics, and outcomes of CBP apprehensions and ICE detentions.

Border Patrol Data

For our analysis of Border Patrol data, we used "apprehensions" as our unit of analysis, instead of the number of individuals apprehended, because an individual may have been apprehended multiple times in the same year.[85] We identified a small number of Border Patrol apprehension records that had the same date of apprehension and unique identifier ("A-number"). It is possible that these apprehension records represented one apprehended individual that Border Patrol agents processed as two apprehensions. These records comprised less than one percent of the more than 2.3 million apprehension records we analyzed. We included these apprehension records in our analysis because Border Patrol considers them unique apprehensions and because their small number did not materially affect our analysis.

In addition, Border Patrol did not systematically track family relationships in its data systems until fiscal year 2016, as we have previously reported.[86] Therefore, our analysis of Border Patrol apprehensions of family unit members processed under expedited removal proceedings is for fiscal years 2016 through the first two quarters of 2019.[87]

Further, according to Border Patrol officials, Border Patrol did not record reasonable fear cases in its automated data system before April 2016. Therefore, we are reporting the number of reasonable fear cases

---

[85] For our analysis, we only included apprehensions for deportable noncitizens as opposed to any U.S. citizens or other non-deportable individuals apprehended by the Border Patrol.

[86] GAO, *Unaccompanied Children: Agency Efforts to Reunify Children Separated from Parents at the Border*, GAO-19-163 (Washington, D.C.: Oct. 9, 2018).

[87] Consistent with CBP's October 2015 *National Standards on Transport, Escort, Detention, and Search*, for the purposes of this chapter, we define a "family unit" as a group of apprehended individuals that includes one or more non-U.S. citizen juvenile(s) accompanied by their parent(s) or legal guardian(s).

recorded by the Border Patrol in its automated system from fiscal year 2017 (the first full year for which Border Patrol recorded this information in its system) through the second quarter of fiscal year 2019. We did not include the 860 reasonable fear cases that Border Patrol recorded in its automated system for fiscal year 2016, since this number represents only partial -year data. According to Border Patrol officials, prior to April 2016, these reasonable fear cases would likely have been recorded under other case dispositions in their automated system, such as one indicating the reinstatement of a prior removal order.

We determined that Border Patrol data are sufficiently reliable to describe the numbers and demographic characteristics of individuals and family unit members apprehended from fiscal year 2014 through the second quarter of fiscal year 2019.

OFO Data

For our analysis of OFO data, we used "apprehensions" as our unit of analysis, instead of the number of individuals apprehended.

We excluded approximately 13 percent of all apprehension records (including single adults, unaccompanied alien children, and parents and children that arrived as part of a family unit) from our analyses because we could not confirm an A-number for those apprehensions. Among the apprehension records missing an A-number, 44 percent were cases in which OFO officers paroled the individuals and, according to OFO officials, officers are not required to assign an A-number to these individuals.[88] In addition, 47 percent of the records with a missing A-number were cases that involved the individual withdrawing their application for admission into the United States, in which OFO officers have discretion whether to assign an A-number.[89] According to OFO

---

[88] Parole generally refers to permitting an individual to enter the United States for a limited purpose, such as to be placed in removal proceedings or to allow the individual to apply for asylum.

[89] OFO officials stated that officers have discretion as to whether or not they assign an A-number for those individuals who have withdrawn their application for admission into the United

officials, additional records with missing A-numbers may be due to data entry errors or problems with the data system saving this information in the database that OFO used to pull the data. Finally, we collapsed 182,266 apprehension records into 86,597 apprehension records because we determined that they were duplicate records for the same individual and the same apprehension, based on factors such as alien number, birth date, and date and time of apprehension.

As a result, we determined that we could not present precise figures for analyses that include OFO data and instead provided approximations throughout the report. We rounded all data and figures on OFO apprehensions down to the hundreds place and described relevant data using modifiers such as "at least" because of possible missing information.

In addition, according to OFO officials, OFO does not capture information in its automated data system on individuals who were processed under expedited removal with a reasonable fear claim. OFO officials stated that, since OFO has historically processed a relatively small number of such apprehensions, it does not collect automated data on reasonable fear claims.

With the previously-described modifications, we determined that OFO data are sufficiently reliable to generally describe the numbers and demographic characteristics of individuals and family unit members apprehended from fiscal year 2014 through the second quarter of fiscal year 2019.

ICE Data

To report on ICE detentions of adults and family unit members, we obtained and analyzed ICE detention data from fiscal years 2014 to 2018, the most current data available at the time of our review.[90] The ICE data

---

States so that the apprehension event does not affect the individual's future applications for admission to the United States.

[90] The data for all fiscal years is current as of May 2019 and includes unique individuals detained by ICE for each fiscal year.

we obtained contained information on whether adults and family members booked-in to an ICE detention facility had a fear claim recorded in ICE's data system as of the date our data were pulled.[91] Specifically, we divided our analysis of ICE detention data into two parts. First, we obtained data on all individuals (all adults and children without consideration of any family relationships) detained from fiscal year 2014 through fiscal year 2018. Second, we obtained data specifically on family unit members apprehended by CBP and housed at the four ICE family residential centers from fiscal year 2014 through fiscal year 2018.[92]

Regarding our analysis of family unit members who made a fear claim in one of ICE's family residential centers, we excluded less than one percent of all detention records from our analyses because we could not confirm a unique identifier for the individual. In addition, for individual family unit members who were detained more than once in a fiscal year, we included the most recent record for the individuals in our analyses to report on the most recent information available about each individual. This accounted for less than one percent of all detention records in our time period of analysis.

We determined that the data were sufficiently reliable to describe the numbers of individuals (adults and family unit members) who were apprehended by CBP and recorded by ICE as having made a credible fear claim.

To address our second objective, in addition to our aforementioned interviews and site visits, we reviewed relevant laws and regulations governing the credible and reasonable fear screening process. We collected and analyzed documentation on key USCIS oversight mechanisms related

---

91 According to ICE officials, fear claims in ICE's data system are identified by the "case category" recorded for each individual. The officials explained that these case categories may be updated as the person moves through the immigration process. Therefore, our data reflect the fear claim status for each individual as of May 2019—the date our data were pulled by ICE.

92 For family unit members, we analyzed detention records for individuals apprehended by CBP and housed in one of ICE's four family residential centers. During the time period covered by our data, ICE detained families at four family residential centers for varying periods between fiscal year 2014 and fiscal year 2019. These family residential centers included Artesia Family Residential Center, Berks Family Residential Center, Karnes Family Residential Center, and the South Texas Family Residential Center.

to credible and reasonable fear screenings— supervisory review, asylum officer training, and quality assurance reviews. In particular, we reviewed the *Credible Fear Procedures Manual, and the Reasonable Fear Procedures Manual,* standard operating procedures, training and quality assurance records and materials, and guidance on conducting credible and reasonable fear screenings for families in ICE detention.

Specifically, we reviewed USCIS asylum officer basic training materials from RAIO and the Asylum Division, and training materials for officers from outside the Asylum Division who screen credible and reasonable fear cases. In particular, we reviewed USCIS Asylum Division quarterly training reports for fiscal year 2018 and used them to analyze the weekly training activities in each asylum office for each week of the reporting quarter. We compared RAIO and Asylum Division training materials with federal internal control standards related to developing competent individuals qualified to carry out assigned responsibilities.[93] We also reviewed documents associated with the quality assurance reviews that the Asylum Division conducted, including those reviews conducted in collaboration with RAIO. Specifically, we reviewed standard operating procedures, reviewer checklists, and resulting reports and analysis for three RAIO nationwide reviews of credible and reasonable fear cases and for the six periodic reviews of credible and reasonable fear cases the Asylum Division conducted at asylum offices and at the family residential centers between November 2017 and May 2018. We compared these policy documents and their role in providing oversight of the credible and reasonable fear process against federal internal control standards related to ongoing monitoring activities and evaluation of results. We also reviewed USCIS standard operating procedures, requirements, and training materials for processing family members, and corresponding data on applicant family relationships. We then compared the procedures, requirements and data against federal internal control standards related to obtaining high quality data.[94]

---

[93] GAO, *Standards for Internal Control in the Federal Government*, GAO-14-704G (Washington, D.C.: September 2014).

[94] GAO-14-704G.

To address our third objective, we reviewed USCIS and EOIR documents and data, and interviewed relevant officials to evaluate the extent to which USCIS and EOIR have process for managing their respective credible and reasonable fear-related workloads.

USCIS

In particular, we reviewed USCIS documentation and spoke with officials from Asylum Division headquarters and local asylum offices regarding the Asylum Division's staffing allocation model for the credible and reasonable fear workload. In addition, we obtained and analyzed record-level data from USCIS's automated case management system to identify processing times and case delays for credible and reasonable fear cases between fiscal year 2014 through the second quarter of fiscal year 2019 (March 2019). We included cases that had a fear determination that was served or an administrative closure for both detained and nondetained individuals.

In this chapter, we present information on both credible and reasonable fear case receipts and analysis of processing times for the cases using the "clock-in" date recorded in USCIS's automated case management system. However, while USCIS relies on the "clock -in" date to track case processing times, according to an Asylum Division official USCIS tracks and reports the number of credible and reasonable fear case receipts based on the date cases are input into, or "created" in, its automated system. According to the official, these "created" and "clock-in" dates are often the same, but can differ slightly.[95] Therefore, the number of case receipts tracked and reported by USCIS may differ slightly from those presented in this chapter.

[95] According to the Asylum Division official, USCIS uses the automated system's "clock-in" date to denote the date on which ICE refers the case to USCIS and when case processing begins, thus establishing USCIS jurisdiction over the case. However, the official added that the date USCIS establishes jurisdiction over the credible or reasonable fear referral (and is reflected by the system's "clock-in" date) may differ slightly from the date the case is data-entered and "created" in the case management system.

Regarding credible fear cases, we determined case processing times by calculating the difference between the beginning and end dates for credible fear cases. We considered credible fear case processing times for detained individuals to begin on the day when USCIS receives referral documents and records a "clock-in" date in the automated case management system, as noted previously.[96] For nondetained individuals, the clock starts for credible fear cases when a USCIS asylum office conducts the interview for a credible fear screening.[97] We used the starting clock date for detained and nondetained individuals provided by USCIS for our analysis. We considered credible fear case processing times to end on the day when cases either had a fear determination that was served or an administrative closure.[98] We included credible fear cases that had a fear determination that was served or an administrative closure for detained and nondetained individuals.[99] We also reviewed USCIS's publicly-reported data on credible fear processing times during this time period.

Regarding reasonable fear cases, we used USCIS data to count the number of processing days and percent of cases completed in certain time intervals. We determined reasonable fear processing times by calculating the difference between the beginning and end dates for reasonable fear cases. We considered reasonable fear case processing times for detained individuals to begin on the day when USCIS receives referral documents and records a "clock-in" date in the automated case management system, as noted previously. For nondetained individuals, the clock starts for reasonable fear cases when a USCIS asylum office conducts the interview

---

[96] According to USCIS documents, the clock automatically starts for credible fear cases when USCIS receives a referral for individuals in expedited removal proceedings. ICE is responsible for referring any fear claims to USCIS for a fear screening after individuals enter detention. For nondetained individuals, the clock starts for credible fear cases when a USCIS asylum office conducts the interview for a fear screening.

[97] According to USCIS documents, a nondetained individual's interview date is used as the starting clock date.

[98] We identified 1,187 credible fear cases that received both a fear determination and administrative closure. For calculating processing times for those credible fear cases, we selected the earlier of the two dates.

[99] We identified 57 credible fear cases for individuals with unknown detention status and included these cases in our analyses.

for a reasonable fear screening.[100] We used the starting clock date for detained and nondetained individuals provided by USCIS for our analysis. We calculated reasonable fear processing times in court days by excluding weekends and federal holidays.[101] USCIS may also pause the clock when processing reasonable fear cases in certain circumstances.[102] We excluded approximately 13 percent of reasonable fear cases that had at least one pause in case processing time from our analysis because in conducting our analysis we could not systematically confirm the appropriate order of dates for those cases.[103] We considered reasonable fear case processing times to end on the day when cases either had a fear determination that was served or administrative closure.[104] We also included reasonable fear cases that were served a fear determination or received an administrative closure for detained and nondetained individuals.[105]

To identify the reasons for delays in credible and reasonable fear cases during the time period of our analysis, we identified the fields that USCIS's case management system tracks for case delays related to the credible and reasonable fear workload. In addition, we reviewed USCIS's manuals and documentation on its case management system. We compared USCIS's recording and tracking of data on case delays to federal internal control standards related to obtaining data on a timely basis for

---

100 According to USCIS documents, the clock automatically starts for detained reasonable fear cases when USCIS receives a referral for individuals in expedited removal proceedings. ICE is responsible for referring any fear claims to USCIS for a fear screening after individuals enter detention. According to USCIS documents, a nondetained individual's interview date is used as the starting clock date.

101 According to the Alfaro-Garcia settlement agreement, reasonable fear processing times are measured in court days. See Alfaro Garcia v. Johnson, No. 14-1775 (N.D. Cal. Oct. 27, 2015) (settlement agreement and release). According to USCIS officials, court days are equivalent to business days.

102 USCIS policy states that officers may pause reasonable fear cases in limited circumstances, such as if the applicant or the applicant's representative requests to defer the interview, the applicant refuses to participate in the interview or accept service of a fear determination, or in exceptional circumstances.

103 The 13 percent of reasonable fear cases with pauses includes reasonable fear cases that had at least one clock stop and restart, or other combinations of clock stops and restarts.

104 We identified 162 reasonable fear cases with no pauses in processing time that received both a fear determination and administrative closure. For calculating processing times for those reasonable fear cases, we selected the earlier of the two dates.

105 We identified 30 reasonable fear cases for individuals with unknown detention status and included these cases in our analysis.

management to use for effective monitoring and that data should be processed into high quality information.[106] We determined that the USCIS data we reviewed on credible and reasonable fear processing times and case delays were sufficiently reliable for our purposes.

EOIR

To evaluate EOIR's process for managing its credible and reasonable fear-related workload, we interviewed EOIR officials about their practices to manage the credible and reasonable fear workload, including immigration judge hiring, oversight of credible and reasonable fear review processing times, infrastructure requirements for credible and reasonable fear reviews, and the use of video teleconferencing by judges to conduct credible and reasonable fear reviews. We reviewed publicly available data about EOIR's workload and case adjudications, including data about the number of credible and reasonable fear reviews EOIR judges completed and data about judges hired from fiscal year 2014 through fiscal year 2019. We also reviewed guidance documents, such as EOIR's 2018 Case Priorities and Performance Measures memorandum, which established performance measures for credible and reasonable fear reviews. In addition, we used EOIR data to analyze the timeliness of EOIR's completion of credible and reasonable fear reviews and compared EOIR's processing times for fiscal year 2014 through the third quarter of fiscal year 2019 with required time frames. By reviewing documentation on EOIR's case management system and interviewing officials with knowledge about EOIR's case management system and the methodology used to calculate the publicly-reported data, we determined that the EOIR data we reviewed on credible and reasonable fear review processing times and outcomes was sufficiently reliable for analyzing the number of credible and reasonable fear reviews completed and pending, and the duration of the reviews.

---

[106] GAO-14-704G.

We conducted this performance audit from November 2018 to February 2020 in accordance with generally accepted government auditing standards. Those standards require that we plan and perform the audit to obtain sufficient and appropriate evidence to provide a reasonable basis for our findings and conclusions based on our audit objectives. We believe that the evidence obtained provides a reasonable basis for our findings and conclusions based on our audit objectives.

APPENDIX II: ELIGIBILITY, SCREENING STANDARDS, AND POSSIBLE SCREENING OUTCOMES FOR CREDIBLE AND REASONABLE FEAR CASES

This appendix provides detailed information on eligibility, screening standards, and possible screening outcomes for both credible fear and reasonable fear cases.[107] Noncitizens placed into expedited removal who make fear claims will be referred to U.S. Citizenship and Immigration Services (USCIS) for a credible fear screening by an asylum officer or, if the individual has been issued a final administrative removal order after conviction for an aggravated felony or has a prior order of removal that is reinstated, and expressed a fear of return, for a reasonable fear screening.[108] Table 8 below describes the eligibility and screening standards, as well as the potential outcomes for USCIS's credible fear screening cases. Similarly, Table 9 details eligibility, screening standards, and potential outcomes for reasonable fear screening cases.

---

107 See 8 C.F.R. §§8 C.F.R. §§ 208.13(c) (establishing a number of grounds for mandatory denial of asylum, including, among others, conviction of certain crimes, being reasonably regarded as a danger to security of the United States, and the third country asylum bar); 208.30-208.31.

108 See 8 U.S.C. §§ 1225(b), 1228, 1231(a)(5). An "asylum officer" is defined as "an immigration officer who has had professional training in country conditions, asylum law, and interview techniques comparable to that provided to full-time adjudicators of [asylum applications] and is supervised by an officer who has had such training and has had substantial experience adjudicating asylum applications." See 8 U.S.C. § 1225(b)(1)(E). We use this term to refer to any officer conducing credible and reasonable fear screenings.

Table 8. Eligibility, Screening Standards, and Possible Screening Outcomes for Credible Fear as Provided in Federal Law and Regulation[a]

Eligibility	• Under the Immigration and Nationality Act, individuals placed into expedited removal are subject to credible fear screening if the individual expresses a fear of returning to his or her country or last habitual residence (if stateless), a fear of persecution or torture, or intent to apply for asylum. This is because, unlike full removal proceedings, where individuals may apply for relief from removal or other protection, including asylum, before an immigration judge, if noncitizens are placed into expedited removal proceedings instead of full removal proceedings, they are to be ordered removed from the United States without further hearing before an immigration judge unless they indicate either an intention to apply for asylum or a fear of return, a fear of persecution or torture (referred to throughout this chapter as making a "fear claim").[b] With some exceptions, including unaccompanied alien children, noncitizens present in the United States without being admitted or paroled who are encountered by an immigration officer within 100 air miles of any U.S. international land border, and who have not established to the satisfaction of an immigration officer that they have been physically present in the United States continuously for 14 days may be placed into expedited removal.[c]	
Screening standard	**Prior to September 2019a** • Asylum officers are to assess whether there is a "significant possibility" that the individual can establish in a hearing before an immigration judge that he or she has been persecuted or has a well-founded fear of persecution on account of race, religion, nationality, particular social group, or political opinion if returned to his or her country. They are also to assess whether there is a "significant possibility" that he or she would be tortured in his or her country of removal, or, if the applicant is stateless, the applicant's country of last habitual residence.	**Amended Process Effective Nationwide as of September 2019a** • Asylum officers are to first assess whether or not the noncitizen is subject to a new mandatory bar to asylum known as the "third country transit bar." Under the interim final rule, any noncitizen who enters, attempts to enter, or arrives in the United States across the southern land border on or after July 16, 2019, after transiting through at least one country outside the noncitizen's country of citizenship, nationality or last lawful habitual residence en route to the United States, that individual must be found ineligible for asylum unless the noncitizen demonstrates that he or she falls under an exception to the third country transit bar.[d]

Screening standard		• If the asylum officer determines that the noncitizen is subject to the third country transit bar, the officer is then to determine if there is a "reasonable possibility" the individual would be persecuted on account of his or her race, religion, nationality, membership in a particular social group or political opinion, or a "reasonable possibility" that he or she would be tortured in his or her country of removal. According to Department of Homeland Security (DHS) U.S. Citizenship and Immigration Services (USCIS) policy, this is a higher standard than the "significant possibility" standard. • If the asylum officer determines that the noncitizen is not subject to the third country transit bar, the asylum officer is to assess whether there is a "significant possibility" that the individual can establish in a hearing before an immigration judge that he or she has been persecuted or has a well-founded fear of persecution on account of race, religion, nationality, membership in a particular social group, or political opinion if returned to his or her country. They are also to assess whether there is a "significant possibility" that he or she would be tortured in his or her country of removal.
Possible screening outcomes	**Prior to September 2019a** • **Positive determination:** USCIS is to issue a "notice to appear" to the individual to appear before an immigration court where his or her case will be heard in full removal proceedings.	**Amended Process Effective Nationwide as of September 2019a** • **Not subject to third country bar – positive determination of "significant possibility" of persecution:** USCIS is to issue a "notice to appear" to the individual to appear before an immigration court where his or her case will be heard in full removal proceedings.

Table 8. (Continued)

Possible screening outcomes	• During these proceedings, the person may apply for asylum or other forms of relief or protection—i.e., withholding of removal or deferral of removal (deferral applies if the person has a bar that would prevent them being eligible for asylum or withholding). • **Negative determination:** USCIS is to notify U.S. Immigration and Customs Enforcement (ICE) of the determination. ICE is to initiate the removal process for the individual. The individual may request a review by a Department of Justice (DOJ) immigration judge in which case USCIS will issue a Notice of Referral. The immigration judge can reverse (or "vacate") the USCIS decision and enter the person into full removal proceedings before the court where he or she may then apply for asylum or other forms of relief. If the immigration judge agrees with the negative fear determination (or the individual decides not to ask for review of the asylum officer's negative determination), ICE will remove the individual from the United States	• During these proceedings, the person may apply for asylum or other forms of relief or protection—i.e., withholding of removal or deferral of removal (deferral applies if the person has a bar that would prevent them being eligible for asylum or withholding). • **Subject to third country bar – positive determination of "reasonable possibility" of persecution:** USCIS is to issue a "notice to appear" to the individual to appear before an immigration court where his or her case will be heard in full removal proceedings. During these proceedings, the immigration court may determine the individual's eligibility for relief or protection, such as withholding of removal or deferral of removal, (deferral applies if the person has a bar that would prevent them being eligible for asylum or withholding). • **Negative determination:** USCIS is to notify ICE of the determination. ICE is to initiate the removal process for the individual.

Possible screening outcomes		• The individual may request a review by an immigration judge who can reverse (or "vacate") the USCIS decision and place the person into full removal proceedings before the court where he or she may then apply for asylum or other forms of relief, as appropriate. If the immigration judge agrees with the negative fear determination (or the individual decides not to ask for review of the asylum officer's negative determination), ICE will remove the individual from the United States

Source: GAO analysis of 8 C.F.R. § 208.30, as amended, and DHS and DOJ documentation. I GAO-20-250.

[a]The regulations governing the credible fear process were amended by an interim final rule published by DHS on July 16, 2019, which became effective on the date of publication. See 84 Fed. Reg. 33,829 (July 16, 2019) (codified as amended at 8 C.F.R. §§ 208.13, 208.30). However, in a lawsuit filed to challenge the interim final rule, the district court for the Northern District of California granted a nationwide preliminary injunction, preventing DHS from taking any action to implement the Rule. See East Bay Sanctuary Covenant v. Barr, No. 19-04073 (N. D. Cal. July 24, 2019) (order granting preliminary injunction). This injunction was then briefly limited to the jurisdiction of the court of appeals for the Ninth Circuit before it was ultimately appealed to the Supreme Court of the United States, which allowed the interim final rule to go into effect nationwide on September 11, 2019, pending further proceedings in the district court and court of appeals for the Ninth Circuit. See Barr v. East Bay Sanctuary Covenant, No. 19- A230 (U.S. September 11, 2019) (opinion staying nationwide injunction). As of November 2019, this litigation is still ongoing. Additionally, on November 19, 2019, DHS published an interim final rule, which became effective on publication, to modify existing regulations, including credible fear regulations, to provide for the implementation of Asylum Cooperative Agreements that the United States enters with other countries. See 84 Fed. Reg. 63994 (Nov.19, 2019). This table does not reflect amendments to the credible fear process as a result of this new rulemaking.

[b]See 8 U.S.C. §§ 1225(b); 1229a.

[c]See 69 Fed. Reg. 48,877, 48,880 (Aug. 11, 2004); see also 6 U.S.C. § 279(g)(2) (defining "unaccompanied alien child"). DHS published a notice designating additional noncitizens as eligible for expedited removal on July 23, 2019, including eliminating the 100 air miles requirement and expanding the 14-day time frame to two years. See 84 Fed. Reg. 35,409 (July 23, 2019). This rulemaking was enjoined by the district court for the District of Columbia on September 27, 2019 and as of November 2019, litigation was ongoing. Make the Road New York v. McAleenan, No. 19-2369 (D. D.C. Sept. 27, 2019) (order granting preliminary injunction).

[d]See 8 C.F.R. § 208.13(c)(4). These exceptions are: (1) if the noncitizen demonstrates that he or she applied for protection from persecution or torture in at least one country outside the noncitizen's country of citizenship, nationality, or last lawful habitual residence through which the noncitizen transited en route to the United States, and received a final judgment denying protection in such country; (2) the noncitizen demonstrates the he or she meets the definition of "victim of a severe form of trafficking in persons (as defined in 8 C.F.R. § 214.11 to generally mean either commercial sex trafficking or involuntary servitude or slavery); (3) or the countries through which the noncitizen transited en route to the United States were not, at the time of transit, parties to international refugee and humanitarian protection agreements.

Table 9. Eligibility, screening standards, and possible screening outcomes for reasonable fear as provided in federal law and regulation[a]

Eligibility	• The individual is either (1) subject to the reinstatement of a prior order of removal from the United States, or (2) has been issued a final administrative order of removal after conviction for certain serious crimes that meet the definition of an "aggravated felony" in the Immigration and Nationality Act. The individual must also have received a final administrative removal order and expressed a fear of return to their country.[a]
Screening standard	• Department of Homeland Security's (DHS) U.S. Citizenship and Immigration Services (USCIS) is to determine if there is a "reasonable possibility" the individual would be persecuted on account of his or her race, religion, nationality, membership in a particular social group or political opinion, or a "reasonable possibility" that he or she would be tortured in his or her country of removal. According to USCIS policy, this is a higher standard than the "significant possibility" standard.
Possible screening outcomes	• **Positive determination:** USCIS issues a Notice of Referral to an immigration judge for removal proceedings to consider the applicants' eligibility for withholding of removal or deferral of removal.[b] Individuals in reasonable fear cases are not eligible for asylum. • **Negative determination:** Individuals who receive a negative reasonable fear determination may request immigration judge review of the determination by USCIS. For these cases, USCIS will issue a Notice of Referral to a Department of Justice (DOJ) immigration judge. U.S. Immigration and Customs Enforcement will remove the individual if the immigration judge upholds USCIS's negative determination or if the person does not request a review. If the immigration judge reverses a negative reasonable fear finding by USCIS, the individual will be placed in proceedings before the immigration judge for a determination on eligibility for withholding of removal or deferral of removal only.

Source: GAO analysis of 8 C.F.R. § 208.31 and DHS and DOJ documentation and DHS and DOJ documentation. I GAO-20-250.

[a]See 8 U.S.C. §§ 1228, 1231(a)(5); 8 C.F.R. § 208.31.

[b]U.S. immigration law provides that noncitizens physically present within the United States, whether or not at a designated port of arrival, may be granted asylum if they are found to be unable or unwilling to return to their home country because of past persecution, or a well-founded fear of future persecution based on their race, religion, nationality, membership in a particular social group, or political opinion (referred to as "protected grounds"). Additionally, if they are precluded from asylum based on, for example, past convictions of serious crimes, but their life or freedom would be threatened based on the protected grounds or would be tortured if removed, they may also seek withholding of removal. See 8 U.S.C. §§ 1101(a)(42), 1157-1159; See 8 U.S.C. § 1231(b)(3); 8 C.F.R. § 208.16 (codifying both withholding of removal under the Immigration and Nationality Act and the Convention Against Torture). For the purposes of this chapter, we refer to withholding of removal under the Immigration and Nationality Act and withholding of removal under the Convention against Torture collectively as "withholding of removal."

APPENDIX III: DATA ON NONCITIZENS APPREHENDED, DETAINED, AND SCREENED FOR CREDIBLE OR REASONABLE FEAR BY DEPARTMENT OF HOMELAND SECURITY

If noncitizens are placed into expedited removal proceedings instead of full removal proceedings,[109] they are to be ordered removed from the United States without further hearing before an immigration judge unless they indicate either an intention to apply for asylum or a fear of persecution or torture or a fear of return to their country (referred to throughout this appendix as making a "fear claim").[110] This appendix provides information on the number and dispositions (such as full removal proceedings or expedited removal proceedings, among others) of noncitizens who were apprehended by the Department of Homeland Security's (DHS) U.S. Customs and Border Protection's (CBP) U.S. Border Patrol (Border Patrol) and Office of Field Operations (OFO) at or between U.S. ports of entry from fiscal year 2014 through the second quarter of fiscal year 2019.[111] It also includes U.S. Immigration and

---

[109] CBP's October 2015 National Standards on Transport, Escort, Detention, and Search defines a "family unit" to include one or more non-U.S. citizen juvenile(s) accompanied by their parent(s) or legal guardian(s). Therefore, in this chapter, we generally use the term "noncitizen" to refer to individuals who would meet the definition of "alien." The Immigration and Nationality Act defines the term "alien" as "any person not a citizen or national of the United States." See 8 U.S.C. § 1101(a)(3). In addition, for the purposes of this chapter, we use the term "parent" to refer to "noncitizen parent(s) or legal guardian(s)."

[110] Noncitizens placed into expedited removal who make fear claims will be referred to U.S. Citizenship and Immigration Services (USCIS) for a credible fear screening by an asylum officer or, if the individual has been issued a final administrative removal order after conviction for an aggravated felony or has a prior order of removal that is reinstated, and expressed a fear of return, for a reasonable fear screening. See 8 C.F.R. §§ 208.30-31. We use the terms "credible fear claim" to describe individuals who are referred to USCIS for a credible fear screening and "reasonable fear claim" to describe individuals who are referred to USCIS for a reasonable fear screening.

[111] Within CBP, Border Patrol apprehends individuals at U.S. borders between ports of entry, and the Office of Field Operations encounters individuals that arrive at ports of entry. According to CBP officials, OFO encounters noncitizens instead of apprehending them because the noncitizens have not entered the United States at ports of entry until OFO officers have processed them. For the purposes of this chapter, we use the term "apprehend" to describe both Border Patrol and OFO's first interactions with noncitizens at the border. In addition,

Customs Enforcement (ICE) data on detentions of noncitizens who made a credible fear claim.[112] For cases in which noncitizens were referred to U.S. Citizenship and Immigration Services (USCIS) for a fear screening, this appendix also provides additional information on the characteristics of these cases, including their country of origin, age, gender, whether they had representation, and location of their screenings.

Case Dispositions for Border Patrol Apprehensions of Noncitizens from Fiscal Years 2014 through the First Two Quarters of Fiscal Year 2019

As shown in Table 10, Border Patrol apprehensions totaled more than 2.3 million from fiscal year 2014 through the second quarter of fiscal year 2019.[113] Further, Border Patrol data indicate that agents processed about 687,000 (or 30 percent) for full immigration proceedings and nearly 931,000 (or 40 percent) under expedited removal proceedings. For those apprehensions that agents processed under expedited removal, more than 197,000 (approximately 9 percent of total apprehensions) included a credible fear claim made in Border Patrol custody. As also shown in Table 10, during fiscal years 2017 through the first two quarters of 2019, Border Patrol apprehended more than 10,000 additional noncitizens who made reasonable fear claims.[114]

---

while OFO typically refers to its officers as "Customs and Border Protection officers," we use the term "OFO officers" in this chapter for clarity.

[112] We report the numbers of detentions rather than the number of noncitizens detained as our unit of analysis because the individual may have been detained multiple times in the same year. Further, upon initial book-in to a detention facility, ICE personnel will record a specific case category in the automated system for instances where the noncitizen is making a credible fear claim.

[113] We used "number of apprehensions," rather than number of noncitizens apprehended, as our unit of analysis for Border Patrol data because an individual may have been apprehended multiple times in the same year.

[114] Border Patrol did not begin recording reasonable fear claims in its automated database until April 2016. Therefore, the first full fiscal year for which we have reasonable fear data from the Border Patrol is 2017.

Table 10. U.S. Border Patrol (Border Patrol) apprehensions[a] and processing dispositions, fiscal years 2014 through first two quarters of fiscal year 2019

Fiscal year	Total apprehensions	Given a notice to appear (NTA) before an immigration court	Total apprehensions placed in expedited removal (ER)	Number placed in ER with credible fear claims	Number of reasonable fear claims[b]	Other case dispos-itions[c]
2014	486,651	118,753	199,161	16,122	—	168,737
2015	337,116	64,775	148,148	16,894	—	124,193
2016	415,816	93,146	186,292	48,365	—	136,378
2017	310,531	88,315	126,498	36,265	2,200	95,718
2018	404,136	116,427	175,321	51,389	3,810	112,388
2019 (first 2 quarters)	365,148	205,369	95,226	28,262	4,296	64,553
Total	2,319,398	686,785	930,646	197,297	10,306	701,967

Source: GAO analysis of Border Patrol data. | GAO-20-250.

Notes: With some exceptions, including unaccompanied alien children, individuals apprehended by Border Patrol may be placed into administrative removal proceedings before an immigration judge or, if the individual is an arriving noncitizen or encountered within 14 days and 100 miles of entry and is inadmissible based on fraud or misrepresentation, may be placed into expedited removal. Individuals placed into expedited removal are to be ordered removed from the United States without further hearing unless the individual indicates either an intention to apply for asylum or a fear of persecution or torture, or a fear of return, in which case they are to be referred to the Department of Homeland Security's U.S. Citizenship and Immigration Services for credible fear of persecution screening, as appropriate. See 8 U.S.C. § 1225(b); 8 C.F.R. § 208.30. For the purposes of this chapter, we use the term "credible fear claim" to describe individuals who are referred to USCIS for a credible fear screening.

[a]We use the number of apprehensions, rather than number of noncitizens apprehended, as our unit of analysis because an individual may have been apprehended multiple times in the same year.

[b]Noncitizens issued a final administrative order of removal after conviction for crimes that meet the definition of an "aggravated felony" in the Immigration and Nationality Act or whose prior removal order is reinstated may be placed into streamlined removal proceedings where they cannot apply for asylum. However, if they express a fear of return, they are to be screened for "reasonable fear," which is a screening for withholding or deferral of removal, more limited forms of humanitarian protection. See 8 C.F.R. §§ 208.31, 208.16. For the purposes of this chapter, we use the term "reasonable fear claim" to describe individuals who are referred to USCIS for a reasonable fear screening. Border Patrol did not record reasonable fear cases in its automated data system before April 2016. Therefore, this table presents Border Patrol's data on reasonable fear cases for fiscal year 2017 through the first two quarters of fiscal year 2019 only—the most complete fiscal year data at the time of our analysis.

[c]Other case dispositions in the Border Patrol data include a reinstatement of a prior order of removal (without an associated fear claim) and voluntary returns (meaning the process by which an individual at the border admits being unlawfully present in the United States and is allowed to return to his or her country of citizenship in lieu of full removal proceedings), among other dispositions.

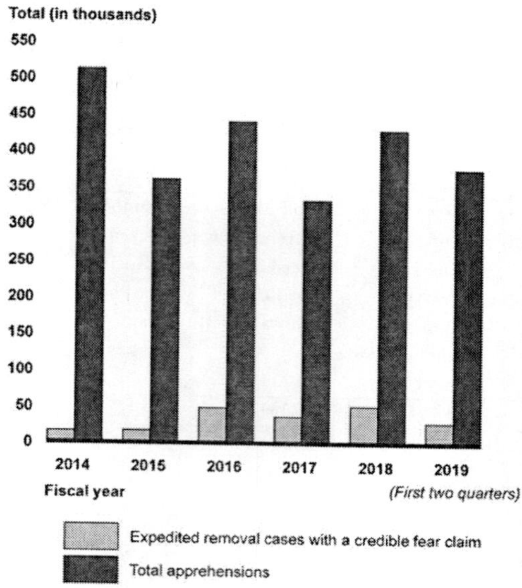

Source: GAO analysis of Border Patrol data. | GAO-20-250.

Notes: With some exceptions, including unaccompanied alien children, individuals apprehended by Border Patrol may be placed into administrative removal proceedings before an immigration judge or, if the individual is an arriving noncitizen or encountered within 14 days and 100 miles of entry and is inadmissible based on fraud or misrepresentation, may be placed into expedited removal. Individuals placed into expedited removal are to be ordered removed from the United States without further hearing unless the individual indicates either an intention to apply for asylum or a fear of persecution or torture, or a fear of return, in which case they are to be referred to the Department of Homeland Security's U.S. Citizenship and Immigration Services for credible fear of persecution screening, as appropriate. See 8 U.S.C. § 1225(b); 8 C.F.R. § 208.30. For the purposes of this chapter, we use the term "credible fear claim" to describe individuals who are referred to USCIS for a credible fear screening.

Figure 7. U.S. Border Patrol's (Border Patrol) Apprehensions of Noncitizens Placed into Expedited Removal Proceedings with a Credible Fear Claim, Fiscal Years 2014 through First Two Quarters of Fiscal Year 2019.

As shown in Figure 7, the number of Border Patrol apprehensions of individuals who were placed into expedited removal proceedings with a credible fear claim increased from more than 16,000 apprehensions in fiscal year 2014 to more than 51,000 in fiscal year 2018. These apprehensions of individuals claiming fear ranged from 3 percent to 13 percent of total apprehensions during these fiscal years.

Characteristics of Noncitizens Apprehended by Border Patrol Processed under Expedited Removal Who Claimed Fear

Border Patrol data include various characteristics of each apprehension such as age, gender, and whether a noncitizen was a member of a family unit. For example, of the nearly 208,000 apprehensions processed under expedited removal with a credible or reasonable fear claim during fiscal years 2014 through the first half of fiscal year 2019, approximately 166,000 (or 80 percent) were adults age 18 and above with the remaining 42,000 (or 20 percent) encompassing children age 17 and under (see Table 11).

Of the nearly 208,000 apprehensions processed under expedited removal with a credible or reasonable fear claim during fiscal years 2014 through the first half of fiscal year 2019, approximately 117,000 (or 56 percent) were male and the remaining 90,000 (44 percent) were female (see Table 12).

Table 11. U.S. Border Patrol (Border Patrol) apprehensions[a] of noncitizens placed into expedited removal proceedings with credible and reasonable fear claims, by age, fiscal years 2014 through the first two quarters of 2019

Fiscal year	Total Border Patrol fear claims[b]	Adults claiming fear (age 18 and above)	Percentage of total fear claims (adults)	Children claiming fear (age 17 and below)	Percentage of total fear claims (children)
2014	16,121	15,055	93	1,066	7
2015	16,894	14,382	85	2,512	15
2016	48,365	35,482	73	12,883	27
2017	38,465	29,227	76	9,238	24

Table 11. (Continued)

Fiscal year	Total Border Patrol fear claims[b]	Adults claiming fear (age 18 and above)	Percentage of total fear claims (adults)	Children claiming fear (age 17 and below)	Percentage of total fear claims (children)
2018	55,196	43,026	78	12,170	22
2019 (first two quarters)	32,558	28,377	87	4,181	13
Total	207,599	165,549	80	42,050	20

Source: GAO analysis of Border Patrol data. | GAO-20-250.

Notes: With some exceptions, including unaccompanied alien children, individuals apprehended by Border Patrol may be placed into administrative removal proceedings before an immigration judge or, if the individual is an arriving noncitizen or encountered within 14 days and 100 miles of entry and is inadmissible based on fraud or misrepresentation, may be placed into expedited removal. Individuals placed into expedited removal are to be ordered removed from the United States without further hearing unless the individual indicates either an intention to apply for asylum or a fear of persecution or torture, or a fear of return, in which case they are to be referred to the Department of Homeland Security's U.S. Citizenship and Immigration Services for credible fear of persecution screening, as appropriate. See 8 U.S.C. § 1225(b); 8 C.F.R. § 208.30. Noncitizens issued a final administrative order of removal after conviction for crimes that meet the definition of an "aggravated felony" in the Immigration and Nationality Act or whose prior removal order is reinstated may be placed into streamlined removal proceedings where they cannot apply for asylum. However, if they express a fear of return, they are to be screened for "reasonable fear," which is a screening for withholding or deferral of removal, more limited forms of humanitarian protection. See 8 C.F.R. §§ 208.31, 208.16. For the purposes of this chapter, we use the terms "credible fear claim" to describe individuals who are referred to USCIS for a credible fear screening, and "reasonable fear claim" to describe individuals who are referred to USCIS for a reasonable fear screening.

Border Patrol's automated system did not contain dates of birth for four apprehensions during this time period (one apprehension in fiscal year 2014 and three apprehensions in fiscal year 2018). Since this did not allow us to determine whether these noncitizens were adults or children, we did not include those four apprehensions in this table for those years.

[a]We use the number of apprehensions, rather than number of noncitizens apprehended, as our unit of analysis because an individual may have been apprehended multiple times in the same year.

[b]Border Patrol did not record reasonable fear cases in its automated data system before April 2016. Therefore, this table presents Border Patrol's data on reasonable fear cases (as part of overall fear cases along with credible fear) for fiscal year 2017 through the first two quarters of fiscal year 2019 only—the most complete fiscal year data at the time of our analysis.

Table 12. U.S. Border Patrol (Border Patrol) apprehensions[a] of noncitizens placed into expedited removal proceedings with credible and reasonable fear claims, by gender, fiscal years 2014 through the first two quarters of 2019[b]

Fiscal year	Total Border Patrol fear claims	Male	Percentage of total fear claims (male)	Female	Percentage of total fear claims (female)
2014	16,122	9,256	57	6,866	43
2015	16,894	9,875	58	7,019	42
2016	48,365	24,497	51	23,868	49
2017	38,465	20,243	53	18,222	47
2018	55,199	31,629	57	23,570	43
2019 (first two quarters)	32,558	21,739	67	10,819	33
Total	207,603	117,239	56	90,364	44

Source: GAO analysis of Border Patrol data. | GAO-20-250.

Notes: With some exceptions, including unaccompanied alien children, individuals apprehended by Border Patrol may be placed into administrative removal proceedings before an immigration judge or, if the individual is an arriving noncitizen or encountered within 14 days and 100 miles of entry and is inadmissible based on fraud or misrepresentation, may be placed into expedited removal. Individuals placed into expedited removal are to be ordered removed from the United States without further hearing unless the individual indicates either an intention to apply for asylum or a fear of persecution or torture, or a fear of return, in which case they are to be referred to the Department of Homeland Security's U.S. Citizenship and Immigration Services for credible fear of persecution screening, as appropriate. See 8 U.S.C. § 1225(b); 8 C.F.R. § 208.30. Noncitizens issued a final administrative order of removal after conviction for crimes that meet the definition of an "aggravated felony" in the Immigration and Nationality Act or whose prior removal order is reinstated may be placed into streamlined removal proceedings where they cannot apply for asylum. However, if they express a fear of return, they are to be screened for "reasonable fear," which is a screening for withholding or deferral of removal, more limited forms of humanitarian protection. See 8 C.F.R. §§ 208.31, 208.16. For the purposes of this chapter, we use the terms "credible fear claim" to describe individuals who are referred to USCIS for a credible fear screening, and "reasonable fear claim" to describe individuals who are referred to USCIS for a reasonable fear screening.

[a]We use the number of apprehensions, rather than number of noncitizens apprehended, as our unit of analysis because an individual may have been apprehended multiple times in the same year.

[b]Border Patrol did not record reasonable fear cases in its automated data system before April 2016. Therefore, this table presents Border Patrol's data on reasonable fear cases (as part of overall fear cases along with credible fear) for fiscal year 2017 through the first two quarters of fiscal year 2019 only—the most complete fiscal year data at the time of our analysis.

Table 13. Number of family unit members among U.S. Border Patrol apprehensions[a] who were placed into expedited removal proceedings with credible and reasonable fear claims, fiscal years 2016 through the first two quarters of 2019

Fiscal year	Total family unit members	Family unit members placed in expedited removal	Family unit members with credible fear claims	Family unit members with reasonable fear claims[b]
2016	77,376	37,373	22,942	NA[c]
2017	75,738	27,262	16,799	701
2018	112,339	40,901	23,163	1,361
2019 (first two quarters)	190,212	14,492	7,602	2,372
Total	455,665	120,028	70,506	4,434

Source: GAO analysis of Border Patrol data. | GAO-20-250.

Notes: With some exceptions, including unaccompanied alien children, individuals apprehended by Border Patrol may be placed into administrative removal proceedings before an immigration judge or, if the individual is an arriving noncitizen or encountered within 14 days and 100 miles of entry and is inadmissible based on fraud or misrepresentation, may be placed into expedited removal. Individuals placed into expedited removal are to be ordered removed from the United States without further hearing unless the individual indicates either an intention to apply for asylum or a fear of persecution or torture, or a fear of return, in which case they are to be referred to the Department of Homeland Security's U.S. Citizenship and Immigration Services for credible fear of persecution screening, as appropriate. See 8 U.S.C. § 1225(b); 8 C.F.R. § 208.30. Noncitizens issued a final administrative order of removal after conviction for crimes that meet the definition of an "aggravated felony" in the Immigration and Nationality Act or whose prior removal order is reinstated may be placed into streamlined removal proceedings where they cannot apply for asylum. However, if they express a fear of return, they are to be screened for "reasonable fear," which is a screening for withholding or deferral of removal, more limited forms of humanitarian protection. See 8 C.F.R. §§ 208.31, 208.16. For the purposes of this chapter, we use the terms "credible fear claim" to describe individuals who are referred to USCIS for a credible fear screening, and "reasonable fear claim" to describe individuals who are referred to USCIS for a reasonable fear screening.

[a]We use the number of apprehensions, rather than number of noncitizens apprehended, as our unit of analysis because an individual may have been apprehended multiple times in the same year.

[b]Border Patrol did not record reasonable fear cases in its automated data system before April 2016. Therefore, this table presents Border Patrol's data on reasonable fear cases for fiscal year 2017 through the first two quarters of fiscal year 2019 only—the most complete fiscal year data at the time of our analysis.

[c]Not applicable.

As shown in Table 13, for fiscal years 2016 through the first two quarters of 2019, Border Patrol apprehended nearly 456,000 noncitizens who were members of families.[115] Of these, Border Patrol processed more than 120,000 (or 26 percent) under expedited removal proceedings. Nearly 71,000 apprehensions during this time period (15 percent of total family unit members apprehended and 59 percent of those placed in expedited removal) included a credible fear claim.

Case Dispositions for OFO Apprehensions from Fiscal Years 2014 through the First Two Quarters of Fiscal Year 2019

From fiscal year 2014 through March 2019, OFO apprehensions at ports of entry totaled at least 546,900.[116] Of these 546,900 apprehensions, OFO officers placed at least 193,500 (or 35 percent) into expedited removal proceedings. For those in expedited removal proceedings, OFO data indicate that at least 104,600 apprehensions included a credible fear claim in OFO custody (19 percent of total apprehensions).[117] In addition, OFO issued Notices to Appear before an immigration judge for full immigration proceedings to at least 167,400 (or 31 percent) of the approximately 546,900 total apprehensions (see Figure 8).

---

115 We collected family-specific Border Patrol data for fiscal year 2016 through the second quarter of fiscal year 2019 because the Border Patrol began to systematically collect data on individuals that arrived as part of a family unit in fiscal year 2016.

116 We used "number of apprehensions" rather than number of noncitizens apprehended, as our unit of analysis for OFO data because an individual may have been apprehended multiple times in the same year. According to our analysis of the OFO data, OFO did not have a unique identifier for approximately 13 percent of its apprehension records during the period of our review. As such, we could not independently confirm these records as reliable and excluded them from our analysis. Therefore, we rounded all OFO data in this chapter. Appendix I provides additional details about our methodology for assessing limitations of OFO's data and making rounding decisions.

117 With regard to reasonable fear cases, OFO officials stated they do not systematically track these cases in their automated system. OFO officials explained that, due to the relatively small number of reasonable fear cases they encounter each year, OFO does not have a specific field in its automated database to track reasonable fear cases. OFO officials stated that, in the rare cases where they encounter a reasonable fear claim, OFO officers in the field document that claim in a narrative in the noncitizen's hardcopy file. When transferring noncitizens to ICE custody, OFO field officers are to include information to indicate fear claims by noncitizens subject to reinstatement of a prior removal order.

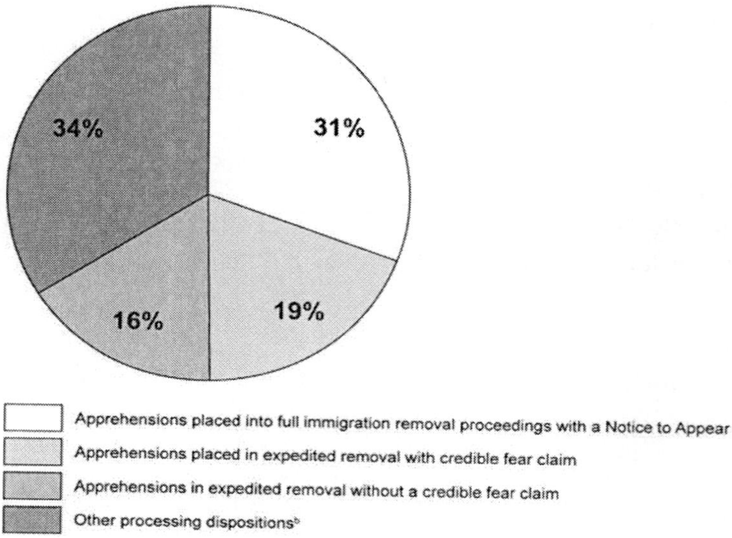

Source: GAO analysis of OFO data. | GAO-20-250. Notes: OFO apprehensions totaled approximately 547,000 at ports of entry during the period covered by this figure. According to OFO officials, due to the relatively small number of reasonable fear cases they encounter each year, OFO does not have a specific field in its automated database to track reasonable fear cases. With some exceptions, including unaccompanied alien children, individuals apprehended by OFO may be placed into administrative removal proceedings before an immigration judge or, if the individual is an arriving alien or encountered within 14 days and 100 miles of entry and is inadmissible based on fraud or misrepresentation, may be placed into expedited removal. Individuals placed into expedited removal are to be ordered removed from the United States without further hearing unless the individual indicates either an intention to apply for asylum or a fear of persecution or torture, or a fear of return, in which case they are to be referred to the Department of Homeland Security's U.S. Citizenship and Immigration Services for credible fear of persecution screening, as appropriate. See 8 U.S.C. § 1225(b); 8 C.F.R. § 208.30. For the purposes of this chapter, we use the term "credible fear claim" to describe individuals who are referred to USCIS for a credible fear screening. [a]We used "number of apprehensions" rather than number of noncitizens apprehended, as our unit of analysis because an individual may have been apprehended multiple times in the same year. According to our analysis of the OFO data, OFO did not have a unique identifier for approximately 13 percent of its apprehension records during the period of our review. As such, we could not independently confirm these records as reliable and excluded them from our analysis. Therefore, we rounded all OFO data in this chapter. [b]Other processing dispositions in the OFO data include, among other dispositions, withdrawals (where an individual is permitted to voluntarily retract an application for admission in the discretion of the Department of Homeland Security in lieu of being placed into removal proceedings) and individuals who are paroled at the ports of entry (on humanitarian, public interest grounds or for a limited purpose such as to attend immigration proceedings through the Migrant Protection Protocols).

Figure 8. Dispositions of U.S. Customs and Border Protection Office of Field Operations (OFO) Apprehensions[a], Including those with Credible Fear Claims, Fiscal Year 2014 through First Two Quarters of Fiscal Year 2019.

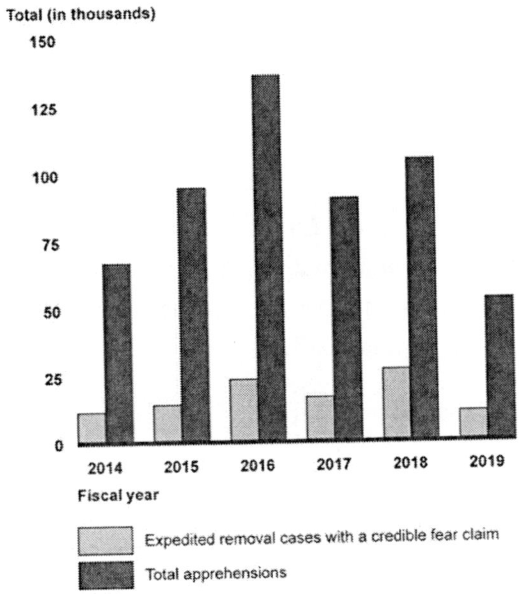

Source: GAO analysis of OFO data. | GAO-20-250.

Notes: According to OFO officials, due to the relatively small number of reasonable fear cases they encounter each year, OFO does not have a specific field in its automated database to track reasonable fear cases. With some exceptions, including unaccompanied alien children, individuals apprehended by OFO may be placed into administrative removal proceedings before an immigration judge or, if the individual is an arriving alien or encountered within 14 days and 100 miles of entry and is inadmissible based on fraud or misrepresentation, may be placed into expedited removal. Individuals placed into expedited removal are to be ordered removed from the United States without further hearing unless the individual indicates either an intention to apply for asylum or a fear of persecution or torture, or a fear of return, in which case they are to be referred to the Department of Homeland Security's U.S. Citizenship and Immigration Services for credible fear of persecution screening, as appropriate. See 8 U.S.C. § 1225(b); 8 C.F.R. § 208.30. For the purposes of this chapter, we use the term "credible fear claim" to describe individuals who are referred to USCIS for a credible fear screening.

[a]We used "number of apprehensions" rather than number of noncitizens apprehended, as our unit of analysis because an individual may have been apprehended multiple times in the same year. According to our analysis of the OFO data, OFO did not have a unique identifier for approximately 13 percent of its apprehension records during the period of our review. As such, we could not independently confirm these records as reliable and excluded them from our analysis. Therefore, we rounded all OFO data in this chapter.

Figure 9. U.S. Customs and Border Protection's Office of Field Operations (OFO) Apprehensions[a] Placed into Expedited Removal with Credible Fear Claims, Fiscal Year 2014 through First Two Quarters of Fiscal Year 2019.

As shown in Figure 9, the number of OFO apprehensions in expedited removal proceedings with a credible fear claim generally increased over this time period from at least 11,600 apprehensions in fiscal year 2014 to at least 27,000 in fiscal year 2018 (the last full year of data available at the time of our analysis). In addition to this overall increase, the percentage of OFO's total apprehensions placed into expedited removal proceedings with a credible fear claim also increased. Specifically, these apprehensions increased from about 17 percent of all apprehensions in fiscal year 2014 to about 26 percent in fiscal year 2018.

Characteristics of Noncitizens Apprehended by OFO and Placed into Expedited Removal Proceedings with a Credible Fear Claim

OFO apprehension data include various characteristics such as age, gender, and whether an apprehension involved a member of a family unit. For example, as shown in Table 14, of the approximately 104,300 OFO apprehensions with credible fear claims, at least 78,500 (or 75 percent) were adults age 18 and above with about 25,700 (or 25 percent) of the remaining credible fear claims encompassing children age 17 and under. Also, for each year during this period, the percentage of adults versus children was generally consistent with this overall percentage with the exception of fiscal year 2019, for which the partial year's data show that about 98 percent of those apprehensions processed under expedited removal with a credible fear claim were adults.[118]

---

[118] According to OFO officials, the drop off in the percentage of children making credible fear claims between fiscal year 2018 and the first two quarters of fiscal year 2019 could possibly be attributed to OFO officers not being required to ask the standard fear questions of noncitizens being referred for full removal proceedings before an immigrations judge. The OFO officials added that another contributing factor could be the fact that this lower percentage is based on partial-year data for fiscal year 2019.

Table 14. U.S. Customs and Border Protection's Office of Field Operations (OFO) apprehensions[a] placed into expedited removal proceedings with credible fear claims, by age, fiscal years 2014 through the first two quarters of 2019

Fiscal year	Total OFO credible fear claims	Adults with credible fear claims (age 18 and above)	Percentage of total credible fear claims (adults)	Children with credible fear claims (age 17 and below)	Percentage of total credible fear claims (children)[b]
2014	11,600	8,600	74	3,000	26
2015	14,300	11,100	78	3,100	22
2016	23,500	16,300	69	7,200	31
2017	16,800	11,800	70	5,000	30
2018	27,000	19,800	73	7,200	27
2019 (first two quarters)	11,100	10,900	98	200	2
Total	104,300	78,500	75	25,700	25

Source: GAO analysis of OFO data. | GAO-20-250.

Notes: According to OFO officials, due to the relatively small number of reasonable fear cases they encounter each year, OFO does not have a specific field in its automated database to track reasonable fear cases. With some exceptions, including unaccompanied alien children, individuals apprehended by OFO may be placed into administrative removal proceedings before an immigration judge or, if the individual is an arriving alien or encountered within 14 days and 100 miles of entry and is inadmissible based on fraud or misrepresentation, may be placed into expedited removal. Individuals placed into expedited removal are to be ordered removed from the United States without further hearing unless the individual indicates either an intention to apply for asylum or a fear of persecution or torture, or a fear of return, in which case they are to be referred to the Department of Homeland Security's U.S. Citizenship and Immigration Services for credible fear of persecution screening, as appropriate. See 8 U.S.C. § 1225(b); 8 C.F.R. § 208.30. For the purposes of this chapter, we use the term "credible fear claim" to describe individuals who are referred to USCIS for a credible fear screening.

[a]We used "number of apprehensions" rather than number of noncitizens apprehended, as our unit of analysis because an individual may have been apprehended multiple times in the same year. According to our analysis of the OFO data, OFO did not have a unique identifier for approximately 13 percent of its apprehension records during the period of our review. As such, we could not independently confirm these records as reliable and excluded them from our analysis. Therefore, we rounded all OFO data in this chapter.

[b]According to OFO officials, the drop off in the percentage of children making credible fear claims between fiscal year 2018 and the first two quarters of fiscal year 2019 could possibly be attributed to OFO officers not being required to ask the standard fear questions of noncitizens being referred for full removal proceedings before an immigrations judge. The OFO officials added that another contributing factor could be the fact that this lower percentage is based on partial-year data for fiscal year 2019.

Table 15. U.S. Customs and Border Protection's Office of Field Operations (OFO) apprehensions[a] placed into expedited removal proceedings with credible fear claims, by gender, fiscal years 2014 through the first two quarters of 2019

Fiscal year	Total OFO fear claims	Male	Percentage of total credible fear claims (male)[b]	Female	Percentage of total credible fear claims (female)[b]
2014	11,600	6,200	53	5,300	46
2015	14,300	8,100	57	6,100	43
2016	23,500	11,900	51	11,500	49
2017	16,800	8,800	52	8,000	48
2018	27,000	13,600	50	13,300	49
2019 (first two quarters)	11,100	7,900	71	3,200	29
Total	104,300	56,500	54	47,400	45

Source: GAO analysis of OFO data. | GAO-20-250.

Notes: According to OFO officials, due to the relatively small number of reasonable fear cases they encounter each year, OFO does not have a specific field in its automated database to track reasonable fear cases. With some exceptions, including unaccompanied alien children, individuals apprehended by OFO may be placed into administrative removal proceedings before an immigration judge or, if the individual is an arriving alien or encountered within 14 days and 100 miles of entry and is inadmissible based on fraud or misrepresentation, may be placed into expedited removal. Individuals placed into expedited removal are to be ordered removed from the United States without further hearing unless the individual indicates either an intention to apply for asylum or a fear of persecution or torture, or a fear of return, in which case they are to be referred to the Department of Homeland Security's U.S. Citizenship and Immigration Services for credible fear of persecution screening, as appropriate. See 8 U.S.C. § 1225(b); 8 C.F.R. § 208.30. For the purposes of this chapter, we use the term "credible fear claim" to describe individuals who are referred to USCIS for a credible fear screening.

Approximately 180 apprehensions in OFO data (0.2 percent of total OFO fear claims) did not indicate gender. According to OFO officials, cases where no gender was recorded in their automated system are potentially attributable to error by the system operator based on the fact that gender may not have been a mandatory field for data entry at the time.

[a]We used "number of apprehensions" rather than number of noncitizens apprehended, as our unit of analysis because an individual may have been apprehended multiple times in the same year. According to our analysis of the OFO data, OFO did not have a unique identifier for approximately 13 percent of its apprehension records during the period of our review. As such, we could not independently confirm these records as reliable and excluded them from our analysis. Therefore, we rounded all OFO data in this chapter.

[b]Percentages in some years do not equal 100 percent due to rounding.

Table 16. Number of family unit member apprehensions[a] U.S. Customs and Border Protection's Office of Field Operations (OFO) placed into expedited removal proceedings with credible fear claims, fiscal years 2016 through the first two quarters of 2019

Fiscal year	Total family unit members	Family unit members placed in expedited removal	Family unit members with credible fear claims
2016	42,900	13,600	12,100
2017	29,300	9,900	8,300
2018	48,400	14,500	12,100
2019 (first 2 quarters)	23,500	1,100	400
Total	144,100	39,100	32,900

Source: GAO analysis of OFO data. | GAO-20-250.

Notes: According to OFO officials, due to the relatively small number of reasonable fear cases they encounter each year, OFO does not have a specific field in its automated database to track reasonable fear cases. With some exceptions, including unaccompanied alien children, individuals apprehended by OFO may be placed into administrative removal proceedings before an immigration judge or, if the individual is an arriving alien or encountered within 14 days and 100 miles of entry and is inadmissible based on fraud or misrepresentation, may be placed into expedited removal. Individuals placed into expedited removal are to be ordered removed from the United States without further hearing unless the individual indicates either an intention to apply for asylum or a fear of persecution or torture, or a fear of return, in which case they are to be referred to the Department of Homeland Security's U.S. Citizenship and Immigration Services for credible fear of persecution screening, as appropriate. See 8 U.S.C. § 1225(b); 8 C.F.R. § 208.30. For the purposes of this chapter, we use the term "credible fear claim" to describe individuals who are referred to USCIS for a credible fear screening.

[a]We used "number of apprehensions" rather than number of noncitizens apprehended, as our unit of analysis because an individual may have been apprehended multiple times in the same year. According to our analysis of the OFO data, OFO did not have a unique identifier for approximately 13 percent of its apprehension records during the period of our review. As such, we could not independently confirm these records as reliable and excluded them from our analysis. Therefore, we rounded all OFO data in this chapter.

In addition, for fiscal years 2014 through the first two quarters of fiscal 2019, at least 56,500 (or 54 percent) of these apprehensions involving a fear claim were male and at least 47,400 (or 45 percent) were female (see Table 15). Also, for each year during this period, the number of males and females were almost evenly split with the exception of fiscal year 2019, for which the partial year's data show a larger proportion of males claiming fear.

As shown in Table 16, for fiscal years 2016 through the first two quarters of 2019, OFO had a total of at least 144,100 apprehensions involving members of family units.[119] Of these approximately 144,100 apprehensions, OFO placed at least 39,100 (27 percent) into expedited removal proceedings of which at least 32,900 (about 23 percent of total family unit members apprehended and approximately 84 percent of those placed in expedited removal) claimed a credible fear of returning to their country.

Number of Individuals in ICE Detention with a Credible Fear Claim, Fiscal Years 2014 through 2018

The number of individuals in expedited removal proceedings detained in ICE facilities with a credible fear claim increased from fiscal years 2014 to 2018.[120] Specifically, as shown in Table 17, ICE data indicate that the number of individuals in expedited removal proceedings with a recorded credible fear claim while in ICE detention increased from about 37,000 (or 9 percent) in fiscal year 2014 to about 99,000 (or 26 percent) in fiscal year 2018. The period of greatest percentage increase was from fiscal years 2015 to 2016 when the percentage of individuals in expedited removal proceedings with a credible fear claim while in ICE custody increased from approximately 15 percent to 25 percent.

---

[119] We collected family-specific OFO data for fiscal year 2016 through the second quarter of fiscal year 2019 because OFO began to systematically collect data on individuals that arrived as part of a family and families in fiscal year 2016.

[120] The ICE data we obtained included a case category field indicating credible fear claims made by individual noncitizens in ICE detention and denotes their current status at the time our data were pulled by ICE—May 2019. Therefore, these case category data obtained did not include any possible updates made at a later time to the case category such as those reflecting a subsequent fear claim made at another detention facility.

Table 17. Noncitizens in expedited removal proceedings detained in U.S. Immigration and Customs Enforcement (ICE) detention facilities with credible fear claims, fiscal years 2014 through 2018

Fiscal year	Unique individuals detained each year	Number of unique individuals detained with a credible fear claim	Percentage of unique individuals detained with a credible fear claim
2014	396,595	37,180	9.4
2015	290,458	42,593	14.7
2016	337,039	84,537	25.1
2017	309,582	66,606	21.5
2018	384,499	99,065	25.8
Total	1,718,173	329,981	19.2

Source: GAO analysis of ICE data. | GAO-20-250.

Notes: With some exceptions, including unaccompanied alien children, apprehended individuals may be placed into administrative removal proceedings before an immigration judge or, if the individual is an arriving alien or encountered within 14 days and 100 miles of entry and is inadmissible based on fraud or misrepresentation, may be placed into expedited removal. Individuals placed into expedited removal are to be ordered removed from the United States without further hearing unless the individual indicates either an intention to apply for asylum or a fear of persecution or torture, or a fear of return, in which case they are to be referred to the Department of Homeland Security's U.S. Citizenship and Immigration Services for credible fear of persecution screening, as appropriate. See 8 U.S.C. § 1225(b); 8 C.F.R. § 208.30. For the purposes of this chapter, we use the term "credible fear claim" to describe individuals who are referred to USCIS for a credible fear screening.

The ICE data we obtained included a case category field indicating credible fear claims made by individual noncitizens in ICE detention and denotes their current status at the time our data were pulled by ICE—May 2019. Therefore, these case category data obtained did not include any possible updates made at a later time to the case category such as those reflecting a subsequent fear claim made at another detention facility.

Numbers in the table are unique individuals detained in each fiscal year. Therefore, the totals are likely overstated due to the possibility that some individuals were detained across more than one fiscal year.

Table 18. Noncitizen family unit members in expedited removal proceedings housed in U.S. Immigration and Customs Enforcement (ICE) family residential centers with credible fear claims, fiscal years 2014 through 2018

Fiscal year	Unique individual family unit members in family residential centers	Number of family unit members in family residential centers with a credible fear claim	Percentage of family unit members in family residential centers with a credible fear claim
2014	2,047	1,441	70.4
2015	12,541	8,594	68.5
2016	43,163	35,588	82.5
2017	37,490	28,018	74.7
2018	45,904	40,557	88.4
Total[a]	141,145	114,198	80.9

Source: GAO analysis of ICE data. | GAO-20-250.

Notes: With some exceptions, including unaccompanied alien children, apprehended individuals may be placed into administrative removal proceedings before an immigration judge or, if the individual is an arriving alien or encountered within 14 days and 100 miles of entry and is inadmissible based on fraud or misrepresentation, may be placed into expedited removal. Individuals placed into expedited removal are to be ordered removed from the United States without further hearing unless the individual indicates either an intention to apply for asylum or a fear of persecution or torture, or a fear of return, in which case they are to be referred to the Department of Homeland Security's U.S. Citizenship and Immigration Services for credible fear of persecution screening, as appropriate. See 8 U.S.C. § 1225(b); 8 C.F.R. § 208.30. For the purposes of this chapter, we use the term "credible fear claim" to describe individuals who are referred to USCIS for a credible fear screening.

The ICE data we obtained included a case category field indicating credible fear claims made by individual noncitizen family unit members in ICE detention and denotes their current status at the time our data were pulled by ICE—May 2019. Therefore, these case category data obtained did not include any possible updates made at a later time to the case category such as those reflecting a subsequent fear claim made at another detention facility.

For family unit members, we analyzed detention records for individuals apprehended by CBP and housed in one of ICE's four family residential centers. During the time period covered by our data, ICE detained families at four family residential centers for varying periods between fiscal year 2014 and fiscal year 2019. These family residential centers included Artesia Family Residential Center, Berks Family Residential Center, Karnes Family Residential Center, and the South Texas Family Residential Center.

[a]Numbers in the table are unique individuals detained in each fiscal year. Therefore, the totals are likely overstated due to the possibility that some individuals were detained across more than one fiscal year.

Table 19. Noncitizen adults and children in expedited removal proceedings housed in U.S. Immigration and Customs Enforcement (ICE) family residential centers with credible fear claims, fiscal years 2014 through 2018

Fiscal year	Number of family unit members in family residential centers with a credible fear claim	Number and percentage of adult family unit members with a credible fear claim[a]	Number and percentage of children among family unit members with a credible fear claim[a]
2014	1,441	623 (43)	818 (57)
2015	8,594	3,674 (43)	4,920 (57)
2016	35,588	15,534 (44)	20,054 (56)
2017	28,018	12,697 (45)	15,321 (55)
2018	40,557	18,732 (46)	21,825 (54)
Total	114,198	51,260 (45)	62,938 (55)

Source: GAO analysis of ICE data. | GAO-20-250.

Notes: With some exceptions, including unaccompanied alien children, apprehended individuals may be placed into administrative removal proceedings before an immigration judge or, if the individual is an arriving alien or encountered within 14 days and 100 miles of entry and is inadmissible based on fraud or misrepresentation, may be placed into expedited removal. Individuals placed into expedited removal are to be ordered removed from the United States without further hearing unless the individual indicates either an intention to apply for asylum or a fear of persecution or torture, or a fear of return, in which case they are to be referred to the Department of Homeland Security's U.S. Citizenship and Immigration Services for credible fear of persecution screening, as appropriate. See 8 U.S.C. § 1225(b); 8 C.F.R. § 208.30. For the purposes of this chapter, we use the term "credible fear claim" to describe individuals who are referred to USCIS for a credible fear screening.

The ICE data we obtained included a case category field indicating credible fear claims made by individual noncitizen family unit members in ICE detention and denotes their current status at the time our data were pulled by ICE—May 2019. Therefore, these case category data obtained did not include any possible updates made at a later time to the case category such as those reflecting a subsequent fear claim made at another detention facility.

For family unit members, we analyzed detention records for individuals apprehended by U.S. Customs and Border Protection and housed in one of ICE's four family residential centers. During the time period covered by our data, ICE detained families at four family residential centers for varying periods between fiscal year 2014 and fiscal year 2019. These family residential centers included Artesia Family Residential Center, Berks Family Residential Center, Karnes Family Residential Center, and the South Texas Family Residential Center.

[a]Percentages do not equal 100 percent due to rounding.

For fiscal years 2014 through 2018, the majority of family unit members in ICE's four family residential centers had a credible fear claim (81 percent), as demonstrated in Table 18.[121] The number of family unit members with a fear claim ranged from approximately 69 percent in fiscal year 2015 to 88 percent in fiscal year 2018.

For fiscal years 2014 through 2018, slightly more than half of all family unit members in ICE's four family residential centers with a credible fear claim were children under the age of 18 (55 percent). As also shown in Table 19, the division between adults and children with fear claims varied little each year.

Nationalities of Noncitizens Referred to USCIS for Credible or Reasonable Fear Screenings from Fiscal Year 2014 through the First Two Quarters of Fiscal Year 2019

As shown in Figure 10, the majority of credible fear cases referred to USCIS for screening from fiscal year 2014 through the first two quarters of fiscal year 2019 had applicants who were nationals of El Salvador, Honduras, Guatemala, or Mexico.[122] Citizens of these countries accounted for 74 percent of all credible fear cases during this time period (approximately 306,000 referrals).

---

[121] For family unit members, we analyzed detention records for individuals apprehended by CBP and housed in one of ICE's four family residential centers. During the time period covered by our data, ICE detained families at four family residential centers for varying periods between fiscal year 2014 and fiscal year 2019. These family residential centers included Artesia Family Residential Center, Berks Family Residential Center, Karnes Family Residential Center, and the South Texas Family Residential Center.

[122] USCIS's automated system did not record citizenship for nearly 700 credible fear cases (0.2 percent of total credible fear cases). According to USCIS officials, these are likely cases where the individual's citizenship was unknown.

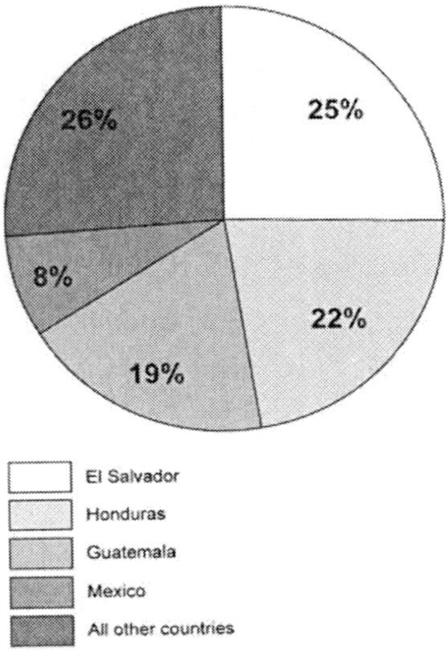

Source: GAO analysis of USCIS data. | GAO-20-250.

Notes: With some exceptions, including unaccompanied alien children, apprehended individuals may be placed into administrative removal proceedings before an immigration judge or, if the individual is an arriving alien or encountered within 14 days and 100 miles of entry and is inadmissible based on fraud or misrepresentation, may be placed into expedited removal. Individuals placed into expedited removal are to be ordered removed from the United States without further hearing unless the individual indicates either an intention to apply for asylum or a fear of persecution or torture, or a fear of return, in which case they are to be referred to USCIS for credible fear of persecution screening, as appropriate. See 8 U.S.C. § 1225(b); 8 C.F.R. § 208.30.

USCIS received approximately 413,000 credible fear referrals during the period covered by this graphic.

We use the number of cases, rather than number of individual noncitizens screened by USCIS, as our unit of analysis because an individual noncitizen may have claimed fear and been screened more than once during the time period covered by our data. Percentages do not equal 100 percent due to rounding.

USCIS's automated system did not record citizenship for nearly 700 credible fear cases (0.2 percent of total credible fear cases). According to USCIS officials, these are likely cases where the individual's citizenship was unknown.

Figure 10. Top Four Countries of Nationality for U.S. Citizenship and Immigration Services (USCIS) Credible Fear Cases, Fiscal Year 2014 through the First Two Quarters of Fiscal Year 2019.

As shown in Table 20, El Salvador had the most credible fear referrals to USCIS each year from fiscal year 2014 through fiscal year 2017.[123] However, beginning in fiscal year 2018, Honduras accounted for the most credible fear referrals to USCIS among these four countries.

Table 20. Top four countries of nationality for U.S. Citizenship and Immigration Services (USCIS) credible fear cases, fiscal years 2014 through the first two quarters of fiscal year 2019

Fiscal Year	El Salvador	Honduras	Guatemala	Mexico	All Other countries	Total cases
2014	18,305	7,563	6,196	4,131	11,449	47,754
2015	14,299	7,635	7,151	7,250	11,647	48,089
2016	32,386	19,513	14,820	7,432	17,250	91,598
2017	20,114	16,652	15,738	4,904	20,160	77,698
2018	13,471	25,874	24,502	6,855	27,234	98,083
2019 (first two quarters)	6,035	14,242	8,511	2,039	19,262	50,091
Total	104,610	91,479	76,918	32,611	107,002	413,313

Source: GAO analysis of USCIS data. | GAO-20-250.

Notes: With some exceptions, including unaccompanied alien children, apprehended individuals may be placed into administrative removal proceedings before an immigration judge or, if the individual is an arriving alien or encountered within 14 days and 100 miles of entry and is inadmissible based on fraud or misrepresentation, may be placed into expedited removal. Individuals placed into expedited removal are to be ordered removed from the United States without further hearing unless the individual indicates either an intention to apply for asylum or a fear of persecution or torture, or a fear of return, in which case they are to be referred to USCIS for credible fear of persecution screening, as appropriate. See 8 U.S.C. § 1225(b); 8 C.F.R. § 208.30.

We use the number of cases, rather than number of individual noncitizens screened by USCIS, as our unit of analysis because an individual noncitizen may have claimed fear and been screened more than once during the time period covered by our data.

USCIS's automated system did not record citizenship for nearly 700 credible fear cases (0.2 percent of total credible fear cases). According to USCIS officials, these are likely cases where the individual's citizenship was unknown.

[123] USCIS's automated system did not record citizenship for nearly 700 credible fear cases (0.2 percent of total credible fear cases). According to USCIS officials, these are likely cases where the individual's citizenship was unknown.

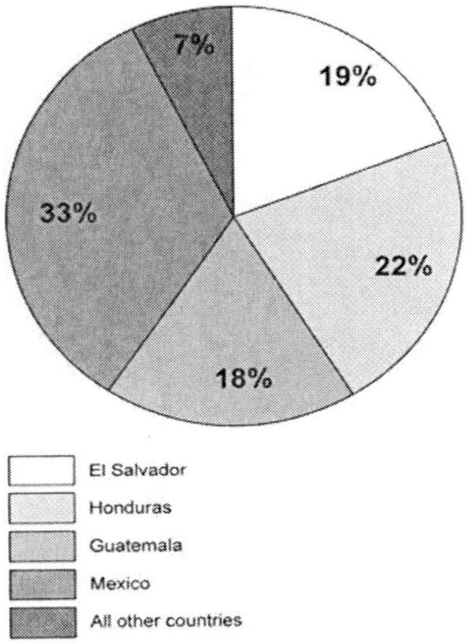

Source: GAO analysis of USCIS data. | GAO-20-250.

Notes: Noncitizens issued a final administrative order of removal after conviction for crimes that meet the definition of an "aggravated felony" in the Immigration and Nationality Act or whose prior removal order is reinstated may be placed into streamlined removal proceedings where they cannot apply for asylum. However, if they express a fear of return, they are to be screened for "reasonable fear," which is a screening for withholding or deferral of removal, more limited forms of humanitarian protection. See 8 C.F.R. §§ 208.31, 208.16.

USCIS received approximately 52,000 reasonable fear referrals during the period covered by this graphic.

We use the number of cases, rather than number of individual noncitizens screened by USCIS, as our unit of analysis because an individual noncitizen may have claimed fear and been screened more than once during the time period covered by our data. Percentages do not equal 100 percent due to rounding.

USCIS's automated system did not record citizenship for nearly 500 reasonable fear cases (0.9 percent of reasonable fear cases). According to USCIS officials, these are likely cases where the individual's citizenship was unknown.

Figure 11. Top Four Countries of Nationality for U.S. Citizenship and Immigration Services (USCIS) Reasonable Fear Cases, Fiscal Years 2014 through the First Two Quarters of Fiscal Year 2019.

As shown in Figure 11, applicants from the countries of Mexico, Honduras, El Salvador, and Guatemala accounted for all but approximately 7 percent of the reasonable fear cases screened by USCIS for fiscal years 2014 through the first two quarters of fiscal year 2019.[124] Overall, Mexican nationals accounted for the largest number of reasonable fear cases among these four countries (33 percent of total reasonable fear cases).

As shown in Table 21, Mexico had the most reasonable fear referrals to USCIS each year from fiscal years 2014 through the first two quarters of fiscal year 2019.

Table 21. Top four countries of nationality for U.S. Citizenship and Immigration Services (USCIS) reasonable fear cases, fiscal years 2014 through the first two quarters of fiscal year 2019

Fiscal year	Mexico	Honduras	El Salvador	Guatemala	All other countries	Total cases
2014	2,835	1,649	1,744	1,509	686	8,602
2015	2,943	1,423	1,685	1,302	551	8,000
2016	2,956	1,903	2,200	1,537	587	9,274
2017	3,281	2,097	1,989	1,792	588	9,792
2018	3,638	2,621	1,672	2,132	590	10,697
2019 (first two quarters)	1,796	1,777	868	1,223	456	6,121
Total	17,449	11,470	10,158	9,495	3,458	52,486

Source: GAO analysis of USCIS data. | GAO-20-250.

Notes: Noncitizens issued a final administrative order of removal after conviction for crimes that meet the definition of an "aggravated felony" in the Immigration and Nationality Act or whose prior removal order is reinstated may be placed into streamlined removal proceedings where they cannot apply for asylum. However, if they express a fear of return, they are to be screened for "reasonable fear," which is a screening for withholding or deferral of removal, more limited forms of humanitarian protection. See 8 C.F.R. §§ 208.31, 208.16.

We use the number of cases, rather than number of individual noncitizens screened by USCIS, as our unit of analysis because an individual noncitizen may have claimed fear and been screened more than once during the time period covered by our data.

USCIS's automated system did not record citizenship for nearly 500 reasonable fear cases (0.9 percent of total reasonable fear cases). According to USCIS officials, these are likely cases where the individual's citizenship was unknown.

---

[124] USCIS's automated system did not record citizenship for nearly 500 reasonable fear cases (0.9 percent of total reasonable fear cases). According to USCIS officials, these are likely cases where the individual's citizenship was unknown.

Outcomes of USCIS Credible Fear and Reasonable Fear Screenings Based on the Presence of Representation at the Applicant's Interview

Table 22. Outcomes for U.S. Citizenship and Immigration Services (USCIS) credible fear cases where the applicant had a representative present (attorney or other consultant) during the interview, fiscal years 2014 through the first two quarters of 2019

Fiscal year	Percentage of positive determinations when the applicant has representation	Percentage of positive determinations when the applicant does not have representation
2014	82.5	69.5
2015	81.3	69.7
2016	86.1	78.3
2017	86.1	74.8
2018	86.5	75.8
2019 (first two quarters)	89.7	75.9
Total	84.9	74.9

Source: GAO analysis of USCIS data. | GAO-20-250.

Notes: The data presented in this table on representation are based on the number of credible fear cases for which USCIS's automated case management system indicates the individual had either an attorney or consultant present at the interview.

With some exceptions, including unaccompanied alien children, apprehended individuals may be placed into administrative removal proceedings before an immigration judge or, if the individual is an arriving alien or encountered within 14 days and 100 miles of entry and is inadmissible based on fraud or misrepresentation, may be placed into expedited removal. Individuals placed into expedited removal are to be ordered removed from the United States without further hearing unless the individual indicates either an intention to apply for asylum or a fear of persecution or torture, or a fear of return, in which case they are to be referred to USCIS for credible fear of persecution screening, as appropriate. See 8 U.S.C. § 1225(b); 8 C.F.R. § 208.30.

According to USCIS, a consultant may be a relative, friend, clergy person, attorney, or representative. We use the number of cases, rather than number of individual noncitizens screened by USCIS, as our unit of analysis because an individual noncitizen may have claimed fear and been screened more than once during the time period covered by our data.

As Table 22 shows, noncitizens making credible fear claims who had representation present at their interviews with asylum officers more often received positive determinations of fear by the asylum officer. Overall, during this time period, the number of positive determinations in cases with representation was nearly 10 percentage points greater than those without representation.

As Table 23 shows, similar to credible fear cases, noncitizens making reasonable fear claims who had representation present at their interviews with asylum officers more often received positive determinations of fear by the asylum officer. Overall, during this time period, the number of positive determinations in cases with representation was over 20 percentage points greater than those without representation.

Table 23. Outcomes for U.S. Citizenship and Immigration Services (USCIS) reasonable fear cases where the applicant had a representative present (attorney or other consultant) during the interview, fiscal years 2014 through the first two quarters of 2019

Fiscal year	Percentage of positive determinations when the applicant has representation	Percentage of positive determinations when the applicant does not have representation
2014	45.8	22.2
2015	45.2	24.0
2016	49.3	27.7
2017	48.6	24.7
2018	48.7	23.3
2019 (first two quarters)	53.6	26.6
Total	47.9	24.7

Source: GAO analysis of USCIS data. | GAO-20-250.

Notes: The data presented in this table on representation is based on the number of reasonable fear cases for which USCIS's automated case management system indicates the individual had either an attorney or consultant present at the interview.

Noncitizens issued a final administrative order of removal after conviction for crimes that meet the definition of an "aggravated felony" in the Immigration and Nationality Act or whose prior removal order is reinstated may be placed into streamlined removal proceedings where they cannot apply for asylum. However, if they express a fear of return, they are to be screened for "reasonable fear," which is a screening for withholding or deferral of removal, more limited forms of humanitarian protection. See 8 C.F.R. §§ 208.31, 208.16.

We use the number of cases, rather than number of individual noncitizens screened by USCIS, as our unit of analysis because an individual noncitizen may have claimed fear and been screened more than once during the time period covered by our data.

ICE Detention Facilities and Family Residential Centers Making the Most Credible Fear and Reasonable Fear Referrals to USCIS for Screening during Fiscal Years 2014 through the First Two Quarters of Fiscal Year 2019

Table 24. Top five detention facilities and family residential centers with the highest number of U.S. Citizenship and Immigration Services (USCIS) credible and reasonable fear cases, fiscal years 2014 through the first two quarters of fiscal year 2019

Fiscal Year	Dilley Family Residential Center[a]	Karnes Family Residential Center[b]	Pearsall Detention Complex	Hutto Residential Center	Port Isabel Service Processing Center	All other facilities	Top five facilities as percent of all facilities
2014	—	620	3,920	5,080	2,099	42,995	21
2015	6,680	2,943	3,729	3,303	2,941	31,566	38
2016	27,275	14,681	4,327	3,820	3,207	45,786	54
2017	21,223	10,389	5,348	3,340	3,068	38,219	53
2018	32,114	11,453	6,069	4,751	3,622	48,485	54
2019 (first two quarters)	10,057	2,945	2,741	2,345	2,274	35,337	37
Total	97,349	43,031	26,134	22,639	17,211	242,388	46

Source: GAO analysis of USCIS data. | GAO-20-250.

Notes: With some exceptions, including unaccompanied alien children, apprehended individuals may be placed into administrative removal proceedings before an immigration judge or, if the individual is an arriving alien or encountered within 14 days and 100 miles of entry and is inadmissible based on fraud or misrepresentation, may be placed into expedited removal. Individuals placed into expedited removal are to be ordered removed from the United States without further hearing unless the individual indicates either an intention to apply for asylum or a fear of persecution or torture, or a fear of return, in which case they are to be referred to USCIS for credible fear of persecution screening, as appropriate. See 8 U.S.C. § 1225(b); 8 C.F.R. § 208.30. Noncitizens issued a final administrative order of removal after conviction for crimes that meet the definition of an "aggravated felony" in the Immigration and Nationality Act or whose prior removal order is reinstated may be placed into streamlined removal proceedings where they cannot apply for asylum. However, if they express a fear of return, they are to be screened for "reasonable fear," which is a screening for withholding or deferral of removal, more limited forms of humanitarian protection. See 8 C.F.R. §§ 208.31, 208.16.

We use the number of cases, rather than number of individual noncitizens screened by USCIS, as our unit of analysis because an individual noncitizen may have claimed fear and been screened more than once during the time period covered by our data.

[a]U.S. Immigration and Customs Enforcement (ICE) housed families at the South Texas Family Residential Center in Dilley, Texas from November 2014 to present.

[b]ICE housed families at the Karnes Family Residential Center in Karnes, Texas from July 2014 to March 2019 and October 2019 to present.

As Table 24 shows, two of ICE's family residential centers (Dilley and Karnes family residential centers) accounted for the highest number of credible and reasonable fear referrals, among the top five facilities making these referrals, from fiscal years 2014 through the first two quarters of fiscal year 2019.

Reasonable Fear Referrals to USCIS from ICE's Family Residential Centers, and Related Positive Outcomes, during Fiscal Years 2014 through the First Two Quarters of Fiscal Year 2019

As shown in Table 25, reasonable fear screenings for those in ICE family residential centers comprised 6 percent of all such cases referred to USCIS during this same period with the percentage of positive determinations (77 percent) higher than that for all reasonable fear cases nationwide (30 percent).

Table 25. Reasonable fear referrals to U.S. Citizenship and Immigration Services (USCIS) from U.S. Immigration and Customs Enforcement's (ICE) family residential facilities, and related positive outcomes, fiscal years 2014 through first two quarters of 2019

Fiscal year	Total reasonable fear referrals to USCIS	Total reasonable fear referrals from ICE's family residential centers	Percentage of reasonable fear referrals from ICE's family residential centers	Total and percentage of positive determinations for all reasonable fear referrals	Total and percentage of positive determination from ICE's family residential centers
2014	8,602	87	1	2,493 (29)	62 (71)
2015	8,000	374	5	2,423 (30)	285 (76)
2016	9,274	964	10	3,005 (32)	717 (74)
2017	9,792	550	6	2,942 (30)	417 (76)

Fiscal year	Total reasonable fear referrals to USCIS	Total reasonable fear referrals from ICE's family residential centers	Percentage of reasonable fear referrals from ICE's family residential centers	Total and percentage of positive determinations for all reasonable fear referrals	Total and percentage of positive determination from ICE's family residential centers
2018	10,697	703	7	3,014 (28)	557 (79)
2019 (first two quarters)	6,121	425	7	1,913 (31)	358 (84)
Total	52,486	3,103	6	15,790 (30)	2,396 (77)

Source: GAO analysis of USCIS data. | GAO-20-250.

Notes: With some exceptions, including unaccompanied alien children, apprehended individuals may be placed into administrative removal proceedings before an immigration judge or, if the individual is an arriving alien or encountered within 14 days and 100 miles of entry and is inadmissible based on fraud or misrepresentation, may be placed into expedited removal. Individuals placed into expedited removal are to be ordered removed from the United States without further hearing unless the individual indicates either an intention to apply for asylum or a fear of persecution or torture, or a fear of return, in which case they are to be referred to USCIS for credible fear of persecution screening, as appropriate. See 8 U.S.C. § 1225(b); 8 C.F.R. § 208.30. Noncitizens issued a final administrative order of removal after conviction for crimes that meet the definition of an "aggravated felony" in the Immigration and Nationality Act or whose prior removal order is reinstated may be placed into streamlined removal proceedings where they cannot apply for asylum. However, if they express a fear of return, they are to be screened for "reasonable fear," which is a screening for withholding or deferral of removal, more limited forms of humanitarian protection. See 8 C.F.R. §§ 208.31, 208.16.

Number of Credible Fear and Reasonable Fear Cases Screened, by USCIS Asylum Office, for Fiscal Years 2014 through the First Two Quarters of Fiscal Year 2019

As shown in Table 26, the Houston asylum office screened two-thirds (67 percent) of credible fear cases from fiscal year 2014 through the first two quarters of fiscal year 2019.

Also, over this same time period, USCIS's Los Angeles asylum office screened the second most credible fear cases (11 percent). However, since fiscal year 2018, USCIS's Asylum Pre-Screening Center has screened the second most credible fear cases after Houston.[125]

Table 26. U.S. Citizenship and Immigration Services (USCIS) credible fear cases by Asylum office, Fiscal Years (FY) 2014 through the first two quarters of 2019

Asylum Office	FY 2014	FY 2015	FY 2016	FY 2017	FY 2018	FY 2019 (first two quarters)	Total	Percent of total credible fear cases for all years
Asylum Pre-Screening Center[a]	—	—	3	1,357	11,024	6,956	19,340	4.7
Arlington	1,776	1,749	3,060	3,550	3,481	1,621	15,237	3.7
Boston Sub Office[b]	—	1	—	141	240	104	486	0.1
Chicago	1,199	529	1,873	1,410	1,502	1,091	7,604	1.8
Houston	26,845	28,248	64,631	52,442	69,032	33,868	275,066	66.6
Los Angeles	8,620	9,199	11,039	9,911	4,854	2,718	46,341	11.2
Miami	2,010	1,707	3,464	1,672	815	786	10,454	2.5
Newark	5,247	3,447	4,643	2,719	1,970	493	18,519	4.5
New York	147	84	96	390	91	125	933	0.2
New Orleans Sub Office[c]	—	—	1	1,696	2,059	1,084	4,840	1.2

[125] The Asylum Pre-Screening Center is co-located with the Arlington asylum office in Arlington, VA. USCIS established the Asylum Pre-Screening Center in fiscal year 2016 to provide additional support for the credible and reasonable fear caseload. As of April 2019, the Asylum Pre-Screening Center and the Arlington Asylum Office together had jurisdiction over 27 ICE detention centers across the United States. According to USCIS officials, asylum officers from the Arlington asylum office may also be assigned to screen credible and reasonable fear cases that are under the jurisdiction of the Asylum Pre-Screening Center.

Asylum Office	FY 2014	FY 2015	FY 2016	FY 2017	FY 2018	FY 2019 (first two quarters)	Total	Percent of total credible fear cases for all years
San Francisco	1,910	3,125	2,788	2,410	3,015	1,245	14,493	3.5
Total	47,754	48,089	91,598	77,698	98,083	50,091	413,313	—

Source: GAO analysis of USCIS data. | GAO-20-250.

Notes: With some exceptions, including unaccompanied alien children, apprehended individuals may be placed into administrative removal proceedings before an immigration judge or, if the individual is an arriving alien or encountered within 14 days and 100 miles of entry and is inadmissible based on fraud or misrepresentation, may be placed into expedited removal. Individuals placed into expedited removal are to be ordered removed from the United States without further hearing unless the individual indicates either an intention to apply for asylum or a fear of persecution or torture, or a fear of return, in which case they are to be referred to USCIS for credible fear of persecution screening, as appropriate. See 8 U.S.C. § 1225(b); 8 C.F.R. § 208.30.

We use the number of cases, rather than number of individual noncitizens screened by USCIS, as our unit of analysis because an individual noncitizen may have claimed fear and been screened more than once during the time period covered by our data.

[a]The Asylum Pre -Screening Center, which is located in Arlington, Virginia, became operational in fiscal year 2016.

[b]The Boston office, a sub-office under the Newark asylum office, did not receive credible fear cases until fiscal year 2015, had no credible fear cases in fiscal year 2016, and resumed processing credible fear cases for the remainder of the time period covered by our data.

[c]The New Orleans office, a sub-office under Houston's jurisdiction, did not receive credible fear cases until fiscal year 2016 and reasonable fear cases until fiscal year 2017.

Table 27. U.S. Citizenship and Immigration Services (USCIS) reasonable fear cases, by Asylum Office, Fiscal Years (FY) 2014 through the first two quarters of Fiscal Year 2019

Asylum Office	FY 2014	FY 2015	FY 2016	FY 2017	FY 2018	FY 2019 (first two quarters)	Total	Percent of total reasonable fear cases for all years
Asylum Pre-Screening Center[a]	—	—	—	408	1,781	1,008	3,197	6.1
Arlington	758	715	823	1,164	1,342	702	5,504	10.5
Boston Sub Office[b]	—	—	—	8	82	52	142	0.3
Chicago	534	439	498	576	607	410	3,064	5.8

Table 27. (Continued)

Asylum Office	FY 2014	FY 2015	FY 2016	FY 2017	FY 2018	FY 2019 (first two quarters)	Total	Percent of total reasonable fear cases for all years
Houston	3,537	3,507	5,220	4,132	4,392	2,649	23,437	44.7
Los Angeles	1,375	1,381	1,223	1,473	488	323	6,263	11.9
Miami	395	303	184	222	283	162	1,549	3.0
Newark	862	606	551	549	368	194	3,130	6.0
New York[c]	30	49	6	—	149	28	262	0.5
New Orleans Sub Office[d]	—	—	—	334	565	326	1,225	2.3
San Francisco	1,111	1,000	769	926	640	267	4,713	9.0
Total	8,602	8,000	9,274	9,792	10,697	6,121	52,486	—

Source: GAO analysis of USCIS data. | GAO-20-250.

Notes: Noncitizens issued a final administrative order of removal after convection for crimes that meet the definition of an "aggravated felony" in the Immigration and Nationality Act or whose prior removal order is reinstated may be placed into streamlined removal proceedings where they cannot apply for asylum. However, if they express a fear of return, they are to be screened for "reasonable fear," which is a screening for withholding or deferral of removal, more limited forms of humanitarian protection. See 8 C.F.R. §§ 208.31, 208.16.

We use the number of cases, rather than number of individual noncitizens screened by USCIS, as our unit of analysis because an individual noncitizen may have claimed fear and been screened more than once during the time period covered by our data.

[a]The Asylum Pre-Screening Office, which is located in Arlington, VA, did not receive any records of reasonable fear cases for FY 2014 and FY 2015 because the Asylum Pre-Screening Office became operational in fiscal year 2016.

[b]The Boston office, a sub-office under the Newark asylum office, did not receive reasonable fear cases until fiscal year 2017.

[c]The New York office did not receive any reasonable fear cases in fiscal year 2017.

[d]The New Orleans office, a sub-office under Houston's jurisdiction, did not receive credible fear cases until fiscal year 2016 and reasonable fear cases until fiscal year 2017.

As shown in Table 27, the Houston asylum office screened nearly half (approximately 45 percent) of reasonable fear cases from fiscal year 2014 through the first two quarters of fiscal year 2019. Also, over this same time period, USCIS's Los Angeles asylum office screened the second most reasonable fear cases (12 percent). However, since fiscal year 2018, USCIS's Asylum Pre-Screening Center has screened the second most reasonable fear cases after Houston.

APPENDIX IV: COMMENTS FROM THE DEPARTMENT OF HOMELAND SECURITY

U.S. Department of Homeland Security
Washington, DC 20528

Homeland Security

January 29, 2020

Rebecca Gambler
Director, Homeland Security and Justice
U.S. Government Accountability Office
441 G Street, NW
Washington, DC 20548

Re: Management Response to Draft Report GAO-20-250, "IMMIGRATION: Actions Needed to Strengthen USCIS's Oversight and Data Quality of Credible and Reasonable Fear Screenings"

Dear Ms. Gambler:

Thank you for the opportunity to review and comment on this draft report. The U.S. Department of Homeland Security (DHS) appreciates the U.S. Government Accountability Office's (GAO) work in planning and conducting its review and issuing this report.

The Department appreciates the GAO's reporting of DHS's credible and reasonable fear screening programs. During Fiscal Year (FY) 2019, U. S. Citizenship and Immigration Services (USCIS) received historic levels of both credible fear and reasonable fear cases with more than 105,000 and 13,000 cases respectively, surpassing records set in previous years. The USCIS Asylum Division was assisted by refugee officers and former asylum officers from USCIS, as well as U.S. Border Patrol Agents (BPAs) from U.S. Customs and Border Protection, in order to complete the record number of credible fear and reasonable fear cases received. DHS remains committed to conducting credible fear and reasonable fear cases in a thorough and timely manner to fulfill international and domestic protection laws and obligations while also ensuring that the U.S. border is secure.

As noted in the draft report, starting in June 2019, BPAs were assigned to a credible fear task force to complete credible fear interviews and determinations. More than 75 BPAs have completed training and have conducted credible fear interviews throughout the United States. Starting in September 2019, the BPAs have primarily been assigned to conduct credible fear interviews at the Family Residential Center (FRC) in Dilley, Texas.

Throughout FY 2019, USCIS continued to improve its new case management system for tracking credible fear and reasonable fear case processing, conducted user interviews with staff to gain valuable feedback, and implemented new tools within the case management system to assist with tracking and increasing efficiency. For example, USCIS implemented the uploading of working documents into the case management system to allow more flexibility with case assignments and less dependence on paper files and e-mail. In addition, USCIS began using electronic signatures for officers and supervisors and exploring improved document generation to support the credible and reasonable fear caseload.

The draft report contained four recommendations with which the Department concurs. Attached find our detailed responses to each recommendation. DHS previously submitted technical comments under a separate cover.

Again, thank you for the opportunity to review and comment on this draft report. Please feel free to contact me if you have any questions. We look forward to working with you again in the future.

Sincerely,

JIM H. CRUMPACKER, CIA, CFE
Director
Departmental GAO-OIG Liaison Office

Attachment: Management Response to Recommendations Contained in GAO-20-250

GAO recommended that the Director of USCIS:

Recommendation 1: Ensure that, in addition to USCIS's basic asylum officer training, all asylum offices provide pre-departure training on credible and reasonable fear processes before their officers begin screening cases at the family residential centers.

Response: Concur. USCIS Directorate for Refugee, Asylum & International Operations (RAIO) staff already provides family processing training to all USCIS officers and Border Patrol Agents (BPAs) detailed to its Asylum Division. In addition, for more than a decade USCIS has required weekly training for USCIS asylum officers on a variety of adjudication topics. In the future, USCIS will provide a refresher training to all staff conducting asylum-related screening. In addition, USCIS will develop a standardized pre-departure training and provide this training to all detailees prior to deployment to the family residential centers (FRCs). Estimated Completion Date (ECD): September 30, 2020.

Recommendation 2: Develop and implement more specific guidance on requirements for documenting results of Asylum Division periodic quality assurance reviews.

Response: Concur. USCIS RAIO will create a results template to ensure that the outcomes of periodic quality assurance reviews involving similar case types are documented in a consistent manner to better track trends across the asylum offices. Staff assigned to participate in these reviews will be trained on how to use this template. ECD: June 30, 2020.

Recommendation 3: Ensure asylum officers systematically record in USCIS's automated case management system if individuals receive credible fear determinations as principal applicants, dependents, or in the interest of family unity, pursuant to regulation or USCIS policy.

Response: Concur. USCIS RAIO will explore ways to modify its case management system so that asylum officers can record whether the individual received a positive credible fear determination as a principal, dependent, or in the interest of family unity. USCIS will make any appropriate changes in the case management system and will train asylum officers on these changes. ECD: December 31, 2020.

Recommendation 4: Collect and analyze additional information on case delays, including specific reasons for delays and how long they last, that asylum officers may face when screening credible and reasonable fear cases.

Response: Concur. As noted in the draft report, USCIS does track limited information about some case delays. However, USCIS will explore ways to collect additional information on credible and reasonable fear case delays in the case management system. Once USCIS has identified ways to collect the additional information, it will modify the case management system, as appropriate, instruct users on the changes, and begin collecting and analyzing the information. ECD: December 31, 2020.

APPENDIX V: ACCESSIBLE DATA

Data Tables

Data Table for Figure 2. Outcomes of U.S. Citizenship and Immigration Services (USCIS) credible fear screenings, Fiscal Years 2014 through the first two quarters of 2019

Fiscal Year	Positive Determination	Negative Determination	Administrative Closure	Pending Resolution
2014	73.085	18.187	8.7008	0.0272
2015	72.7734	16.2158	10.9713	0.0395
2016	79.6841	10.0766	10.2131	0.0262
2017	76.6828	10.5305	12.7519	0.0347
2018	76.9481	9.4746	13.5028	0.0744
2019	77.5469	10.7265	11.6009	0.1258

Data Table for Figure 3. Outcomes of U.S. Citizenship and Immigration Services (USCIS) reasonable fear screenings, Fiscal Years 2014 through the first two quarters of 2019

Fiscal Year	Positive Determination	Negative Determination	Administrative Closure	Pending Resolution
2014	28.9816	28.7026	42.3157	0
2015	30.2875	34.425	35.2875	0
2016	32.4024	32.8661	34.7315	0
2017	30.0449	33.221	36.7341	0
2018	28.1761	34.9257	36.8234	0.07479
2019	31.2531	33.8343	34.8636	0.04901

Data Table for Figure 7. U.S. Border Patrol's (Border Patrol) apprehensions of noncitizens placed into expedited removal proceedings with a credible fear claim, Fiscal Years 2014 through first two quarters of Fiscal Year 2019

Fiscal Year	Credible Fear Cases	Total Apprehensions
2014	16.124	512.038
2015	16.895	361.241
2016	48.366	440.469
2017	36.27	333.205
2018	51.397	429.03
2019	28.452	375.78

Data Table for Figure 9. U.S. Customs and Border Protection's Office of Field Operations (OFO) apprehensionsa placed into expedited removal with credible fear claims, Fiscal Year 2014 through first two quarters of Fiscal Year 2019

Fiscal Year	Expedited Removal Cases with a Credible Fear Claim	Total Apprehensions
2014	11.654	67.044
2015	14.316	94.96
2016	23.592	136.206
2017	16.845	90.65
2018	27.061	104.941
2019	11.178	53.237

In: Immigration
Editor: Klonimir Jović

ISBN: 978-1-53618-183-8

Chapter 2

IMMIGRATION DETENTION: CARE OF PREGNANT WOMEN IN DHS FACILITIES*

United States Government Accountability Office

ABBREVIATIONS

CBP	U.S. Customs and Border Protection
CRCL	Office for Civil Rights and Civil Liberties
DHS	Department of Homeland Security
FRS	Family Residential Standards
ICE	U.S. Immigration and Customs Enforcement
IIDS	ICE Integrated Decision Support
IGA	intergovernmental agreement
IGSA	intergovernmental service agreement
IHSC	ICE Health Service Corps
NCCHC	National Commission on Correctional Health Care

* This is an edited, reformatted and augmented version of United States Government Accountability Office; Report to Congressional Requesters, Publication No. GAO-20-330, dated March 2020.

NDS	National Detention Standards
NGO	nongovernmental organization
OB-GYN	obstetrician-gynecologist
OFO	Office of Field Operations
PBNDS	Performance Based National Detention Standards
USMS	U.S. Marshals Service

WHY GAO DID THIS STUDY

In December 2017, the Department of Homeland Security (DHS) updated its policy on pregnant women, removing language that stated that pregnant women would generally not be detained except in extraordinary circumstances or as mandated by law. Within DHS, CBP temporarily holds individuals in its facilities and processes them for further action, such as release or transfer to ICE. ICE manages the nation's immigration detention system. ICE utilizes various facility types to detain individuals, such as those owned and operated by ICE and contract facilities. GAO was asked to review issues related to the care of pregnant women in DHS facilities.

This chapter examines (1) what available data indicate about pregnant women detained or held in DHS facilities, (2) DHS policies and standards that address the care of pregnant women, and (3) what is known about the care provided to pregnant women in DHS facilities.

GAO analyzed available DHS data and documents from calendar years 2015 through 2019, including detention data, inspection reports and data, and complaints; reviewed policies related to the care of pregnant women; and interviewed agency officials and three national non-governmental organizations.

GAO also interviewed a non- generalizable sample of 14 pregnant women detained or released by DHS and five non-governmental organizations in four field locations that had the greatest number of detentions of pregnant women, among other things.

What GAO Found

GAO's analyses of U.S. Immigration and Customs Enforcement (ICE) and U.S. Customs and Border Protection (CBP) data on pregnant women found:

- ICE detained pregnant women over 4,600 times from calendar year 2016 through 2018, with more than 90 percent resulting from CBP arrests.
- Sixty-eight percent of these detentions were for 1 week or less, while 10 percent were for more than 30 days.
- Seventy-eight percent of these initial detentions occurred at facilities staffed with ICE medical personnel.

ICE has policies and detention standards that address a variety of topics regarding the care of pregnant women, such as pregnancy testing requirements, for which non-governmental organizations, professional associations, and federal agencies have issued recommended guidance. However, some facility types— which vary based on who owns, operates, and provides medical care at the facility—did not address all these pregnancy-related topics in their policies and standards, such as prenatal vitamins, as of December 2019. ICE has plans to address the gaps GAO identified in these facility types, including updating some of its policies and detention standards in February 2020. In regards to CBP, its facilities are designed for holding individuals for no more than 72 hours, and therefore are not equipped to provide long-term care. Nonetheless, CBP has some policies and standards regarding pregnant women for its short-term facilities, including those related to nutrition and the circumstances in which restraints could be used.

GAO's analyses of inspections and complaint mechanisms offered the following insights into the care provided to pregnant women:

- ICE inspections found 79 percent or greater compliance with most of its pregnancy-related performance measures. For example, inspections found 91 percent of pregnant woman were seen by an obstetrician-gynecologist within 30 days of pregnancy confirmation, from December 2016 through March 2019. According to ICE officials and agency documentation, ICE has processes in place to address non-compliance. Additional inspections identified pregnancy-related issues at 13 facilities from January 2015 through July 2019. The facilities or ICE have taken actions to address the issues.

- CBP generally relies on offsite care for pregnant women, and as a result has limited information on care CBP provided. However, CBP has efforts underway to enhance medical support at selected facilities.
- Over 100 complaints were filed about ICE's and CBP's care of pregnant women from January 2015 through April 2019. Of these complaints, 3 were substantiated or partially substantiated, and 24 were unsubstantiated or partially unsubstantiated. In most cases there was not enough information for the investigating agency to determine whether proper care had been provided.

March 24, 2020
Congressional Requesters:

The health and safety of pregnant women in the custody of the Department of Homeland Security (DHS) have been a concern in recent years for a number of policymakers, medical associations, and advocacy groups. For example, a March 2018 letter written to DHS by various medical groups[1] noted their concerns about the health risks associated with detaining pregnant women. The letter reported that the maternal psychological state in detention can negatively affect fetal and child development and that shackling during pregnancy can have serious physical and mental health impacts on pregnant women. In addition, some

---

[1] Medical associations included the American Academy of Pediatrics, the American College of Obstetricians and Gynecologists, and the American Academy of Family Physicians.

Members of Congress have introduced bills to, in part, limit the use of restraints on pregnant women, set healthcare standards, and require the use of alternatives to detention for pregnant women.[2]

In 2017, the President issued a series of executive orders related to border security and immigration, including an Executive Order that addressed DHS's immigration enforcement priorities. Specifically, on January 25, 2017, the President issued an Executive Order instructing federal agencies, including DHS, to employ all lawful means to ensure the enforcement of the immigration laws of the United States against all removable foreign nationals.[3] On February 20, 2017, the Secretary of Homeland Security issued a memorandum implementing the Executive Order.[4] In accordance with the Executive Order and memorandum, DHS is no longer required to allocate resources according to tiered immigration enforcement priorities, which had previously placed threats to national security, border security, and public safety in the highest priority category. Instead, various categories of removable individuals are general priorities for removal, and DHS is authorized to take action against any removable foreign national, including pregnant women, encountered during its law enforcement operations. The memorandum states that DHS components may allocate resources to prioritize enforcement activities, such as by prioritizing enforcement against convicted felons or gang members.

---

[2] A recent example is the Alternatives to Detention Act of 2019, two versions of which have been introduced in the House (H.R. 532), in January 2019, and the Senate (S. 1894) in June 2019. In addition, the Stop Shackling and Detaining Pregnant Women Act (H.R. 3563) was introduced in the House in June 2019.

[3] *Enhancing Public Safety in the Interior of the United States*, Exec. Order No. 13768, 82 Fed. Reg. 8799 (Jan. 25, 2017). The term "foreign national" in this chapter is synonymous with the term "alien" in the Immigration and Nationality Act, i.e., a person who is not a citizen or national of the United States. See 8 U.S.C. § 1101(a)(3),(a)(22). A foreign national may be removable on statutory grounds of inadmissibility, Immigration and Nationality Act (INA) § 212(a), 8 U.S.C. § 1182(a), if they have no prior lawful admission, or deportability, INA § 237, 8 U.S.C. § 1227, if they were previously lawfully admitted. See 8 U.S.C. § 1229a(e)(2). The lawfulness of a prior admission may be at issue in removal proceedings. See 8 U.S.C. §§ 1182(a)(6)(C)(i) (inadmissibility for having fraudulently obtained admission into the United States), 1227(a)(1)(A) (deportability for having been inadmissible at the time of entry).

[4] Department of Homeland Security, *Enforcement of the Immigration Laws to Serve the National Interest* (February 2017).

DHS cannot practicably pursue immigration enforcement action against all persons who may be subject to removal from the United States,[5] and, therefore, DHS must continue to exercise prosecutorial discretion in the enforcement of U.S. immigration law, given the administration's removal priorities and available resources.[6] At the time the Executive Order and February 2017 memo were issued, the U.S. Immigration and Customs Enforcement (ICE) was also operating under an August 2016 memo, titled *Identification and Monitoring of Pregnant Detainees*, that stated that pregnant women would generally not be detained except in extraordinary circumstances or as mandated by law.[7] For example, ICE would be required to detain a pregnant woman if she fell within one of the law's mandatory detention categories, which includes foreign nationals deemed inadmissible for certain criminal convictions or terrorist activity, or those who have been ordered removed.[8] This August 2016 memo was superseded in December 2017 by a memo under the same title that removed the language stating that absent extraordinary circumstances or a legal requirement, pregnant women will generally not be detained by ICE.

---

[5] DHS estimated in 2015 that the total foreign national population in the United States was about 27.3 million, and of that number, about 12 million foreign nationals were without lawful status or presence. DHS's *Population Estimates: Illegal Alien Population Residing in the United States: January 2015* is the most recent report that DHS issued on this population. According to DHS, the remaining approximately 15.3 million foreign nationals includes lawful permanent residents (13.2 million), resident nonimmigrants (2 million), and individuals granted refugee or asylee status (0.1 million), as of 2015. DHS reported data on lawful permanent residents and those without lawful presence or status as of January 2015, and data for resident nonimmigrants and refugees or asylees as of September 2015. Data on foreign national populations come from DHS's Office of Immigration Statistics, see DHS Office of Immigration Statistics, *Population Estimates: Lawful Permanent Resident Population in the United States: January 2015* (Washington, D.C.: May 2019); *Nonimmigrants Residing in the United States: Fiscal Year 2015* (Washington, D.C.: September 2017); *Refugees and Asylees: 2015* (Washington, D.C.: November 2016); and *Population Estimates: Illegal Alien Population Residing in the United States: January 2015* (Washington, D.C.: December 2018).

[6] Prosecutorial discretion is the longstanding authority of an agency charged with enforcing a law to decide how to use its resources in the enforcement of the law.

[7] This is in accordance with a 2014 DHS memorandum, entitled *Policies for the Apprehension, Detention and Removal of Undocumented Immigrants* (Nov. 20, 2014).

[8] For mandatory detention categories, see 8 U.S.C. §§ 1225, 1226(c), 1226a, 1231.

In December 2019, we reported that the number of detentions of pregnant women increased from calendar year 2016 to calendar year 2018.[9]

You asked us to review issues related to DHS's detention of pregnant women. This chapter examines (1) what available data indicate about pregnant women detained or held in DHS facilities; (2) policies and standards that DHS has to address the care of pregnant women, and the extent to which they are applicable across all facilities; and (3) what is known about the care provided to pregnant women in DHS facilities.

To address all three objectives, we interviewed DHS officials from ICE and U.S. Customs and Border Protection (CBP) in headquarters and four field locations, pregnant detainees, and non-governmental organizations (NGO) to obtain their perspectives on the care of pregnant women in DHS custody. We selected locations based on ICE detention facilities that had the greatest number of detentions of pregnant women from fiscal years 2014 through 2017,[10] which included a mix of facility types.[11] For each of our site visits, we observed the facility operations and conducted semi-structured interviews with ICE and contract officials responsible for oversight or management of the facility, as well as ICE or contract medical staff.[12] In addition, we interviewed 10 pregnant women who were detained at three of the four ICE facilities we visited.[13] We

---

[9] GAO, *Immigration Enforcement: Arrests, Detentions, and Removals and Issues Related to Selected Populations*, GAO-20-36 (Washington, D.C.: Dec. 5, 2019).

[10] These were the most recent data available at the time of our site selection. Although some data were available in 2014, ICE did not begin collecting data on all pregnant women until June 2015.The four ICE facilities we visited in California and Texas collectively accounted for 87 percent of initial book-ins and 53 percent of detention days for pregnant women during this time period.

[11] Specifically, we selected ICE detention facilities to include a variety of facility types, based on who owns and operates the facility, who provides the medical services, and what detention standards they have in place. We discuss ICE detention facilities and standards later in this chapter.

[12] In total, we conducted 16 interviews with ICE and contract staff, and some interviews involved multiple officials. Specifically, we conducted 12 interviews with ICE and contract officials responsible for oversight or management of the facility, and four interviews with ICE and contract medical staff.

[13] With the consent of these women, we conducted structured interviews to obtain insight into the care they received at their respective ICE facility. According to ICE, these were the only adult pregnant women detained at these facilities during the time of our visits. At the time of our site visits, ICE identified a total of 10 pregnant women detained at three of the four facilities, and there were no pregnant women detained at the fourth ICE facility at the time

interviewed an additional four pregnant women at a local shelter in Texas after their release from DHS custody.[14] We also observed facility operations and conducted six semi-structured interviews with CBP officials at four Border Patrol facilities and four Office of Field Operations (OFO) ports of entry that were located in the four locations we selected. Moreover, we conducted semi-structured interviews with officials from five local and three national NGOs to obtain their perspectives on the care of pregnant women in DHS custody.[15] While these site visits and interviews with field officials, pregnant women, and NGOs are not generalizable and may not be indicative of the care provided at all detention facilities, they provided us with perspectives on the care provided to pregnant women.

To address the first objective, we reviewed data sources that ICE uses to track pregnant women in detention from calendar years 2016 through 2018 and matched these data with various ICE databases.[16] Specifically, we matched ICE records for pregnant women with data from ICE's individual-level detention dataset to determine the total number of detentions of pregnant women, as well as the length of detention, facility location, case status, arresting agency, gestation of pregnancy, and whether there is an associated criminal conviction (criminality). We reported on total detentions since a pregnant woman may have been detained multiple times during a calendar year. Our analysis is based on over 4,600 detainee records we were able to match, including 1,377 for 2016; 1,150 for 2017; and 2,094 for 2018.[17] We also merged the detention data with data from

---

of our visit. We interviewed detainees in Spanish, and we used a translation service for interviews conducted in other languages.

[14] All of these women spoke Spanish, and as such, we used an interpreter provided by our staff and staff at the shelter.

[15] We selected local NGOs or coalitions based on their representation of detained populations located near our site visit locations and their coordination with ICE and CBP. We selected national NGOs based on their healthcare expertise and publication of recommended guidance for the care of detained pregnant women. National NGOs included the American College of Obstetricians and Gynecologists, National Commission on Correctional Health Care, and American Correctional Association.

[16] We selected these years since ICE first collected data on all pregnant women beginning in June 2015, and 2018 was the last full year of available data for our audit.

[17] ICE collected data for 1,437 pregnant detainees in 2016; 1,170 in 2017; and 2,126 in 2018. We excluded 60 of the unique pregnant detainee records for 2016; 20 for 2017; and 32 for 2018

ICE's weekly facility list report, as of February 2019,[18] to determine characteristics of the facilities in which our study population were detained—such as who owned and operated the facility, who provided medical services, and in what state the facility was located. Finally, we also analyzed ICE data on pregnancy outcomes— abortions, births, stillbirths, and miscarriages—from 2015 through June 2019—which includes, but is not limited to, our study population of over 4,600 detentions from 2016 through 2018. To determine the number of pregnant women held by CBP, we analyzed summary data for the most recent data available.[19] We also analyzed CBP's significant incident reports to identify pregnancy outcomes from 2015 through February 2019.[20] We assessed the reliability of the data used in each of our analyses by reviewing relevant information about these systems, interviewing knowledgeable agency officials, and conducting electronic tests to identify missing data, anomalies, or potentially erroneous values. We determined the data were sufficiently reliable for describing general information on pregnant women in DHS custody.

To address the second objective, we analyzed ICE and CBP policies and standards and training documents that address the care of pregnant women. Policies and detention standards we analyzed included (1) ICE policies and detention standards that govern the conditions of confinement at ICE detention facilities, and (2) CBP policies for Border Patrol and OFO, and CBP's national standards.[21] Furthermore, we developed 16 pregnancy-related topics—such as pregnancy testing requirements,

---

because we were unable to match these records to individual-level detention data. A detainee could have more than one detention.

18 At the time that we merged the data sets, the February 2019 list was the most recent report.

19 In March 2018, OFO began collecting self-reported data on pregnant women held at its ports of entry. We analyzed these data from this date through September 2019. In March 2017, Border Patrol began collecting self-reported data on pregnant women in two of its nine southwest border sectors, including gestation data. We analyzed these data from this date through March 2019.

20 CBP has requirements for reporting certain types of incidents, such as deaths. According to CBP officials, although there is no requirement to report miscarriages and births, some are reported at the discretion of CBP officials. As such, it is possible that not all information was reported. The data include reports only involving foreign nationals.

21 U.S. Customs and Border Protection, *National Standards on Transport, Escort, Detention, and Search* (October 2015).

prenatal care, and the use of restraints—and categorized agency policies and standards accordingly.[22] We analyzed the extent to which ICE facility types had a policy or detention standard that addressed each of these 16 topics. For this analysis, facility type was based on who owns and operates the facility and provides medical care. Further, for each of these topics, we summarized recommended guidance published by NGOs, professional associations, and federal agencies, and assessed the extent to which each ICE facility type had a policy or detention standard that generally aligned with recommended guidance.[23] We spoke with ICE and CBP officials in headquarters and the selected field locations noted above to obtain their perspectives on policies, detention standards—including any planned updates—and related training.

To address the third objective, we analyzed inspections results, agency data, and complaint information. Specifically, we analyzed reports and data from five ICE inspections that address compliance with pregnancy-related policies and detention standards from 2015 through July 2019.[24] We also analyzed ICE documentation on corrective actions that facilities reported taking to address inspection findings. Further, we reviewed and categorized complaints that detainees, family members, NGOs, or other parties submitted through various complaint systems from January 2015 through April 2019—the latest available complaints at the time of our

---

[22] We developed these pregnancy-related topics based on our review of guidance from professional associations and NGOs, NGO complaints and media reports, ICE's and CBP's policies and detention standards, and reports issued by federal agencies. Further, we did not include recommended guidance that was not directly relevant to the care of pregnant women once detained, such as guidance on detention determinations and child care.

[23] We selected this guidance based on our research and review of non-governmental and agency documents and recommendations from NGO officials. Recommended guidance is from American College of Obstetricians and Gynecologists, National Commission on Correctional Health Care, and the American Correctional Association, as well as other relevant organizations including the United Nations, the National Women's Law Center, American Civil Liberties Union, and working groups assembled by both the Departments of Justice and Homeland Security. Because the specificity of the guidance varies across entities, we summarized the recommended guidance for our report purposes. NGO officials we spoke with said that although their recommended guidance was designed to apply in a criminal incarceration setting, their recommended guidance is also applicable to immigration detention.

[24] These were the most recent data available at the time of our review. We selected these inspections because they review some aspect of the care provided to pregnant women. CBP officials told us that they did not have inspections that address the care of pregnant women.

review—regarding ICE's and CBP's care of pregnant women. We selected these complaint systems because they contained relevant information on the care of pregnant women, according to DHS officials. In addition, we analyzed agency documentation on the extent to which complaints could be substantiated, and any corrective actions that agencies and facilities reported taking to address complaints. We also reviewed ICE medical data from calendar year 2016 through 2018.[25] We also reviewed significant incident reports that CBP documented for incidents that involved a pregnant woman being sent to a hospital from 2015 through February 2019.[26] We assessed the reliability of the data used in each of our analyses by reviewing relevant information about these systems, interviewing knowledgeable agency officials, and conducting electronic tests to identify missing data, anomalies, or potentially erroneous values. We determined the data were sufficiently reliable for our purposes of understanding what is known about the care of pregnant women in DHS custody. Further, we interviewed ICE and CBP officials in headquarters and selected field locations, as previously described. We interviewed pregnant women who were detained, as well as representatives of NGOs, to obtain their perspectives on the care of pregnant women in DHS custody. Appendix I describes our analyses of ICE data, inspections, and complaints in greater detail.

We conducted this performance audit from August 2018 to March 2020 in accordance with generally accepted government auditing standards.

Those standards require that we plan and perform the audit to obtain sufficient, appropriate evidence to provide a reasonable basis for our findings and conclusions based on our audit objectives. We believe that the evidence obtained provides a reasonable basis for our findings and conclusions based on our audit objectives.

---

[25] As mentioned previously, 2016 was the first year that ICE collected data on all pregnant women.

[26] These were the most recent data available at the time of our request.

BACKGROUND

Federal Roles and Responsibilities

Within DHS, ICE is responsible for immigration enforcement and removal operations. This entails, among other duties, identifying, arresting, and detaining foreign nationals for the administrative purpose of facilitating their appearance during removal proceedings, and for processing, and preparing them for removal from the United States, among other things. As such, ICE manages the nation's immigration detention system, which houses foreign nationals detained while their immigration cases are pending or after being ordered removed from the country. ICE generally has broad discretion in determining whether to detain removable foreign nationals or release them under various conditions, unless the law specifies that detention is mandatory.[27] Additionally, foreign nationals arriving at the U.S. border or a port of entry without valid entry documents and placed into expedited removal proceedings[28] are required to be detained while awaiting an inadmissibility determination and, as applicable, any subsequent credible fear decision.[29] Except in cases where detention is mandatory, ICE may release an individual pending the outcome of removal proceedings and has various release options for doing so, including the Alternatives to Detention program.[30]

---

[27] See 8 U.S.C. § 1226. Conditions of release include bond, conditional parole, terms of supervision, or other alternatives to detention.

[28] Expedited removal under Immigration and Nationality Act (INA) § 235(b) is the process by which a DHS immigration officer may, subject to statutory criteria, order arriving and other designated foreign nationals removed from the United States without formal removal proceedings under INA § 240. See 8 U.S.C. § 1225(b).

[29] Foreign nationals may indicate an intention to apply for asylum or express a credible fear of persecution or torture if they are returned to their home country. After a credible fear referral, screening and determination, aliens are generally to be detained pending review of such determination, their removal, or a decision on any subsequent asylum application. Individuals found to have a credible fear and referred to immigration court for an asylum hearing may receive a bond hearing and therefore be eligible for release on bond, conditional parole, terms of supervision or other alternatives to detention.

[30] We have previously issued work on ICE's Alternatives to Detention program, and the extent of its cost effectiveness. See GAO, *Alternatives to Detention: Improved Data Collection and Analyses Needed to Better Assess Program Effectiveness*, GAO-15-26 (Washington, D.C., Nov. 13, 2014). Further, as reported in GAO-20-36, ICE does not track specific

While foreign nationals are detained, ICE is responsible for providing accommodations and medical care to individuals in detention with special needs or vulnerabilities, such as those who are pregnant.[31] ICE's December 2017 memo, *Identification and Monitoring of Pregnant Detainees,* sets forth policy and procedures to ensure pregnant detainees in ICE custody are identified, monitored, tracked, and housed in an appropriate facility.

CBP is a component within DHS and the lead federal agency charged with a dual mission of facilitating the flow of legitimate travel and trade at our nation's borders while also keeping terrorists and their weapons, criminals and their contraband, and inadmissible foreign nationals out of the country. CBP temporarily holds individuals to complete general processing and determine the appropriate course of action, such as transferring them to a court, jail, prison, or another agency; relocating them into ICE detention facilities; removing them from the country; or releasing them—as CBP has discretion to release individuals with a notice to appear in court. Within CBP, individuals, including pregnant women, could be held by Border Patrol or OFO.[32]

---

characteristics of individuals enrolled in its Alternatives to Detention program, including pregnant women. In addition, we have previously reported on the challenges with identifying medical costs at ICE detention facilities. See GAO, *Immigration Detention: Additional Actions Needed to Strengthen Management and Oversight of Detainee Medical Care*, GAO-16-231 (Washington, D.C., Feb. 29, 2016) and GAO, *Immigration Detention: Additional Actions Needed to Strengthen Management and Oversight of Facility Costs and Standards,* GAO-15-153 (Washington, D.C., Oct. 10, 2014). Specifically, for some facilities, we reported that costs for medical care are typically included in each facility's per diem rate for housing detainees and ICE pays a set fee per day per detainee. As such, medical care costs are not tracked separately.

31 ICE includes pregnant women as one of its vulnerable populations.

32 Border Patrol operates between the ports of entry, while OFO operates at the ports of entry. Border Patrol has 20 sectors while OFO operates 328 land, air, and sea ports of entry—which provides for the controlled entry into or departure from the United States. Specifically, a port of entry is any officially designated location (seaport, airport, or land border location) where DHS officers or employees are assigned to clear passengers and merchandise, collect duties, and enforce customs laws, and where DHS officers inspect persons entering or applying for admission into, or departing the United States pursuant to U.S. immigration and travel controls.

ICE Detention Facility Types, Detention Standards, and Medical Care

ICE detains individuals in both under-72-hour and over-72-hour detention facilities.[33] Detention facilities may be for male only, female only, or both; and some are specifically reserved for family units (also known as family residential centers). ICE uses various types of detention facilities to hold detainees for more than 72-hours. These include ICE owned and operated detention facilities, also known as service processing centers,[34] as well as facilities that ICE oversees but the day-to-day operations are generally run by another entity,[35] as follows:

- contract detention facilities owned and operated by a private company under direct ICE contract that exclusively houses ICE detainees,
- facilities owned by state or local government or private entity, operating under an intergovernmental service agreement (IGSA), that exclusively houses ICE detainees or houses ICE detainees and other confined populations,[36] and
- facilities owned by state or local government or private entity, operating under an intergovernmental agreement (IGA), or contract, with U.S. Marshals Service (USMS), that exclusively houses ICE detainees or houses ICE detainees and other confined populations.[37]

---

[33] In addition to detention facilities, ICE may detain an individual in a hold room. Hold rooms are used for detention of individuals awaiting removal, transfer, immigration hearings, medical treatment, intra-facility movement, or other processing into or out of a facility. According to ICE, an individual may not be confined in a facility's hold room for more than 12 hours.

[34] According to ICE officials, contract staff may operate at these facilities.

[35] ICE personnel have a presence at these facilities to carry out ICE responsibilities—such as making detention determinations—and to provide oversight.

[36] All of ICE's family residential centers are operated under an IGSA.

[37] ICE may be a rider on an USMS contract—which allows ICE to use a facility for the purpose of detaining individuals in ICE custody. USMS has no role in the oversight of ICE detainees in these facilities, according to ICE officials. Further, ICE officials stated that ICE would not have USMS transport or escort any of its DHS immigration detainees, and CBP officials stated that USMS may escort a DHS detainee during federal criminal court proceedings but that this would be rare. Individuals in DHS custody—which may include pregnant

ICE detention facilities are generally required to adhere to one of four sets of detention standards. The detention standards vary depending on the contract or agreement.[38] As we have previously reported, ICE's detention standards are based on the American Correctional Association's expected practices and have been updated when ICE identified issues of heightened concern or gaps in agency procedures.[39] Some detention facilities used by ICE are not obligated to adhere to ICE's detention standards—because, for example, ICE is a rider on the contract and the facility may be held to other standards.[40]

Further, on-site medical care may be directly provided by ICE Health Service Corps (IHSC) or other entities at these detention facilities.[41] IHSC provides direct on-site medical services in 20 ICE facilities authorized to house detainees for over 72 hours. In addition to any applicable detention standards, IHSC staff must also adhere to IHSC policies. At detention facilities that are not staffed with IHSC personnel (non-IHSC facilities),

---

women—could be referred to the Department of Justice for criminal prosecutions. USMS detains those individuals who have been remanded to their custody by a federal judge. USMS also provides courtroom security for federal criminal court proceedings. We have ongoing work on pregnant women in Bureau of Prisons and USMS custody.

[38] Our prior work has examined ICE's efforts to have all contracted facilities operating or inspected under the newest detention standards, see GAO-15-153 (Washington, D.C., Oct. 10, 2014). We have ongoing work on ICE's detention contracts.

[39] See GAO-15-153. The American Correctional Association develops expected practices for correctional facilities, and correctional facilities can apply to be accredited by the American Correctional Association. According to the American Correctional Association, its expected practices represent correctional practices that ensure staff and inmate safety and security; enhance staff morale; improve record maintenance and data management capabilities; assist in protecting the agency against litigation; and improve the function of the facility or agency at all levels. According to officials from the American Correctional Association, their expected practices are applicable to immigration detention.

[40] Although they may not be obligated to adhere to one of the four sets of detention standards, according to ICE officials, facilities used by ICE to house single adults for more than 60 days are inspected against one of the four sets of detention standards.

[41] Facilities serviced by IHSC include service processing centers, contract detention facilities, IGSA facilities, and family residential centers. IHSC personnel include Commissioned Corps officers of the Department of Health and Human Services' Public Health Service. IHSC provides direct care at designated facilities to include medical, dental mental health, and public health services. In addition, IHSC also has the authority to provide health care to detainees, as well as to authorize treatment of detainees in hospitals outside of detention facilities while in ICE custody. See 42 U.S.C. § 249; 42 C.F.R. § 34.7(a).

medical care is provided onsite by local government staff or private contractors and overseen by IHSC.[42]

ICE inspects "authorized" detention facilities against detention standards and any applicable IHSC policies.[43] Table 1 details information on each of the detention standards, the number of authorized facilities contractually obligated to each standard, the percent of the average daily population at each, and the presence of IHSC staff.

Table 1. U.S. Immigration and Customs Enforcement (ICE) detention standards, number of authorized facilities, percent of the average daily population, and ICE Health Service Corps (IHSC) presence, as of February 2019

Detention standard	Description	Number of authorized facilities obligated to adhere to standard	Percent of average daily population, fiscal year 2019	Number of authorized facilities that are also staffed by IHSC[a]
2000 National Detention Standards (NDS)[b]	The 2000 NDS are a set of standards intended to govern the conditions of confinement at ICE detention facilities. They dictate how facilities should operate to ensure safe, secure, and humane confinement for immigration detainees, laying out requirements that covered facilities must meet to remain in operation.	73	11.1	0

[42] IHSC is to provide medical case management and oversight for detainees housed at non-IHSC facilities.

[43] According to ICE officials, authorized facilities are those facilities that are used on a frequent and regular basis. Facilities that are not used on a frequent basis are deemed non-authorized and are not inspected by ICE. Non-authorized facilities could include hold rooms, staging facilities, and hospitals.

Detention standard	Description	Number of authorized facilities obligated to adhere to standard	Percent of average daily population, fiscal year 2019	Number of authorized facilities that are also staffed by IHSC[a]
2007 Family Residential Standards[b]	ICE approved the Family Residential Standards in 2007 to apply to its facilities that house families in detention. The standards are based on ICE analysis of family detention operations and state statutes that affect children.	4	5.2	3
2008 Performance-Based National Detention Standards (PBNDS)	ICE revised its standards to align with the fourth edition of the *American Correctional Association's Performance-Based Standards for Adult Local Detention Facilities*. This version introduces expected outcomes, or results that the required procedures found in the standards are expected to accomplish.	14	8.3	1
2011 PBNDS[c]	The 2011 version of the standards, like the 2008 PBNDS, outline expected outcomes for each standard. This version also introduces provisions, which are non-mandatory, and which represent optimal levels of compliance with the standards. The standards were updated in 2016, and are referred to as the 2011 PBNDS with 2016 revisions.	40	63.9	14

Table 1. (Continued)

Detention standard	Description	Number of authorized facilities obligated to adhere to standard	Percent of average daily population, fiscal year 2019	Number of authorized facilities that are also staffed by IHSC[a]
Obligated to other standards	Some facilities are not obligated to adhere to ICE's detention standards. However, facilities used by ICE to house single adults for more than 60 days are inspected against one of its detention standards. For example, U.S. Marshals Service intergovernmental agreement facilities are under agreements to adhere to Department of Justice detention standards. Facilities under private contract with the U.S. Marshals Service are to adhere to the Federal Performance-Based Detention Standards, which incorporate elements of American Correctional Association expected practices, Department of Justice standards, and the 2000 NDS.	78	11.6	0

Detention standard	Description	Number of authorized facilities obligated to adhere to standard	Percent of average daily population, fiscal year 2019	Number of authorized facilities that are also staffed by IHSC[a]
	For ICE inspection purposes, ICE holds facilities affiliated with the U.S. Marshals Service to one of its national standards listed above.			

Source: GAO analysis of ICE documentation. | GAO-20-330.

Note: This table includes authorized facilities, which, according to ICE officials, are those facilities that are used on a frequent and regular basis. Authorized facilities are inspected by ICE. The table does not include non-authorized facilities—such as hold rooms, staging facilities, and hospitals—or facilities that ICE no longer utilizes as of February 2019.

[a]Two additional facilities—staging facilities—are non-authorized but staffed by IHSC.

[b]ICE updated its 2000 NDS in December 2019 and ICE officials stated that facilities will be inspected against the 2019 standards starting March 1, 2020. Further, officials stated that they are in the process of updating the 2007 Family Residential Standards.

[c]Whether a 2011 PBNDS facility is contractually required to adhere to the 2016 revision is dependent upon the contract language negotiated in each agreement. As of September 2019, ICE had 47 facilities operating under 2011 PBNDS, of which 31 were contractually required to meet the 2016 revision when ICE begins inspecting for compliance under the revised standards.

CBP Facilities, Standards, and Medical Care

CBP operates all of its short-term holding facilities and hold rooms, and does not utilize contract services for the management of individuals in CBP custody. In October 2015, CBP issued its first nationwide standards, which govern CBP's interaction with detained individuals.[44] The standards include requirements regarding transport, escort, detention, and search provisions, as well as care for "at-risk individuals," which includes pregnant women. Given that CBP short-term facilities are intended to hold individuals for no more than 72 hours, CBP historically did not have on-site medical professionals at most of its facilities.[45] However, as a result of

[44] U.S. Customs and Border Protection, *National Standards on Transport, Escort, Detention, and Search* (Washington D.C., October 2015).

[45] We previously reported that although Border Patrol officials from 10 facilities we visited stated that time in custody rarely exceeds 72 hours, we noted that approximately 16 percent of

surges in unaccompanied minors and families crossing the border, CBP issued a directive in January 2019 titled *Interim Enhanced Medical Efforts (January 2019).* According to the directive, enhanced medical services were needed to address growing public health concerns and mitigate risk to, and improve care for, individuals in CBP custody along the southwest border. The January 2019 directive was superseded by a December 2019 directive, *Enhanced Medical Support Efforts,* which also calls for medical support to mitigate risk to, and sustain enhanced medical efforts for persons in CBP custody along the southwest border. A related memo issued by the CBP Commissioner, titled CBP's *Expansion of Existing Medical Services Contracts and Expedited Deployment of Additional Contracted Medical Services Personnel to the Southwest Border,* called for the expansion of CBP's medical services contract to numerous Border Patrol facilities and OFO ports of entry along the southwest border.[46] This effort is discussed later in our report.

DHS HAD OVER 4,600 DETENTIONS OF PREGNANT WOMEN FROM 2016 THROUGH 2018 FOR DIFFERENT LENGTHS OF TIME AND IN VARYING TYPES OF FACILITIES

About Two-thirds of ICE's Detentions of Pregnant Women Were for a Week or Less

Number of Pregnant Women Detentions

From calendar year 2016 through 2018, ICE had over 4,600 detentions of pregnant women.[47] The number of detentions decreased from 1,380 in

---

cases with complete data in fiscal years 2014 and 2015 exceeded this threshold. See GAO, *Immigration Detention: Additional Actions Needed to Strengthen DHS Management of Short-Term Holding Facilities,* GAO-16-514 (Washington, D.C., May 26, 2016).

46 We currently have ongoing work on CBP's care and custody of detainees.

47 We selected these years based on the first year ICE collected data on all pregnant women at both IHSC and non-IHSC staffed facilities (2016) and the most recent full year of data (2018) at the time of our review.

calendar year 2016 to 1,160 in 2017, and then increased to 2,098 in calendar year 2018 (see Figure 1).[48]

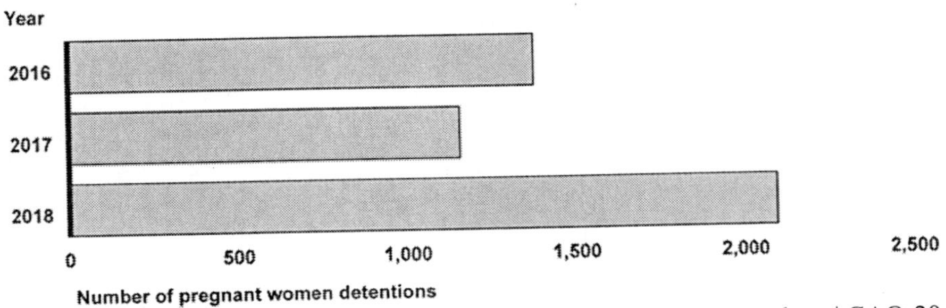

Source: GAO analysis of U.S. Immigration and Customs Enforcement data. | GAO-20-330.

Notes: Our analysis is based on the 1,377 unique pregnant detainee records for 2016; 1,150 for 2017; and 2,094 for 2018 that we were able to match to the detention data. The number of detainees may not equal the number of detentions because a woman may have been detained multiple times during a calendar year.

Figure 1. Immigration and Customs Enforcement Detentions of Pregnant Women, Calendar Years 2016 through 2018.

Of the more than 4,600 detentions of pregnant women from calendar year 2016 through 2018, 32 percent involved pregnant women who were expedited removal cases and were subject to mandatory detention, including those that awaited a credible fear determination.[49] Of the

---

[48] To obtain more information on the characteristics of pregnant women, we analyzed individual pregnant detainee data in conjunction with the ICE detention data. ICE collected data for 1,437 pregnant detainees in 2016; 1,170 in 2017; and 2,126 in 2018. We excluded 60 of the unique pregnant detainee records for 2016; 20 for 2017; and 32 for 2018 because we were unable to match these records using alien number and book-in date (date of intake) combinations. According to ICE officials, this may be due to data entry errors. Our analysis is based on the unique pregnant detainee records we were able to match: 1,377 for 2016; 1,150 for 2017; and 2,094 for 2018. Of those we were able to match, we identified 19 pregnant women that were detained more than once in our time period. ICE also recorded 675 pregnant detainees in 2015; however, we excluded these records from our analysis since ICE did not collect complete data on this population in 2015.

[49] Other pregnant women may have been subject to mandatory detention when they were initially detained, however, ICE updates the status of each individual's record, as they move through immigration proceedings. As such, our data represents the case status at the time ICE extracted these data. For example, some pregnant women that were initially detained and were claiming credible fear—and were subject to mandatory detention, may have

remaining detentions, 49 percent involved pregnant women who were deemed inadmissible and were either awaiting their hearing or an adjudication by an immigration judge, 11 percent involved pregnant women who had a final order of removal, and the remaining detentions (8 percent) involved various other immigration-related circumstances, such as those for which ICE was unable to obtain travel documents. Further, as we reported in December 2019, detentions of non-criminal pregnant women accounted for most of the total detentions of pregnant women each year (ranging from 91 to 97 percent).[50]

Length of Detention

From calendar years 2016 through 2018, 68 percent of ICE detentions of pregnant women were for 7 days or less, 22 percent for 8 to 30 days, and 10 percent for more than 30 days, as shown in Table 2.

Table 2. Length of U.S. Immigration and Customs Enforcement detentions of pregnant women, calendar years 2016 through 2018

Calendar Year	0 -1 day	2 -7 days	8 -15 days	16 -30 days	31 - 90 days	91 - 180 days	181 - 270 days	271 -334 days	Total detentions[a]
2016	627	600	61	42	41	9	0	0	1,380
2017	328	449	117	144	108	14	0	0	1,160
2018	523	644	316	338	261	13	1	1	2,097

Source: GAO analysis of Immigration and Customs Enforcement data. | GAO-20-330.

Note: Our analysis is based on the 1,377 unique pregnant detainee records for 2016; 1,150 for 2017; and 2,094 for 2018 that we were able to match to the detention data. The number of detainees may not equal the number of detentions because a woman may have been detained multiple times during a calendar year.

[a]We were unable to determine the length of detention for one record because the individual had an ongoing detention, as of May 2019. As such, the total detentions for 2018 in this table, is listed as 2,097 rather than 2,098.

---

subsequently received their credible fear determination from DHS, and their case and custody status would change accordingly.

[50] See GAO-20-36. For the purposes of that report, we referred to potentially removable individuals without criminal convictions known to ICE as "non-criminals" and individuals with criminal convictions known to ICE as "convicted criminals." According to ICE, ICE officers electronically request and retrieve criminal history information from the FBI's National Crime Information Center database, which maintains a repository of federal and state criminal history information, and other sources. We used ICE's determination on criminality for our analysis.

According to ICE officials, individual circumstances of each case dictate how long they detain a pregnant woman. For example, ICE may determine not to release a pregnant woman from ICE custody if her case is adjudicated quickly, she is ordered removed, and she is cleared to travel by a medical professional.

Pregnancy Outcomes

Our analysis of ICE data shows that from January 2015 through July 2019, 58 pregnant women in ICE custody experienced a miscarriage, two had an abortion, and one gave birth.[51] Of those, 37 miscarriages and one birth involved women detained at IHSC-staffed facilities at the time of the outcome.[52] Some of these women were in our study population of over 4,600 detentions from calendar years 2016 through 2018, but some were pregnant women detained in 2019.

Most ICE Detentions of Pregnant Women Were at IHSC-Staffed Facilities; and Some Data on Gestation of Pregnancy Were Available

Detention Facility

Our analyses of ICE data found that of the over 4,600 detentions of pregnant women, 78 percent of detentions of pregnant women were initially detained at an IHSC-staffed facility.[53] See appendix II for more

---

[51] According to some ICE policies and detention standards, in the event of a threat to a woman's life from carrying a pregnancy to term, or else in cases of rape or incest, ICE must bear the cost of a detainee's decision to terminate a pregnancy; otherwise the woman must bear the cost. In addition to these outcomes, we identified 24 women for which there was a concern about a potential miscarriage or premature labor; however records did not indicate that a miscarriage or labor occurred.

[52] According to ICE officials, they generally do not detain women in their third trimester. This could contribute to the lower number of births. We were unable to determine the facility for two miscarriages.

[53] Facility information is based on ICE's February 2019 facility list report. It is possible that facilities may change over time, including if they are staffed by IHSC, among other things. For example, between 2016 and 2018, two facilities became IHSC-staffed facilities and one was no longer staffed by IHSC.

details on these data. According to ICE officials, pregnant women may first learn about their pregnancy when a test is performed during their intake into a detention facility. These over 4,600 detentions of pregnant women resulted in approximately 50,300 detention days with more than 66 percent of total detention days spent at IHSC-staffed facilities (see App. II).[54]

Table 3. Detention days spent by pregnant women at each U.S. Immigration and Customs Enforcement (ICE) facility type, calendar years 2016 through 2018

Facility type and ICE Health Service Corps (IHSC) presence	Total detention days	Minimum number of days	Maximum number of days	Average number of days
Contract detention facility/IHSC	11,239	1	332	24
Contract detention facility/ non-IHSC	747	1	156	36
Service processing center/ IHSC	7,900	1	128	3
U.S. Marshals Service intergovernmental agreement/ non-IHSC	3,660	1	161	12
Intergovernmental service agreement/IHSC[a]	13,923	1	147	9
Intergovernmental service agreement/non- IHSC[a]	11,809	1	170	13
Other[b]/IHSC	284	1	3	2
Other[b]/non-IHSC	778	6	41	6
Total	50,340	1	332	7

Source: GAO analysis of ICE data. | GAO-20-330.

Notes: Our analysis is based on the 1,377 unique pregnant detainee records for 2016; 1,150 for 2017; and 2,094 for 2018 that we were able to match to the detention data. We were unable to determine the length of detention for one record which is generally due to an ongoing detention. If a woman was detained in more than one facility on the same day, we counted this as 2 days—1 day in each facility.

[a]Includes family residential centers.

[b]"Other" facilities include Bureau of Prisons, hold rooms, staging facilities, and hospitals, among other facilities.

[54] If a woman was detained in more than one facility on the same day, we counted this as 1 day in each facility.

Some facilities may have a large number of detention days associated with the intake of pregnant women, but may not detain women for a long period of time before releasing or transferring them. For example, at a facility that had one of the largest number of detention days for pregnant women, officials stated that they generally release women once the pregnancy is confirmed. Further, according to ICE officials, ICE will try to transfer pregnant women from their initial detention facility to an IHSC-staffed detention facility or a family residential center—if she is part of a family unit—to ensure they are provided the appropriate accommodations and care. For example, ICE may transfer a pregnant woman awaiting a credible fear determination, as these cases may take longer to process and result in longer detention stays. However, an IHSC official also stated that ICE may detain pregnant women at non-IHSC facilities if ICE believes that the facility can provide the appropriate level of care.[55] Nearly 70 percent of pregnant women's detention days were spent at an IHSC-staffed facility or a family residential center. Contract detention facilities—both IHSC-staffed and non-IHSC—had the highest average number of days for the detention of pregnant women, as shown in Table 3.

Gestation of Pregnancy

Of the 1,450 detentions of pregnant women for which gestation data were available, 49 percent were for women in their first trimester and 41 percent were for women in their second trimester at the time of intake.[56] Ten percent were for women in their third trimester at the time of intake. Of the detentions involving pregnant women in their third trimester, 75 percent were released within one week or less, 9 percent between 8 and 15

---

[55] According to our analysis of ICE data, of the over 4,600 detentions of pregnant women, 37 percent involved a pregnant woman that had at least one transfer during her detention.

[56] We analyzed available gestation data from calendar years 2016 through 2018. Of the over 4,600 detentions of pregnant women, data for 1,450 detentions were available.

Specifically, data on estimated delivery date were readily available for pregnant women detentions at non-IHSC facilities. More limited gestation data were available on detentions at IHSC-staffed facilities. IHSC–staffed facilities began to collect these data more consistently in June 2018—similar to non-IHSC facilities. ICE does not require these data to be collected. However, this information would be available in medical records prior to this date because, according to an IHSC official, gestation can be calculated using other data, such as last menstrual cycle.

days, and the remaining 16 percent between 16 and 90 days. According to ICE officials, ICE does not detain pregnant woman in their third trimester or a pregnant woman who is unlikely to be removed. However, officials stated that there are instances when it takes ICE time to gather information prior to making a custody determination— such as when it needs to collect criminal conviction data to making a custody determination—which could result in detained pregnant women who are nearing or in their third trimester. This is consistent with what ICE officials told us during our visits to facilities in all four locations—that they generally do not detain pregnant women in their third trimester.[57] However, some explained, that pregnant women in their third trimester may be detained if, for example, they are subject to mandatory detention.

CBP Has Data on Pregnant Women in Certain Locations and Has Taken Action that Could Provide Additional Information on Pregnant Women at Other Locations

Number of Pregnant Women

Because of CBP facilities' short-term nature and limited on-site medical care, CBP does not routinely conduct pregnancy tests of women in their custody, and as such, has limited data on pregnancy.[58] However, ICE data provide insight into CBP encounters with pregnant women.

---

[57] Further, CBP officials in the four locations we visited—which include Border Patrol and OFO facilities—generally all stated that ICE will not take pregnant women in their third trimester, or in some cases, at all. They stated that ICE will either release the woman without taking physical custody from CBP, or CBP will have to use their discretion to release the women if they can no longer hold them. In addition, our prior work found similar results, as we reported in GAO-20-36 that ICE officials in all six areas of responsibility we visited stated that they are less likely to detain and may release a woman who is having a high risk pregnancy or in the third trimester of herpregnancy.

[58] CBP has not historically had medical personnel onsite at most of its locations, as previously stated. Some CBP detention facilities had contracts or agreements for medical services during the time period covered in our review, but CBP officials stated that they generally refer individuals to local medical providers in their area, as appropriate and for all emergent or serious issues—including concerns presented by pregnant women. In addition, if CBP needed to provide a pregnancy test to a woman in its custody, officials stated that they would take the woman to an offsite medical provider.

Specifically, our analysis of ICE data from calendar years 2016 through 2018 indicated that nearly 4,400 of ICE's over 4,600 detentions of pregnant women resulted from CBP arrests.

In addition, OFO and Border Patrol collected some data on women in their custody who reported being pregnant. OFO reported holding over 3,900 pregnant women from March 2018 through September 2019 at its ports of entry.[59] At the two sectors where Border Patrol is required to collect such data, Border Patrol reported holding over 750 pregnant women in its facilities from March 2017 through March 2019.[60]

Table 4. Number and percent of women that reported to be pregnant, by trimester, March 2017 through March 2019 in two southwest Border Patrol sectors

Trimester	Count	Percent
First trimester	138	18
Second trimester	331	44
Third trimester	283	38
Total	752	100

Source: GAO analysis of Border Patrol data. | GAO-20-330.

Notes: These data represent women that self-reported being pregnant at two Border Patrol sectors. Border Patrol has 20 sectors, nine of which are southwest border sectors. It is possible that some women in their first trimester may not be aware that they are pregnant. According to U.S. Immigration and Customs Enforcement (ICE) officials, many of the pregnant women that they detained first learned about their pregnancy upon taking a pregnancy test during the intake process at an ICE detention facility.

---

[59] In March 2018, OFO began collecting self-reported data on pregnant women they hold at ports of entry—which includes 328 land, air, and sea ports of entry. OFO, at all ports of entry, uses a standard form when processing an individual that includes a question about pregnancy. Of these pregnant women held by OFO, almost 2,100 women were held at southwest border land ports of entry from March 2018 through March 2019.

[60] In March 2017, Border Patrol began collecting self-reported data on pregnant women in two of its nine southwest border sectors (Yuma and Tucson). Border Patrol began collecting these data due to a court order, see *Unknown Parties v. Johnson*, Order Granting Motion for Preliminary Injunction, Doc. 244, No. CV-15-00250 (D. Az. Nov. 18, 2016). These women may have been transferred to ICE and may also be included in the count of pregnant women detained by ICE. Yuma Sector accounted for 60 percent of these total apprehensions. Border Patrol agents at other sectors may inquire about pregnancy but this is not required.

As shown in Table 4, most of these women reported being in their second or third trimester. These women may have been transferred to ICE and may also be included in the count of pregnant women detained by ICE.

In accordance with its January 2019 directive, *Interim Enhanced Medical Efforts (January 2019),* CBP developed a standardized health interview form that can be used by Border Patrol and OFO. The form includes a question about pregnancy and nursing[61] which could allow for additional data on the number of women in CBP custody that report being pregnant. In December 2019, CBP officials told us that they distributed the form to its field locations.[62]

Pregnancy Outcomes

In addition, we reviewed CBP significant incident reports to determine if any pregnant woman encountered or held by CBP had experienced a birth, stillbirth, or miscarriage during calendar year 2015 through February 2019. Our analysis of CBP reports during this time frame found that pregnant women encountered or apprehended by CBP experienced 43 births, three miscarriages, and six stillbirths after being taken to the hospital by CBP.[63] In some of these incidents, Border Patrol agents encountered pregnant women in the field and took them directly to the hospital. In these cases, the pregnant woman was not in a Border Patrol facility directly prior to being taken to the hospital.[64]

---

[61] According to a December 2019 directive, which superseded the January 2019 directive, the form is required, at a minimum, for all individuals under the age of 18 in custody along the southwest border.

[62] We currently have ongoing work on CBP's care and custody of detainees.

[63] These data were obtained from CBP significant incident reports. CBP has requirements for reporting certain types of incidents, such as deaths. According to CBP officials, although there is no requirement to report miscarriages and births, some are reported at the discretion of CBP officials. As such, it is possible that not all information was reported.

[64] Specifically, 17 of the 37 births and two of the three stillbirths reported by Border Patrol involved pregnant women taken to the hospital after being encountered in the field and prior to be taken to a CBP facility.

DHS Policies and Detention Standards that Address the Care of Pregnant Women Vary by Facility Type and Component

ICE Policies and Detention Standards Address a Range of Pregnancy-Care Topics that Vary across Facility Types; ICE Has Planned Updates to Address Gaps

ICE has policies and detention standards that address a variety of pregnancy-related topics regarding the care of pregnant women, such as pregnancy testing requirements, the use of restraints, and prenatal care. However, we identified certain facility types that did not address all pregnancy-related topics in their policies or detention standards as of December 2019, which ICE is taking actions to address.[65] Appendix III details ICE's policies and detention standards related to the care of pregnant women in detention. For the purpose of our analysis, the facility type is based on contractually obligated detention standards and the presence of IHSC staff, as these factors dictate which detention standards the facility type is required to adhere to and whether IHSC policies apply.[66]

Specifically, we identified 16 topics related to the care of pregnant women and found that in most facility types, ICE had at least one policy or detention standard that addressed many of these topics.[67] Further, we found that if the facility type had policies or detention standards in place regarding a specific topic on the care of pregnant women, at least one of the policies or detention standards generally aligned with recommended

---

[65] ICE may have more general policies at some of these facility types that address these topics, such as HIV care, but they are not specific to pregnant women.

[66] In addition to detention standards and IHSC policies, ICE issues agency-wide policies, such as memos and directives, which are to be followed by ICE personnel, but are not applicable to contracted detention staff unless noted in their contract or agreement. These policies include requirements regarding the identification of pregnant women and the use of restraints during transport.

[67] We reviewed information from associations and organizations, agency policies and detention standards, non-governmental complaints, and media reports to identify and categorize 16 topics related to the care of pregnant women. All 16 topics were addressed in nationally recommended guidance.

guidance from professional associations, NGOs, and federal agencies, (see app. IV for our summary of recommended guidance and associated examples).[68] In addition, we found that from calendar years 2016 through 2018, 64 percent of the detentions of pregnant women were initially detained at the two facility types that had the most policies or detention standards related to each of the pregnancy topics, as of December 2019. Table 5 shows whether policies or detention standards at the various facility types addressed each of the 16 topics, as well as the associated number of detentions of pregnant women—based on the facility in which they were first detained and number of detention days from calendar years 2016 through 2018.

ICE is taking numerous actions to address these gaps in its policies and detention standards. For example, according to ICE officials, ICE has updated, or is in the process of updating, its policies and detention standards, and these updates will address many of the gaps that we identified for the pregnancy-related topics. Specifically, ICE revised its 2000 NDS in December 2019 and the 2007 Family Residential Standards are under revision and will be sent to management for review in February 2020.[69] According to IHSC officials, the revised standards will address all of the gaps we identified for 2007 Family Residential Standards and 2000 NDS facility types.[70] Further, IHSC officials stated that they are revising

---

[68] Recommended guidance is from American College of Obstetricians and Gynecologists, National Commission on Correctional Health Care, and the American Correctional Association, as well as other relevant expert and medical organizations including the United Nations, the National Women's Law Center, American Civil Liberties Union, and working groups assembled by both the Departments of Justice and Homeland Security. We summarized the recommended guidance for our report purposes. Further, we did not include recommended guidance that was not directly relevant to the care of pregnant women once detained, such as guidance on detention determinations and child care. For example, recommended guidance generally states pregnant women should not be detained except in extraordinary circumstances.

[69] These 2000 NDS revised standards are called the 2019 National Detention Standards for Non-Dedicated Facilities. The standards generally cover the pregnancy-related topics. According to ICE officials, facilities will be inspected against the 2019 standards starting March 1, 2020, giving them approximately 60 days for implementation. ICE will be initiating contract modifications for affected facilities during that time.

[70] After the standards are finalized, ICE will implement the revised standards through individual contract modifications with individual facilities. According to ICE officials, this can require detailed and lengthy negotiations with contractors, so the implementation process may last several months.

IHSC's Women's Health Directive and guidance on care for chronic conditions to include required and recommended vaccines for pregnant women and HIV care, respectively—which will address these gaps at IHSC-staffed facilities. Finally, according to ICE officials, facility types operating under the 2008 PBNDS will be modified to either the 2019 NDS 2019 or 2011 PBNDS.

In addition to these updates, in accordance with ICE's December 2017 memo on *Identification and Monitoring of Pregnant Detainees,* ICE is to ensure pregnant detainees receive appropriate medical care, and ensure detention facilities are aware of their obligations regarding directives and detention standards that apply to pregnant detainees, among other things.[71] ICE has mechanisms for maintaining oversight of pregnant detainees, as required by policy. Specifically, ICE collects data to monitor the condition of pregnant women in its custody, and according to ICE officials, ensures that the facility can accommodate the woman. In addition, IHSC conducts weekly reviews that focus on high-risk pregnancies, pregnancies in the third trimester, and recent miscarriages. According to an IHSC official, ICE inspections can contribute to IHSC's understanding of the care of pregnant women at a given facility.[72] Further, although ICE officials stated that it does not have training dedicated to the care of pregnant women in ICE detention specifically, its basic training includes instruction on pregnant detainees. This training is in addition to the professional qualifications of medical staff onsite.[73]

---

[71] In addition, IHSC officials are to (a) ensure proper notification that a pregnant woman has been detained; (b) recommend when a pregnant detainee's transfer to another facility is necessary for appropriate medical care; (c) monitor and track the condition of pregnant detainees, including any risk factors or concerns; (d) ensure oversight of facility capabilities to ensure a pregnant detainee's needs can be accommodated; and (e) develop and maintain a system for tracking and monitoring all pregnant detainees at IHSC-staffed facilities and non-IHSC facilities.

[72] We discuss facility inspections later in this chapter.

[73] At IHSC-staffed facilities, IHSC officials stated that it conducts training at orientation and during annual competency assessments for its registered nurses and conducts training for mid-level and advanced providers.

Table 5. U.S. Immigration and Customs Enforcement (ICE) pregnancy-related policies or detention standards by facility type, as of December 2019

		Facility type based on contractually obligated detention standard and ICE Health Service Corps (IHSC) presence							
		2000 National Detention Standards (NDS)	2000 NDS +IHSC[b]	2007 Family Residential Standards (FRS)	2007 FRS + IHSC	2008 Performance-Based NDS (PBNDS)	2008 PBNDS +IHSC	2011 PBNDS[c]	2011 PBNDS +IHSC[c]
Pregnant women detentions	Number and percent of pregnant women detentions, initial detention facility, calendar years 2016 through 2018[a]	80 (2)	0	108 (2)	703 (15)	7 (0.2)	0	84 (2)	2,887 (62)
	Number and percent of detention days of pregnant women, calendar years 2016 through 2018[a]	2,450 (5)	0	1,585 (3)	6,793 (14)	202 (0.4)	53 (0.1)	4,077 (8)	26,473 (53)
Pregnancy-related care topic[d]	Intake health screening involving pregnant women		✓		✓	✓	✓	✓	✓
	Pregnancy testing at intake		✓		✓	✓	✓	✓	✓
	Access to abortion[e]		✓		✓		✓	✓	✓
	Provision of prenatal care	✓	✓	✓	✓	✓	✓	✓	✓
	Provision of postnatal care	✓	✓	✓	✓	✓	✓	✓	✓
	Provision of perinatal/labor care							✓	✓
	Mental health services and counseling for pregnant women		✓	✓	✓	✓	✓	✓	✓

		Facility type based on contractually obligated detention standard and ICE Health Service Corps (IHSC) presence							
		2000 National Detention Standards (NDS)	2000 NDS +IHSC[b]	2007 Family Residential Standards (FRS)	2007 FRS + IHSC	2008 Performance-Based NDS (PBNDS)	2008 PBNDS +IHSC	2011 PBNDS[c]	2011 PBNDS +IHSC[c]
Pregnancy-related care topic[d]	Care for pregnant women with substance use disorder		√		√	√	√	√	√
	HIV care for pregnant women							√	√
	Vaccinations for pregnant women[f]								
	Prenatal vitamins							√	√
	Nutrition for pregnant women	√	√	√	√	√	√	√	√
	Special accommodations for pregnant women[g]					√	√	√	√
	Segregation of pregnant women[h]			N/A	N/A			√	√
	Use of restraints on pregnant women	√	√	√	√	√	√	√	√
	Record keeping on pregnant women actions	√	√	√	√		√	√	√

√: Indicates that the facility type had at least one policy or detention standard that addressed the topic, as of December 2019.

■: Indicates that no such policy or standard existed at this facility type, as of December 2019. N/A: not applicable, as family residential centers do not segregate individuals.

Source: GAO analysis of ICE policies and detention standards | GAO-20-330.

Notes: In addition to the policies listed above that are applicable at detention facilities, ICE also has policies that require ICE to provide specific oversight at facilities for some of these topics, such as segregation. Further, ICE has a policy regarding the use of restraints on pregnant women when transporting them to a facility. Prior policies that no longer apply may have been in effect before this date. Further, ICE has revised, or is revising, some of its policies and standards that will address some of the gaps identified in this table.

[a]Percentages do not total to 100 because some ICE facilities are not required to adhere to a set of detention standards—but may be inspected against one—or ICE did not specify the detention standard in its facility list report. Facilities not required to adhere to a set of ICE detention standards may be obligated to other standards such as expected practices by the American Correctional Association. Further, according to ICE officials, ICE's facility list report is intended to generate information for facilities that it inspects, and not for infrequently used facilities. These facility types accounted for about 17 percent of the detention days of pregnant women from calendar years 2016 through 2018. The majority of these detention days were in facility types that, although not contractually obligated to adhere to a set of ICE detention standards, ICE last inspected them against 2000 NDS or 2008 PBNDS.

[b]No IHSC-staffed facilities were obligated to 2000 NDS based on ICE's weekly facility list from February 2019.

[c]These detention standards were revised in 2016, but not all facilities are obligated to adhere to the 2016 revisions. Whether a 2011 PBNDS facility is contractually required to adhere to the 2016 revision is dependent upon the contract language negotiated in each agreement. As of September 2019, ICE has 47 facilities operating under 2011 PBNDS. Of these, 31 are contractually required to meet the 2016 revision and will be inspected for compliance under the revised standards beginning in January 2020.

[d]We reviewed guidance from associations and organizations, agency policies and detention standards, non-governmental organization complaints, and media reports to identify and categorize these topics.

[e]Access to abortion refers to women having the option and access to terminate a pregnancy generally at the detainee's expense. It does not refer to ICE providing abortion services.

[f]At IHSC staffed facilities, IHSC policies exists regarding influenza but not any other vaccinations. Specifically, the January 2018 policy states that pregnant women are recommended to receive the influenza vaccination each year.

[g]Special accommodations for pregnant women include beds low to the ground and adjusted work and leisure schedules.

[h]According to ICE officials, they refer to the segregation of detainees from the general population, as being placed in Special Management Units either administratively or for violating disciplinary policies. Detainees placed into administrative segregation generally have the same privileges as detainees housed in the general population. Detainees housed in disciplinary segregation generally have fewer privileges, but still interact daily with staff, medical personnel, legal advisors, and others.

CBP Has Policies and Standards Regarding Its Short-Term Care of Pregnant Women

CBP has some policies and standards regarding the care of pregnant women held in their short-term facilities. Specifically, CBP has national standards on the transport, escort, detention, and search of detainees, with specific requirements for pregnant women. For example, these standards state that barring exigent circumstances, CBP must not use restraints on pregnant detainees unless they have demonstrated or threatened violent behavior, have a history of criminal or violent activity or an articulable likelihood of escape exists. Further, Border Patrol and OFO have policies that address nutrition and special accommodations for pregnant women. See appendix V for more details on CBP policies related to pregnant women. Although these policies and national standards do not cover the full range of the 16 pregnancy-related care topics we identified, CBP facilities are designed for holding individuals for no more than 72 hours; therefore, CBP's facilities are not equipped to provide long-term care. Specifically, CBP does not routinely conduct pregnancy testing and historically it did not have on-site medical care at all its facilities. For the policies and standards that CBP does have in place regarding pregnant women, we found that they generally aligned with the recommended guidance from expert and professional organizations.

In addition to policies that direct the care of pregnant women, although CBP does not have training dedicated to the care of pregnant women specifically, CBP provides initial and annual refresher training on its national standards for the transport, escort, detention, and search of detainees, which includes requirements for pregnant women.

DHS Inspections, Medical Data, and Complaints Offer Insights into the Care Provided to Pregnant Women

ICE Inspections Found 79 Percent or Greater Compliance with Most of Its Pregnancy-Related Performance Measures

ICE uses various inspections for accessing facilities' compliance with policies and detention standards—the frequency and focus of which vary.[74] Some inspections also include pregnancy-related performance measures, such as a measure assessing whether a pregnancy test was performed at intake. We reviewed results from the five ICE inspections that address compliance with pregnancy-related policies and detention standards from 2015 through June 2019. These inspections vary in their scope and targeted facility types (see app. I for more details on each of these inspections). These inspections—along with available medical data—offer insight into the care of pregnant women.[75] Two inspections include pregnancy-related performance measures, and compliance with these measures ranged from 53 to 100 percent, with most indicating 79 percent or more compliance.

Specifically, one inspection of 129 ICE detention facilities—that included inspections of both IHSC-staffed and non-IHSC facilities—found that compliance was 91 percent or more for each of the six performance measures from December 2016 through March 2019, as shown below.

- Pregnancy testing performed at intake: 93 percent
- Pregnancy testing performed prior to x-rays or initiating medication: 100 percent

[74] We previously reported that ICE officials responsible for detention oversight stated that these various inspections complement one another and serve different purposes. See GAO-15-153.

[75] We selected these inspections because they review some aspect of the care provided to pregnant women. Some of these inspections measure compliance with ICE's recommended practices which may not be covered by policies or detention standards at all facilities. We have ongoing work on oversight of ICE detention facilities, including inspections and complaints.

- Obstetrician-gynecologist (OB-GYN) consult ordered within 7 days of pregnancy confirmation: 98 percent
- Patient seen by OB-GYN within 30 days of pregnancy confirmation: 91 percent
- Prenatal vitamins prescribed: 100 percent
- Screened for HIV, sexually transmitted infections, and viral hepatitis: 95 percent[76]

Instances of non-compliance—which were 9 percent or less for each measure—occurred at 16 detention facilities subject to a range of detention standards. Three of these facilities were IHSC-staffed facilities, and 13 were non-IHSC facilities. IHSC documentation indicates that corrective actions are to be implemented to help address inspection findings. See appendix VI for details on the number of records reviewed during the inspections, and the compliance rates.

Our analysis of available medical data and interviews with pregnant detainees showed similar findings regarding pregnancy testing at intake. Specifically, from calendar year 2016 through 2018, 92 percent of women in ICE detention facilities received a pregnancy test either the same day as intake to the facility or the next day. This could include women who arrived at a detention facility in the evening and are tested the next day.[77] Of the remaining, 3 percent were tested within 2 to 3 days of intake, 4 percent were tested between 4 days and 2 weeks, and 2 percent were tested after 2 weeks of being detained.[78] According to the 10 pregnant women we interviewed who were detained at 3 ICE detention facilities we visited,[79]

---

76 According to ICE officials, screening for HIV, sexually transmitted infections, and viral hepatitis reflects recommended practices, but is not specifically required by policies or detention standards.

77 Of the over 4,600 detentions of pregnant women, we were able to determine when the pregnancy test was provided for about 3,800—based on these women being in an IHSC-staffed facility at some point.

78 Totals do not equal 100 percent due to rounding.

79 We interviewed pregnant detainees at three of the four ICE detention facilities we visited—which include IHSC-staffed and non-IHSC staffed facilities. The fourth facility did not have any pregnant detainees at the time of our visit. In addition, we interviewed four pregnant women at a local shelter after their release from a DHS detention facility. It was not always clear where these women had been detained or held. In some cases, their experiences may

all 10 stated that they received a pregnancy test when they arrived at the facility or within the same day.

For the second inspection that included performance measures related to the care of pregnant women at IHSC-staffed facilities, overall compliance was 79 percent or more for most of the nine performance measures from fiscal years 2015 through 2018.[80] The following shows the minimum level of overall compliance for all facilities during this timeframe.[81]

- OB-GYN consult ordered and documented within 7 days of pregnancy confirmation: 75 percent
- Patient seen by OB-GYN within 30 days: 92 percent
- Prenatal vitamins prescribed: 95 percent
- Detainee education documented at each encounter: 79 percent
- Records reviewed by provider after OB appointment: 79 percent
- Proper diet ordered: 86 percent
- Appropriate labs ordered if not obtained from OB-GYN: 79 percent

---

reflect being held by CBP at a port of entry or Border Patrol facility prior to being transferred to an ICE facility. As a result, their perspectives are not included here. See appendix VII for details on all interviews with pregnant women. We did not verify detainees' claims following these interviews.

[80] The average compliance from fiscal years 2015 through 2018 cannot be determined for all performance measures because the extent to which IHSC collected and reported information varied by year. Therefore, we reported the minimum percent compliance reported during this time period. If a facility did not self-report its data, it was considered to be non-compliant (zero percent). According to ICE officials, they have developed a streamlined set of 15 performance measures for use beginning in calendar year 2019, and two of these measures are related to pregnancy standards—specifically whether pregnancy testing was conducted at intake, and whether pregnant patients were seen by an OB-GYN within 30 days of being in custody. Officials said that these measures will provide a more comprehensive way to determine the quality of care, while reducing data collection and reporting requirements for measures that were of no clinical benefit. Officials said that they have collected three quarters of data and have begun to analyze trends.

[81] The level of compliance for some measures varied from year to year. Furthermore, compliance varied across some facilities during any given year. See appendix VI for additional information on these inspections.

- Pregnant patient screened for HIV, sexually transmitted infections, and viral hepatitis: 81 percent
- Hepatitis B vaccine offered: 53 percent

However, for one measure—whether the Hepatitis B vaccine was offered—compliance was 53 percent. ICE officials stated that this performance measure reflects recommended practices but is not specifically required by policy or detention standards. According to ICE officials, any issues identified during IHSC inspections are handled locally at the field level through facilities' quality improvement processes, which includes developing corrective action plans. See appendix VI for the average annual compliance for each measure from fiscal years 2015 through 2018.

Our analysis of available medical data for IHSC-staffed facilities and interviews with pregnant detainees and NGOs provides additional perspectives regarding these issues on the care of pregnant women. Specifically, our analysis of ICE data showed 422 detentions in which a pregnant woman was in an IHSC-staffed facility at some point received at least one referral to an OB or OB-GYN between calendar year 2016 and 2018. Based on ICE's performance measures, pregnant women are to receive an OB-GYN referral within 7 days of pregnancy confirmation—although available data showed that most pregnant women were being released from detention within 7 days.[82] In addition, our analysis of ICE data showed that detentions in which a pregnant woman was in an IHSC-staffed facility at some point were assigned certain special needs, such as a special diet (1,245), lower bunk (113), no heavy lifting (87), and limitations on the use of restraints (316).[83] In addition, all 7 of the pregnant women we spoke with in IHSC-staffed detention facilities said that they

---

[82] Our analysis of the over 4,600 detentions of pregnant women showed that 68 percent were released from detention within 7 days, which is within the required timeframe for submitting an OB-GYN referral. The remaining 32 percent of pregnant women (nearly 1,500) may have been detained in non-IHSC facilities, for which information may be contained in narrative notes but not structured data fields for which were able to readily analyze.

[83] These data are for IHSC-staffed facilities, while data for non-IHSC facilities may be contained in narrative notes and not structured data fields that we can analyze.

received appropriate accommodations, such as a lower bunk and blankets.[84] Similarly, 6 of the 7 pregnant women we spoke with at IHSC-staffed facilities said that they were provided proper nutrition and snacks. The other pregnant woman did not discuss the adequacy of the nutrition she was provided.[85]

In addition, both of these two inspections provided insights into OB-GYN referrals and prenatal vitamins that were generally similar to the information we obtained from pregnant detainees at the locations we visited. Specifically, the above inspections indicated 75 to 98 percent compliance on performance measures related to access to OB-GYN care. Eight of the 10 pregnant women we spoke with in ICE detention did not express concerns about access to OB-GYN when asked about the sufficiency of medical care. However, two stated that they would like more timely access to an OB-GYN, and they did not know when their appointments would occur.[86] In addition, representatives from three NGOs stated that they heard concerns about pregnant women not having access to OB-GYN care or prenatal vitamins. Further, the above inspections indicated 95 to 100 percent compliance on performance measures related to prescribing prenatal vitamins, and all 10 of the pregnant women we spoke with in ICE detention said that they were provided prenatal vitamins.

Although they did not have specific performance measures, three additional inspections identified 19 findings related to the care of pregnant women.[87] All of the findings occurred at non-IHSC facilities.

---

[84] One woman we spoke with at a non-IHSC facility said that she was frequently cold, and would have liked to receive a sweater, more blankets, and a thicker mattress.

[85] The three pregnant women at the non-IHSC staffed facilities said that they were not provided adequate nutrition and snacks. For example, two of the women said that they did not receive any snacks, while one stated that she did not receive extra snacks because of her pregnancy.

[86] According to an ICE official, the date and time of the appointments are not disclosed for security reasons.

[87] These 19 findings were made at 13 different facilities. These inspections included (1) ICE's Office of Detention Oversight inspections from January 2015 through July 2019, (2) ICE's Enforcement and Removal Operations inspections from January 2015 through March 2019, and (3) IHSC's Field Medical Coordinator inspections from fiscal years 2015 through 2017. We reviewed information that resulted from a total of 854 inspections.

- Three of the 19 findings indicated that medical care was not provided or offered. For example, one pregnant woman was not offered a mental health assessment after reporting that she had a miscarriage at a prior facility.
- Seven included a recommendation to provide additional medical care, such as pregnancy testing.
- Four indicated insufficient documentation, such as medical records that were not transferred between facilities, or no documentation that pregnancy testing had occurred.
- Five indicated that a required policy did not exist or did not specify the required standards of care.

All but one of the facilities inspected took corrective actions to address the findings. For example, one inspection found that the facility's initial health assessment form did not address pregnancy testing. In response, the facility updated its intake screening form to include pregnancy testing. ICE determined that the facility that did not implement corrective actions to address deficiencies identified during the inspection would not be used for the detention of ICE detainees. See appendix VI for additional information on each deficiency, recommendation, and corrective action.

Additionally, our review of available data and interviews with pregnant detainees and officials at the locations we visited provided insight into issues related to segregation and the use of restraints—generally finding that these were rarely used. Specifically, our review of ICE data identified two pregnant women who were initially detained from 2015 through 2018, and segregated at some point during their detention—one for 8 days and one for over 4 months.[88] In both cases, ICE reported the reason for the segregation was that the detainee was a threat to the facility's security. Further, all 10 of the pregnant women we interviewed stated that they had not been segregated, and all the detention officials we interviewed at the four locations we visited stated that they were not aware

[88] One of these women was in our population of the more than 4,600 detentions of pregnant women.

of any instances of pregnant women being segregated.[89] Similarly, none of the 10 pregnant detainees reported being placed in restraints, and the officials we interviewed at the four locations generally stated that pregnant women are not to be restrained except in extreme circumstances, such as risk of violence or escape—which is consistent with ICE policies and standards.[90] One official said that he was aware of an incident where a pregnant woman was restrained when she attempted to harm herself and her child. In addition, officials from five local organizations or coalitions we spoke with stated that they had not heard concerns about instances of the use of restraints or segregation.

CBP Generally Takes Pregnant Women to Offsite Facilities for Care, and Has Plans to Enhance Its Medical Support

CBP generally relies on offsite care for pregnant women, and as a result, has limited available information on care CBP provided to pregnant women. However, they have efforts underway to enhance its medical support at selected facilities. As previously discussed, CBP facilities are designed for short-term care,[91] and CBP does not routinely administer pregnancy tests and generally did not have on-site medical personnel. According to CBP officials, they typically refer individuals to local medical providers in their area, as appropriate and for all emergent or serious issues—including concerns presented by pregnant women. In

---

[89] We conducted 16 interviews at four ICE detention facilities with ICE officials, including medical staff, and contracted detention staff.

[90] Some officials did not specifically discuss the policy on restraints.

[91] CBP field officials we spoke with told us that their facilities were not designed to hold pregnant women, as they have historically held single men, and that they have limited ability to provide special accommodations. For example, officials said that pregnant women are to be provided mats, but that they are not equipped with beds. Reports have also raised concerns about overcrowding at Border Patrol facilities, including facilities where we visited and observed pregnant women. For additional information, see Department of Homeland Security, Office of the Inspector General, *Management Alert– DHS Needs to Address Dangerous Overcrowding and Prolonged Detention of Children and Adults in the Rio Grande Valley*, OIG-19-51 (Washington, D.C.: July 2019).

addition, if CBP needed to provide a pregnancy test to a woman in its custody, it would take the woman to an offsite medical provider.

Our analyses of available data indicate that CBP took pregnant women for a hospital visit or admission at least 168 times from 2015 through 2018.[92] See Table 6 for additional information. Ninety-nine percent of these hospital trips involved Border Patrol, while the remaining 4 percent involved OFO.

Table 6. Number of times U.S. Customs and Border Protection (CBP) reported taking pregnant women to the hospital for a visit or admission, calendar years 2015 through 2018

	Border Patrol	Office of Field Operations	CBP total
2015	26	0	26
2016	56	0	56
2017	37	0	37
2018	47	2	49
Total	166	2	168

Source: GAO analysis of CBP documents. | GAO-20-330.

Note: These data were obtained from significant incident reports. According to CBP officials, it is possible that not all incidents were reported, as some discretion exists as to when to file these reports. There were 168 significant incident reports that involved a pregnant woman being sent to a hospital—of which 62 percent were taken from a CBP facility to the hospital, and the remaining were taken directly to the hospital upon being encountered in the field.

Although CBP generally relies on offsite care for pregnant women, CBP established some on-site medical care and has efforts underway to enhance its medical support at additional Border Patrol facilities and OFO ports of entry.[93] Specifically, one port of entry and three Border Patrol facilities established on-site medical care in 2013 and 2015, respectively. CBP officials at one of these locations told us that they developed on-site

---

92 We identified an additional five incidents where Office of Field Operations took a pregnant woman to the hospital from January through February 2019. As discussed earlier in the report, CBP did not collect comprehensive data on pregnant women during this time period. Further, some of these hospital visits were the result of CBP encountering pregnant women in the field, while in other cases CBP took pregnant women to the hospital from a CBP facility.

93 We currently have ongoing work on CBP's care and custody of detainees.

medical care based on the volume of crossings, as well as the operational costs for transporting individuals to offsite medical facilities and performing hospital watches. Subsequently, CBP's January 2019 memo regarding enhanced medical efforts at CBP facilities included efforts to expand medical support.[94] According to a senior CBP official, the agency had staffed more than 40 Border Patrol facilities and OFO ports of entry along the southwest border with on-site contracted medical care, as of January 2020.[95] According to CBP officials, contracted medical staff provide enhanced medical support through initial health intake interviews, medical assessments, diagnosis, treatment, referral, and follow up for persons in custody, including pregnant women. CBP officials stated that they will continue to rely on offsite care to provide emergency or advanced care.[96]

Over 100 Complaints Were Filed about ICE and CBP's Care of Pregnant Women

DHS has various processes to obtain and address the hundreds of medical care complaints it receives annually.[97] Specifically, an individual can file a complaint directly to facilities, ICE, CBP, and other DHS entities, including the Office of Inspector General and Office for Civil Rights and Civil Liberties (CRCL).[98] We identified 107 unique complaints

---

[94] According to Border Patrol officials, initial locations were selected based on the number of family units and unaccompanied children, the proximity and availability of offsite medical care, and consultations with field officials.

[95] Brian S. Hastings, Chief of Law Enforcement Operations, U.S. Border Patrol, *Assessing the Adequacy of DHS Efforts to Prevent Child Deaths in Custody*, testimony before the House Subcommittee on Border Security, Facilitation & Operations, Committee on Homeland Security, 116th Cong., 2nd sess., January 14, 2020.

[96] If CBP utilizes the health interview form, and a detainee reports being pregnant, then a medical assessment is required according to the December 2019 directive.

[97] GAO-16-231.

[98] The Office of Inspector General and CRCL generally determine whether to take their own action on the complaints or forward them to a DHS component, such as ICE or CBP, for resolution. The Office of Inspector General has the right of first refusal to investigate allegations opened by CRCL for investigation. For our report purposes, we refer to the agency that conducts the investigation as the "investigating agency."

that detainees, family members, NGOs, or other parties submitted to various entities from January 2015 through April 2019—54 that involved ICE's care of pregnant women, 50 that involved CBP, and 3 that involved both.[99] As shown in Figure 2, some of these complaints were under investigation as of August 2019, and some were substantiated; however, in most cases there was not enough information for the investigating agency to determine if proper care had been provided, among other things.[100]

Regarding the complaints against ICE, the most common type was that ICE allegedly did not provide medical care, or that the medical care was not quality or timely. See appendix VIII for additional information about the number and types of complaints submitted.

Eleven of the 54 complaints against ICE remained open as part of an on- going investigation, while the remaining 43 were closed.[101] Of the 43 complaints that were closed:

- An investigation substantiated one complaint that prenatal vitamins had not been provided at an IHSC-staffed facility. In response, ICE reported taking actions to address the complaint.
- Investigations partially substantiated one complaint regarding delays in medical care being provided. According to ICE, the delays had resulted from the time required to get medication approved. In response to the complaint, ICE reported coordinating with the facility to address the issues identified.
- Investigations found that 18 complaints were unsubstantiated. For example, ICE's review of medical records found that appropriate care had been provided.

---

[99] Specifically, we reviewed complaint data from CRCL, DHS's Office of Inspector General, and IHSC. These complaints may have been regarding the over 4,600 detentions of pregnant women that we identified in this chapter, or could have been for pregnant women that were detained before or after our time period. We excluded from our analysis one additional complaint where it was unclear which agency the allegation was being made against.

[100] We did not evaluate the sufficiency of these investigations or the determinations made.

[101] In August 2019, officials from DHS CRCL told us that one of the previously closed complaints had been re-opened as an investigation.

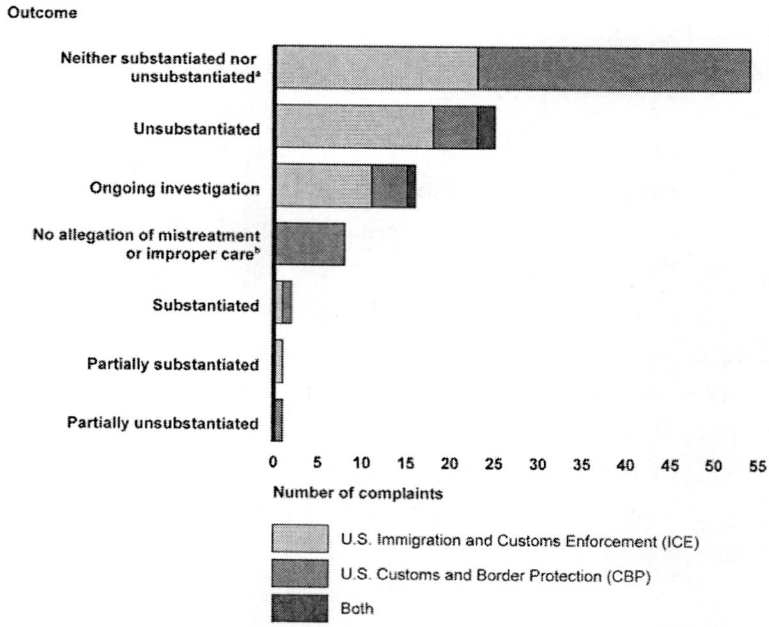

Source: GAO analysis of complaints from ICE Health Service Corps, CBP, Department of Homeland Security Office of Inspector General, and Department of Homeland Security Office for Civil Rights and Civil Liberties. | GAO-20-330.

Notes: These data are based on 107 unique complaints—54 that involved ICE's care of pregnant women, 50 that involved CBP, and 3 that involved both components.

[a]These complaints were not substantiated or unsubstantiated for a variety of reasons. For some complaints, the investigating agency determined that it did not have enough information to conduct an investigation. In other cases, the agency investigated the complaint, but determined that it did not have enough information to establish whether the complaint was substantiated or unsubstantiated, or agency documentation did not clearly specify whether the complaint was substantiated or unsubstantiated.

[b]These complaints described an event that occurred, such as a miscarriage, but the complaint did not allege that mistreatment or improper care had occurred.

Figure 2. Outcomes of Complaints Regarding U.S. Immigration and Customs Enforcement's and U.S. Customs and Border Protection's Care of Pregnant Women, January 2015 through April 2019.

- For the remaining 23 closed complaints, the complaint was not substantiated or unsubstantiated for a variety of reasons. For 11 complaints, the investigating agency determined that it did not have enough information to conduct an investigation, or the agency investigated the complaint but did not have enough information to establish whether the complaint was substantiated or unsubstantiated. For example, the allegation did not contain detailed biographical information, medical records did not contain enough information, or the detainee had been released and the agency could not follow-up. For the remaining 12 complaints, agency documentation did not clearly specify whether the complaint was substantiated or unsubstantiated.[102]

Regarding complaints against CBP, the most common type was that pregnant women had allegedly been physically, verbally, or otherwise mistreated. See appendix VIII for additional information about the number and types of complaints submitted.

Of the 50 complaints against CBP, four remained open as part of an on- going investigation, while the remaining 46 were closed. Of the 46 complaints that were closed:

- An investigation substantiated one complaint that a Border Patrol agent violated social media policy by posting a picture and information about a pregnant woman in custody. In response, CBP reported that the employee was suspended for two days.
- Investigations found that five complaints were unsubstantiated, and one was partially unsubstantiated.[103] For example, an investigation included a review of video footage at a port of entry,

---

[102] For example, according to officials from CRCL, their investigation of complaints may not necessarily result in a determination on whether a complaint is substantiated or unsubstantiated. However, it could lead to other findings—related or unrelated to the complaint—such as whether the agency has sufficient policies and procedures.

[103] For the complaint that was partially unsubstantiated, the agency lacked sufficient information to determine whether the remaining aspects of the complaint were substantiated.

among other things, and found that excessive force had not been used.

- Eight complaints described an event that occurred, such as a miscarriage, but the complaint did not allege that mistreatment or improper care occurred.[104]
- For the remaining 31 closed complaints, the complaint was not substantiated or unsubstantiated—for a variety of reasons. For 10 complaints, the investigating agency determined that it did not have enough information to conduct an investigation, or the agency investigated the complaint but did not have enough information to establish whether the complaint was substantiated or unsubstantiated. For the remaining 21 complaints, agency documentation did not clearly specify whether the complaint was substantiated or unsubstantiated.

With regard to the three complaints that involved allegations against both ICE and CBP, one remained open as part of an on-going investigation, while the other two complaints were found to be unsubstantiated.

AGENCY COMMENTS

We provided a draft of this chapter to DHS for review and comment. DHS provided comments, which are reproduced in appendix IX. DHS also provided technical comments, which we incorporated as appropriate. In addition, we provided relevant excerpts of the report to American College of Obstetricians and Gynecologists, American Correctional Association, and National Commission on Correctional Health Care for review.

[104] For three of these eight complaints, additional documentation indicated whether proper care had been provided during the event. For two of these events, documentation indicated that proper care had been provided. In one case, proper care had been provided, but a CBP official was found to have displayed unprofessional conduct by making insensitive remarks during the event.

Officials from these entities provided technical comments, which we incorporated as appropriate.

As agreed with your offices, unless you publicly announce the contents of this chapter earlier, we plan no further distribution until 30 days from the report date. At that time, we will send copies to the appropriate congressional committees and the Acting Secretary of the Department of Homeland Security.

Sincerely yours,

Gretta L. Goodwin
Director, Homeland Security and Justice Issues

List of Requesters

The Honorable Jerrold Nadler
Chairman
Committee on the Judiciary
House of Representatives

The Honorable Carolyn B. Maloney
Chairwoman
Committee on Oversight and Reform
House of Representatives

The Honorable Karen Bass
House of Representatives

The Honorable Nanette Barragán
House of Representatives

The Honorable Donald S. Beyer Jr.
House of Representatives

The Honorable Tony Cárdenas
House of Representatives

The Honorable André Carson
House of Representatives

The Honorable Katherine Clark
House of Representatives

The Honorable Steve Cohen
House of Representatives

The Honorable J. Luis Correa
House of Representatives

The Honorable Adriano Espaillat
House of Representatives

The Honorable Dwight Evans
House of Representatives

The Honorable Ruben Gallego
House of Representatives

The Honorable Vicente Gonzalez
House of Representatives

The Honorable Raúl M. Grijalva
House of Representatives

The Honorable Eleanor Holmes Norton
House of Representatives

The Honorable Pramila Jayapal
House of Representatives

The Honorable Hakeem Jeffries
House of Representatives

The Honorable Barbara Lee
House of Representatives

The Honorable James P. McGovern
House of Representatives

The Honorable Gwen S. Moore
House of Representatives

The Honorable Frank Pallone, Jr.
House of Representatives

The Honorable Mark Pocan
House of Representatives

The Honorable Jamie Raskin
House of Representatives

The Honorable Lucille Roybal-Allard
House of Representatives

The Honorable Jan Schakowsky
House of Representatives

The Honorable David Scott
House of Representatives

The Honorable Juan Vargas
House of Representatives

The Honorable Nydia M. Velázquez
House of Representatives

The Honorable Bonnie Watson Coleman
House of Representatives

APPENDIX I: METHODOLOGY FOR ANALYSES OF DATA, INSPECTIONS, AND COMPLAINTS

This appendix provides additional details on selected methodologies used to address our questions. Specifically, this includes information on our analyses of U.S. Immigration and Customs Enforcement (ICE) data and inspection findings and Department of Homeland Security (DHS) complaints used to address these questions:

1) What do available data indicate about pregnant women detained or held in DHS facilities?
2) What policies and standards does DHS have to address the care of pregnant women, and to what extent are they applicable across all facilities?
3) What is known about the care provided to pregnant women in DHS facilities?

Analyses of ICE Data

To address our first and third objectives, and provide context for our second objective, we reviewed data sources that ICE uses to track pregnant women in detention from calendar years 2016 through 2018 and matched these data with various ICE databases. We selected these years since ICE first collected data on all pregnant women beginning in June 2015, and 2018 was the last full year of available data for our audit.[105] Specifically, we matched ICE Health Service Corps (IHSC) records for pregnant women detained during calendar years 2016 through 2018 with individual-level detention dataset the ICE Integrated Decision Support (IIDS) database[106] to determine the total number of detentions of pregnant women,[107] as well as the length of detention,[108] facility location, case category status,[109] arresting agency, gestation of pregnancy,[110] when the pregnancy test was

---

105 From August 2013 to June 2015, IHSC collected data on pregnant women at IHSC- staffed facilities only. IHSC staff recorded these pregnancies in IHSC's medical record systems. From June 2015 to January 2016 ICE used a separate pregnancy tracking spreadsheet maintained by field medical coordinators to track pregnancies in non-IHSC staffed facilities. Beginning in January 2016, ICE implemented a new process to track all pregnancies (at both IHSC and non-IHSC staffed facilities). ICE officials stated that they would not document a positive pregnancy test if the individual was released prior to being fully processed, and as such, these women would not be included in our count.

106 According to ICE, IIDS is a data warehouse populated by Enforcement Case Tracking System information related to the investigation, arrest, booking detention, and removal of persons encountered during immigration and criminal law enforcement investigations and operations conducted by certain DHS components, namely ICE and CBP. DHS personnel utilize the Enforcement Case Tracking System applications to enter information into the system.

107 We reported on total detentions since a pregnant woman may have been detained multiple times during a calendar year.

108 To conduct our analysis on length of detention, we compared initial book-in date with the most recent book-out date to calculate the total days in detention for each of our selected populations.

109 Case category provides information on where the individual is in their immigration proceedings. Some of these could be an indicator of mandatory detention, categories of which are enumerated under 8 U.S.C. §§ 1225, 1226(c), 1226a, and 1231. ICE has data fields on mandatory detention, but does not maintain historical data for all mandatory detentions. ICE officials stated that this is only something that they need to track for current detainees. We used case status to help determine whether some women may have been subject to mandatory detention.

110 We analyzed data on the gestation of pregnant women, and found that from calendar years 2016 through 2018, of the over 4,600 detentions of pregnant women, we were able to determine the gestation period for 1,450 detentions. Data on estimated delivery date were readily available for our analyses for pregnant women detentions at non-IHSC facilities, and we had more limited data on detentions at IHSC-staffed facilities. IHSC– staffed facilities began to collect similar structured data in June 2018. ICE does not require these data to be collected. However, this information would be available in medical records prior to this date because, according to an IHSC official, gestation can be calculated using other data, such as last menstrual cycle.

conducted,[111] and whether there is an associated criminal conviction (criminality).[112]

To conduct our analyses, we matched pregnancy data to the IIDS detention data using alien number and excluded additional records we were unable to match. Because individuals may have multiple detentions, we compared the admission or book-in date from each data source with the book-in dates from the IIDS detention data, and excluded additional records with dates more than 30 days apart.[113] ICE collected data for 1,437 pregnant detainees in 2016; 1,170 in 2017; and 2,126 in 2018. We excluded 60 of the unique pregnant detainee records for 2016; 20 for 2017; and 32 for 2018 because we were unable to match these records to the IIDS individual-level detention data using alien number and book-in date combinations. According to ICE officials, this may be due to data entry errors. As a result, our analyses are based on over 4,600 detainee records we were able to match: 1,377 for 2016; 1,150 for 2017; and 2,094 for 2018. In general, this was our study population, unless otherwise noted in the report.

We also merged the detention data with data from ICE's weekly facility list report, as of February 2019, to determine who owned and operated the facility, whether it was staffed by IHSC officials, and in what state the facility was located.[114]

---

[111] Of the over 4,600 detentions of pregnant women, we were able to determine when the pregnancy test was provided for about 3,800—based on these women being in an IHSC-staffed facility at some point.

[112] To conduct our analysis of criminality, we used ICE's determination of criminality— criminal or non-criminal—which ICE determines by conducting electronic criminal history checks. For the purposes of this chapter, we referred to potentially removable individuals without criminal convictions known to ICE as "non-criminals" and individuals with criminal convictions known to ICE as "convicted criminals." According to ICE, ICE officers electronically request and retrieve criminal history information from the FBI's National Crime Information Center database, which maintains a repository of federal and state criminal history information, and other sources.

[113] Of those we were able to match, we identified 19 pregnant women that were detained more than once during the time period covered in our review.

[114] At the time that we merged the data sets, the February 2019 list was the most recent. It is possible that facilities may change over time, including if they are staffed by IHSC, among other things. For example, between 2016 and 2018, two facilities became IHSC- staffed facilities and one was no longer staffed by IHSC.

Further, we merged additional IHSC data with our study population to determine the number of obstetrician-gynecologist referrals and numbers that were assigned certain special needs, such as a special diet, lower bunk, no heavy lifting, and limitations on the use of restraints.[115] We also obtained and analyzed data from ICE's Segregation Review Management System to determine if any of the pregnant women had been segregated.[116]

Finally, we analyzed ICE IHSC data on pregnancy outcomes—abortions, births, stillbirths, and miscarriages.[117] These women who experienced such outcomes while detained may include the same women reported in our study population of more than 4,600 pregnant women detentions from calendar years 2016 through 2018, as well as pregnant women detained in calendar year 2015 and January through June 2019. We did not merge the outcome data with our other data sets, but were able to confirm that most of the outcomes were associated with alien numbers from the over 4,600 detentions in our study population.

We assessed the reliability of the data used in each of our analyses by analyzing available documentation, such as related data dictionaries; interviewing ICE officials knowledgeable about the data; conducting electronic tests to identify missing data, anomalies, or potentially erroneous values; and following up with officials, as appropriate. We determined the data were sufficiently reliable for describing general information on pregnant women detained by ICE, as well as the care provided to them.

---

[115] These data are for detentions in which women were detained at IHSC-staffed facilities at some point. Data on obstetrician-gynecologist referrals and special needs for women that were only detained in non-IHSC facilities may be contained in narrative notes and not structured data fields.

[116] According to ICE officials, data on segregation is documented in this system if (1) individuals are segregated for more than 14 days or 14 days out of any 21-day period or (2) if special vulnerable populations (e.g., pregnant women) are segregated for any period of time. These segregation data were for 2015 through 2018.

[117] We used information available in structured data fields and narrative fields to conduct these analyses—including diagnostic code data and narrative notes.

Analyses of ICE Inspection Results

To address our third objective, we analyzed reports and data from five ICE inspections that address compliance with pregnancy-related policies and detention standards from 2015 through July 2019—the most recent information available at the time of our review.[118] We selected these inspections because they review some aspect of the care provided to pregnant women.[119] Table 7 provides additional information on these inspections.

Table 7. Description of U.S. Immigration and Customs Enforcement (ICE) inspections that include assessments on the care provided to pregnant women

Type of inspection	Description	Inspection results we reviewed
ICE Health Service Corps (IHSC) Quality of Medical Care inspections	Contractor inspections of selected detainee files in IHSC-staffed and non-IHSC facilities that includes pregnancy-related performance measures.	We analyzed performance measure data from inspections of 129 facilities from December 2016 through March 2019.
IHSC Continuous Quality Improvement inspections	Inspections in which IHSC-staffed detention facilities report information, including pregnancy-related performance measures.	We reviewed annual inspection reports from fiscal years 2015 through 2018, which include performance measure data. The number of inspected facilities each year during this timeframe was generally around 20.

---

[118] We reviewed ICE's inspections and excluded from our analysis three ICE inspections that were not in scope because they did not address pregnancy-related care or were not compiled into an electronic format. For example, officials told us that self-assessments conducted by over-72 hour facilities with an average daily population of fewer than 10 detainees are not compiled into an electronic format. We also asked ICE officials responsible for providing oversight at ICE facilities (Detention Service Managers) for information in their weekly reports regarding the care of pregnant women. In response, officials said they identified one issue regarding a pregnant female in Border Patrol custody who was awaiting release, but was not in an ICE detention facility.

[119] For these same five inspections, we also reviewed available site visit inspection reports for facilities we planned to visit during our site visits.

Type of inspection	Description	Inspection results we reviewed
ICE Office of Detention Oversight inspections	Inspections of over-72-hour detention facilities (both IHSC-staffed and non-IHSC facilities) that assess compliance with applicable detention standards, including those related to the care of pregnant women.	We reviewed 131 inspection reports published from 2015 through July 2019.
ICE Enforcement and Removal Operations inspections	Contractor inspections of over-72-hour detention facilities (both IHSC-staffed and non-IHSC facilities) to determine compliance with applicable detention standards, including those related to the care of pregnant women. Inspections also include pre- occupancy reviews to determine whether facility operations and detention conditions are appropriate to house detainees.	We reviewed reports listing any instances where pregnancy-related standards were not met during 479 inspections from January 2015 through March 2019.
IHSC Field Medical Coordinator inspections	Inspections of over-72-hour detention facilities that are not IHSC-staffed, and use a file review and inspection worksheet to access the quality of medical care, including care of pregnant women.	We reviewed reports listing any instances where pregnancy-related standards were not met during 244 inspections from fiscal years 2015 through 2017. ICE did not compile this same information for fiscal year 2018 at the time of our review.

Source: GAO analysis of ICE information. | GAO-20-330.

Note: Some facilities that ICE inspected during these inspections detain only male detainees, and as such, pregnancy-related policies and standards would not be applicable at these facilities.

As noted in the table, two of these inspections contained pregnancy-related performance measures. The remaining three inspections assess compliance and identified findings related to the care of pregnant women, but did not have specific performance measures. For the three inspections that did not contain performance measures, we categorized the nature of each finding, such as a recommendation to provide additional medical care. We developed these categories based on a content analysis of the inspection findings, which involved one analyst categorizing the finding and a second person verifying the categories. If there were differences in analyses, these were reconciled through discussion between the two analysts and a final determination of the appropriate category was made. We also analyzed ICE documentation on corrective actions that facilities reported taking to address inspection findings, and used ICE facility data to determine who provided medical care at these facilities.[120]

To determine the scope and any limitations of inspection reports and data, we spoke with agency officials responsible for managing these inspections and the data systems used for documenting results. We also reviewed relevant documentation, such as data dictionaries and inspection worksheets. We determined that these data were sufficiently reliable for our purposes of describing the results of inspections regarding the care of pregnant women in ICE custody.

Analyses of Complaints

We reviewed and categorized complaints that detainees, family members, non-governmental organizations, or other parties submitted to various entities from January 2015 through April 2019—the latest available complaints at the time of our review—regarding ICE and CBP's care of pregnant women. Specifically, we reviewed complaint data from DHS's Office for Civil Rights and Civil Liberties (CRCL),[121] DHS's Office of Inspector General,[122] and IHSC.[123] We selected these complaint

[120] These facility data include information on, among other things, who owns and operates the facility, who provides the medical services, what populations they detain, and what detention standards they have in place.

[121] CRCL reviews allegations of civil rights and civil liberties violations and abuses by DHS personnel and contractors, including violations of rights while in immigration detention. It receives complaints from a number of sources, including media reports, non-governmental organizations, DHS Office of Inspector General, and a complaint form on its website that can be used by detainees or others on their behalf. Officials told us that they do not receive a large number of allegations related to pregnancy, but of the pregnancy-related complaints they receive, the majority are submitted by non-governmental organizations.

[122] DHS's Office of Inspector General investigates complaints of criminal and non-criminal misconduct by DHS employees and contractors. Anyone can submit a complaint to the Office of Inspector General through information provided on its website. Officials told us that overall they received about 44,000 complaints in 2018 and over 20,000 in 2017.

[123] IHSC reviews and investigates medical care complaints related to immigration detention. These complaints may be submitted by any detainee in custody, family members or other

systems because, according to DHS officials, they contained relevant information on the care of pregnant women, could be queried in an electronic format, and minimized duplicate complaints across systems.[124] We categorized each complaint based on a content analysis of the complaint narrative, which involved one analyst categorizing the complaint and a second person verifying the category. If there were differences in analyses, these were reconciled through discussion between the two analysts and a final determination of the appropriate category was made. We developed categories for 10 pregnancy outcomes, including births or miscarriages at a DHS facility or hospital, as well as 20 categories to describe the nature of the concerns, including physical mistreatment, use of restraints, or medical care not provided. The total number of concerns identified in our analysis exceeds the number of unique complaints filed because each unique complaint may identify more than one area of concern. We also used ICE facility data to determine, for example, who provides medical care at the facilities where the alleged events occurred.[125]

In addition, we analyzed agency documentation on the extent to which complaints could be substantiated, and any corrective actions that agencies and facilities reported taking to address complaints. To determine the scope and any limitations of the complaint information we received, we spoke with agency officials responsible for managing these complaint processes and the data systems used for documenting results. We also reviewed relevant documentation, such as user manuals for complaint systems.

---

detainees on behalf of another detainee, or ICE employees. Officials we spoke with estimated that they receive several thousand complaints per year, while less than 10 percent of these originate from females.

124 Based on these criteria, we excluded three additional complaint systems from our analysis. For example, according to ICE and CBP officials that manage a joint complaint system, they refer complaints that they receive to the Office of the Inspector General for review and these would be duplicative of what we obtained from the Office of the Inspector General. We excluded duplicate complaints from our analysis so that each complaint was counted once. Further, we excluded from our analysis one additional complaint where it was unclear which agency the allegation was being made against. In total, we analyzed 107 unique complaints.

125 Not all complaints included information on the facilities where the alleged events occurred.

Appendix II: Initial Detention Facility and Detention Days for Pregnant Women in U.S. Immigration and Customs Enforcement Facilities

This appendix provides additional details on our analyses of U.S. Immigration and Customs Enforcement (ICE) data from calendar years 2016 through 2018 on (a) where pregnant women were initially detained and (b) facilities that had the largest number of detention days involving pregnant women. In particular, these analyses describe whether the facility has ICE Health Service Corps (IHSC) staff and who owns and operates the facility, based on contracts or agreements.

Initial Detention Facility

Our analyses of ICE data found that of the over 4,600 detentions of pregnant women, in regards to IHSC presence, almost 78 percent of detentions of pregnant women were initially detained at an IHSC-staffed facility.[126] Further, 51 percent were at service processing centers that are owned and primarily operated by ICE, all of which were also staffed by IHSC, as shown in Table 8. According to ICE officials, many pregnant women first learn about their pregnancy when a test is performed during their intake into a detention facility.

Although pregnant women were initially detained in various facility types—based on IHSC presence and who owns and operates the facility, most occurred in eight specific detention facilities located in three states. Specifically, of ICE's over 4,600 pregnant women detentions from calendar year 2016 through 2018, 86 percent were initially detained in one

---

[126] Facility information is based on ICE's February 2019 facility list report. It is possible that facilities may change over time, including if they are staffed by IHSC, among other things. For example, between 2016 and 2018, two facilities became IHSC-staffed facilities and one was no longer staffed by IHSC.

of eight of these detention facilities—with one facility having 45 percent of the intakes of pregnant women.[127]

Table 8. Percent of U.S. Immigration and Customs Enforcement (ICE) detentions of pregnant women by initial detention facility type and ICE Health Service Corps (IHSC) presence, calendar years 2016 through 2018

	IHSC-staffed facility	Non-IHSC facility	Total
Service processing center	51.7	0.0	51.7
Intergovernmental service agreement[a]	17.4	12.4	29.8
Contract detention facility	5.6	0.1	5.7
U.S. Marshals Service intergovernmental agreement	0.0	3.1	3.1
Other[b]	2.8	6.8	9.6
Total[c]	77.6	22.4	100

Source: GAO analysis of Immigration and Customs Enforcement data. | GAO-20-330.

Notes: Our analysis is based on the 1,377 unique pregnant detainee records for 2016; 1,150 for 2017; and 2,094 for 2018 that we were able to match to the detention data. Facility information is based on ICE's February 2019 facility list report and the facility in which the pregnant women were initially detained. They may have been transferred after their initial detention. Of the pregnant women detentions, 37 percent experienced at least one transfer during this time period—which could include transfers to hospitals.

[a]Data include family residential centers.

[b]Other include hold rooms, staging facilities, and hospitals, among other facilities.

[c]Percentage may not sum to totals due to rounding.

Facilities with the Most Number of Detention Days

For these over 4,600 detentions of pregnant women, ICE detained them for a total of almost 50,300 days from calendar year 2016 through 2018.[128] Our analyses of ICE data found that of the 50,300 detention days of pregnant women, in regards to IHSC presence, 66 percent of these days

---

[127] These eight facilities include two service processing centers, four intergovernmental service agreements (including family residential centers), one contract detention facility, and one staging facility. Six of these facilities were IHSC-staffed and two were non-IHSC facilities.

[128] If a pregnant woman was released the same day that she was initially detained, this would count as one day in detention. If a woman was detained in more than one facility on the same day, we counted this as 1 day in each facility.

were at an IHSC-staffed facility. Further, over half were at intergovernmental service agreement facilities—including family residential centers, as shown in Table 9. Some facilities may have a large number of detention days associated with the intake of pregnant women, but these facilities may not detain women for a long period of time before releasing or transferring them. For example, at a facility that had one of the largest number of detention days for pregnant women, officials stated that they generally release women once the pregnancy is confirmed.

Table 9. Percent of detention days of pregnant women, by U.S. Immigration and Customs Enforcement (ICE) detention facility type and ICE Health Service Corps (IHSC) presence, calendar years 2016 through 2018

	IHSC-staffed facility	Non-IHSC facility	Total
Service processing center	15.7	0.0	15.7
Intergovernmental service agreement[a]	27.7	23.5	51.1
Contract detention facility	22.3	1.5	23.8
U.S. Marshals Service intergovernmental agreement	0.0	7.3	7.3
Other[b]	0.6	1.5	2.1
Total	66.2	33.8	100

Source: GAO analysis of Immigration and Customs Enforcement data. | GAO-20-330.

Notes: Our analysis is based on the 1,377 unique pregnant detainee records for 2016; 1,150 for 2017; and 2,094 for 2018 that we were able to match to the detention data. Facility information is based on ICE's February 2019 facility list report. The table above includes over 50,300 detention days. If a woman was detained in more than one facility on the same day, we counted this as 1 day in each facility.

[a]Data include family residential centers.

[b]Other includes hold rooms, staging facilities, and hospitals, among other facilities.

Although pregnant women spent their detention days in various facility types—based on IHSC presence and who owns and operates the facility, most occurred in 19 specific detention facilities located in seven states.

Specifically, of those days that pregnant women were detained by ICE, 89 percent of these days were in one of these 19 detention facilities.[129]

APPENDIX III: U.S. IMMIGRATION AND CUSTOMS ENFORCEMENT POLICIES ON CARE FOR PREGNANT WOMEN

U.S. Immigration and Customs Enforcement (ICE) detention facilities and staff are subject to a variety of policies, including ICE-wide policy directives and memoranda, ICE Health Service Corps (IHSC) policies, and detention standards, as of December 2019.[130] We categorized and summarized these policies and standards, as shown below.

ICE-Wide Policies

ICE-wide policies are directed at ICE staff and officers, and not to contractors or facility staff. The following ICE policies address pregnant detainees and ICE supervision of pregnant detainees:

- ICE Directive 11032.3: Identification and Monitoring of Pregnant Detainees (2017)
- ICE Directive 11065.1: Review of the Use of Segregation for ICE Detainees (2013)
- ICE Directive 11002.1: Parole of Arriving Aliens found to Have a Credible Fear of Persecution or Torture (2010)

---

[129] These 19 facilities include 10 intergovernmental service agreements (including family residential centers), two service processing centers, five contract detention facilities, and one U.S. Marshals Service intergovernmental agreement. Ten of these facilities were IHSC-staffed and nine were non-IHSC facilities.

[130] At the time of our review, ICE had updated, or was in the process of updating, some of its policies and standards. The policies and standards referenced in this appendix were current as of December 2019.

- ICE Memorandum: Use of GPS Monitoring Devices on Persons who are Pregnant or Diagnosed with a Severe Medical Condition (2009)
- ICE ERO [Enforcement and Removal Operations] Policy 11155.1: Use of Restraints (2012)
- Enforcement and Removal Operations National Detainee Handbook (2016)

These ICE-wide policies do not apply to contract or facility staff unless ICE modified the facility's contract or if these are already included in the facility's detention standards to which they are obligated. However, the *National Detainee Handbook* is a resource for detainees at detention facilities operating under ICE detention standards, excluding family residential centers. We categorized these policies and summarized them accordingly.

Intake Health Screening Inquiries about Pregnancy

The policy refers to ICE's responsibility to monitor detention facilities and ensure they meet national detention standard requirements to provide all newly admitted detainees an initial medical screening including pregnancy screening.

- ICE Directive 11032.3: Identification and Monitoring of Pregnant Detainees (2017)

Provision of Prenatal Care

ICE supervisory staff have responsibilities to ensure that pregnant detainees receive appropriate medical care, including transfer to a different facility if necessary. ICE medical staff also have a responsibility to monitor the condition of pregnant detainees and communicate any concerns to supervisory staff.

- ICE Directive 11032.3: Identification and Monitoring of Pregnant Detainees (2017)

- Enforcement and Removal Operations National Detainee Handbook (2016)

Segregation of Pregnant Women

ICE has a responsibility to monitor the use of segregation at detention facilities to ensure that they are adhering to detention standards.[131]

- ICE Directive 11065.1: Review of the Use of Segregation for ICE Detainees (2013)

Use of Restraints on Pregnant Women

Officers should take reasonable precautions to avoid causing discomfort when transporting a restrained detainee. At processing sites or non-ICE detention facilities, ICE personnel shall follow local policies and procedures.

- ICE ERO Policy 11155.1: Use of Restraints (2012)

Record Keeping on Pregnant Women Actions

ICE supervisors should ensure that ICE staff and contracted medical staff have processes to notify them of the arrival of a pregnant woman to a detention facility and ensure staff and facilities are aware of their obligations regarding pregnant detainees. IHSC staff are responsible for monitoring the condition of pregnant women while detained, as well as maintaining their medical records. Any instance of segregation of a pregnant woman must be documented in writing.

- ICE Directive 11032.3: Identification and Monitoring of Pregnant Detainees (2017)

---

131 According to ICE officials, they refer to the segregation of detainees from the general population, as being placed in Special Management Units either administratively or for violating disciplinary policies. Detainees placed into administrative segregation, generally have the same privileges as detainees housed in the general population. Detainees housed in disciplinary segregation generally have fewer privileges, but still interact daily with staff, medical personnel, legal advisors, and others.

- ICE Directive 11065.1: Review of the Use of Segregation for ICE Detainees (2013)

IHSC-Wide Policies

IHSC policies are directed specifically toward IHSC staff at detention facilities where IHSC provides medical services. The following IHSC policies address pregnant detainees:

- ICE Directive 11772.2: Women's Health Services (2017)
- ICE Directive 11741.4: Health Assessment (2016)
- ICE Directive 11742.2: Pre-Screening (2015)
- ICE Directive 11744.2: Intake Screening and Intake Reviews (2016)

We categorized these policies and summarized them accordingly.

Intake Health Screening Inquiries about Pregnancy

Intake screening includes pregnancy testing of women 10 to 56 years of age as well as questioning of pregnancy status.

- ICE Directive 11772.2: Women's Health Services (2017)
- ICE Directive 11742.2: Pre-Screening (2015)
- ICE Directive 11744.2: Intake Screening and Intake Reviews (2016)

Pregnancy Testing at Intake

Intake screening includes pregnancy testing of women 10 to 56 years of age and inquiry of reproductive health including previous pregnancies.

- ICE Directive 11772.2: Women's Health Services (2017)
- ICE Directive 11741.4: Health Assessment (2016)

- ICE Directive 11744.2: Intake Screening and Intake Reviews (2016)

Access to Abortion

In the event of a threat to a woman's life from carrying a pregnancy to term, or else in cases of rape or incest, ICE must bear the cost of a detainee's decision to terminate a pregnancy; otherwise the woman must bear the cost. ICE should offer medical resources to support effective recovery and follow-up care.

- ICE Directive 11772.2: Women's Health Services (2017)

Provision of Prenatal Care

Pregnant women should be seen by medical providers at least once a month while detained. They should also be referred to an obstetric specialist, and their medical records shared with the specialist to facilitate care.

- ICE Directive 11772.2: Women's Health Services (2017)
- ICE Directive 11741.4: Health Assessment (2016)
- ICE Directive 11744.2: Intake Screening and Intake Reviews (2016)

Provision of Postnatal Care

A postpartum detainee must receive postnatal care from a medical provider, in consultation with an obstetric specialist, at least once a month.

- ICE Directive 11772.2: Women's Health Services (2017)

Mental Health Services and Counseling for Pregnant Women

Any female detainee who gave birth, miscarried, or terminated a pregnancy within the last 30 days must receive a mental health evaluation, with the evaluation to occur no later than 72 hours after initial referral.

- ICE Directive 11772.2: Women's Health Services (2017)

Care for Pregnant Women with Substance Use Disorder

Chemically dependent pregnant women are considered high-risk and should be referred to an obstetrician or other appropriate medical provider as soon as they are identified.

- ICE Directive 11772.2: Women's Health Service (2017)
- ICE Directive 11744.2: Intake Screening and Intake Reviews (2016)

Use of Restraints on Pregnant Women

Pregnant detainees or those in postdelivery recuperation should not be restrained except in extraordinary circumstances that are documented by a supervisor or directed by a medical authority, whether in an ICE detention facility, in transport, or at a medical facility. Detainees in active labor or delivery can never be restrained. Even if restraints are used, a pregnant woman should never be restrained face down or on her back, or restrained with a belt that constricts the abdomen or pelvis.

- ICE Directive 11772.2: Women's Health Service (2017)

Record Keeping on Pregnant Women Actions

Intake screenings and assessments including pregnancy test results must be documented, as are risk factors for high risk pregnancies. Any use of restraints or request for abortion services must be documented. ICE supervisory staff must be notified within 72 hours of the arrival at a detention facility of a pregnant woman.

- ICE Directive 11772.2: Women's Health Service (2017)
- ICE Directive 11741.4: Health Assessment (2016)
- ICE Directive 11744.2: Intake Screening and Intake Reviews (2016)

ICE Detention Standards

Entities that have a contract or agreement with ICE to hold immigration detainees are generally contractually obligated to one of four sets of detention standards. These standards address a range of our pregnancy- related categories of care and vary by standard.

- 2000 ICE National Detention Standards (NDS)
- 2007 ICE Family Residential Standards (FRS)
- 2008 ICE Performance-Based National Detention Standards 2008 (2008 PBNDS)
- 2011 ICE Performance-Based National Detention Standards 2011 (2011 PBNDS)

We categorized these standards and summarized them accordingly. The 2011 PBNDS standards received revision in 2016. Whether a 2011 PBNDS facility is contractually required to adhere to the 2016 revision is dependent upon the contract language negotiated in each agreement.[132] Where appropriate, the summaries below note changes to policy as a result of those revisions.

Intake Health Screening Inquiries about Pregnancy

- 2008 PBNDS: Initial screening should be done within 12 hours of arrival and should inquire about the possibility of pregnancy.
- 2011 PBNDS: Initial screening should be done within 12 hours of arrival and should inquire about the possibility of pregnancy. In the 2016 revisions, the evaluation also includes a pregnancy test for women aged 18 to 56.

---

[132] As of September 2019, ICE had 47 facilities operating under 2011 PBNDS, of which 31 were contractually required to meet the 2016 revision when ICE begins inspecting for compliance under the revised standards.

Pregnancy Testing at Intake

- 2008 PBNDS: Initial screening should be done within 12 hours of arrival and should inquire about the possibility of pregnancy.
- 2011 PBNDS: In the 2016 revisions, initial screening includes pregnancy testing of women 18 to 56.

Access to Abortion

- 2011 PBNDS: If the life of the mother is endangered by carrying the fetus to term, or in the case of rape or incest, ICE will assume the costs to terminate the pregnancy. ICE shall arrange the transportation for the medical appointment, and to counseling services if requested in all cases, including those where rape, incest, or risk to life do not apply. Every facility, either directly or via contractor, must provide female detainees with access to counseling for pregnancy planning if the detainee wishes to receive an abortion.

Provision of Prenatal Care

- FRS: Female residents will have access to pregnancy management services including routine prenatal care
- 2008 PBNDS: Female detainees will have access to pregnancy management services including routine prenatal care
- 2011 PBNDS: Pregnant detainees will have access to pregnancy management services including routine prenatal care. They will also receive access to a specialist and receive a health assessment. The 2016 revisions note those actions should occur as soon as appropriate or within two working days. The 2016 revisions also give the medical provider authority to identify pregnant detainees' special needs such as diet or housing requirements and inform all necessary staff and authorities.

Provision of Postnatal Care

- FRS: Female residents will have access to pregnancy management services including postpartum follow-up care.
- 2008 PBNDS: Female detainees will have access to pregnancy management services including postpartum follow-up care.
- 2011 PBNDS: Pregnant detainees will have access to pregnancy management services including postpartum follow-up care. After giving birth, receiving an abortion or miscarrying, mental health assessments should also be offered.

Provision of Perinatal/Labor Care

- 2011 PBNDS: Pregnant detainees will have access to specialized care including labor and delivery.

Mental Health Services and Counseling for Pregnant Women

- FRS: Pregnant females will have access to pregnancy management services that include counseling and assistance.
- 2008 PBNDS: Pregnant females will have access to pregnancy management services that include counseling and assistance.
- 2011 PBNDS: Pregnant detainees will have access to care including counseling and assistance. Detainees can also request transportation to religious, medical and social counseling when considering termination of a pregnancy. In 2016 revisions, intake screening should include education to female detainees about mental health services related to pregnancy and women's health.

Care for Pregnant Women with Substance Use Disorder

- 2008 PBNDS: Female detainees will have access to pregnancy management services that include addiction management.

- 2011 PBNDS: In 2016 revisions, all chemically dependent pregnant detainees are to be considered high risk and referred to an obstetrician or other provider capable of addressing their needs immediately.

HIV Care for Pregnant Women

- 2011 PBNDS: Medical personnel shall provide all detainees diagnosed with HIV/AIDS medical care consistent with national recommendations and guidelines disseminated through the U.S. Department of Health and Human Services, the Center for Disease Control, and the Infectious Diseases Society of America.[133]

Prenatal Vitamins

- 2011 PBNDS: Pregnant detainees will have access to prenatal care including prenatal vitamins.

Nutrition for Pregnant Women

- NDS: Physicians may order snacks or supplemental feedings to increase protein or calories for reasons including pregnancy. In hold rooms, pregnant women should have regular access to snacks, milk, and juice.
- FRS: Physicians may order snacks or supplemental feedings to increase protein or calories for reasons including pregnancy. Pregnant women will have access to pregnancy management services that include nutrition.
- 2008 PBNDS: Physicians may order snacks or supplemental feedings to increase protein or calories for reasons including pregnancy. In hold rooms, pregnant women should have regular

---

[133] These include guidelines for the care of pregnant women with HIV.

access to snacks, milk, and juice. Pregnant women will have access to pregnancy management services that include nutrition.

- 2011 PBNDS: Physicians may order snacks or supplemental feedings to increase protein or calories for reasons including pregnancy. In hold rooms, pregnant women should have regular access to snacks, milk, and juice. Pregnant women will have access to pregnancy management services that include nutrition. Special consideration is given to pregnant women when providing meals and snacks during transportation. In the 2016 revisions, the medical provider is responsible for identifying special needs of pregnant detainees, including diet, and notifying all necessary staff.

Special Accommodations for Pregnant Women

- 2008 PBNDS: In hold rooms, pregnant women will have access to temperature appropriate clothing and blankets and may, depending on facility, have access to bunks, cots, or beds, normally not kept in hold rooms.
- 2011 PBNDS: In hold rooms, pregnant women will have access to temperature appropriate clothing and blankets and may, depending on facility, have access to bunks, cots, or beds, normally not kept in hold rooms. Pregnant detainees should also have access to lactation services in the facility. In the 2016 revisions, the medical provider is responsible for identifying special needs of pregnant detainees and notifying all necessary staff.

Segregation of Pregnant Women

- 2011 PBNDS: In the 2016 revisions, it is stated that women who are pregnant, post-partum, recently had a miscarriage, or recently had a terminated pregnancy should as a general matter not be placed in a Special Management Unit. In very rare situations, a woman who is pregnant, postpartum, recently had a miscarriage, or recently had a terminated pregnancy may be placed in a Special Management Unit as a response to behavior that poses a serious and immediate risk of physical harm, or if the detainee has requested to be placed in protective custody administrative segregation and there are no more appropriate alternatives available. Also in the 2016 revisions, a facility administrator must notify the appropriate field office director in writing as soon as possible, but no later than 72 hours any time a pregnant woman or one who recently had a miscarriage is placed in segregation. In all cases, in the 2016 revisions, this decision must be approved by a representative of the detention facility administration, in consultation with a medical professional, and must be reviewed every 48 hours.

Use of Restraints on Pregnant Women

- NDS: Pregnant detainees should be given special consideration if restrained as a result of a physical encounter. A medical professional should be consulted immediately in the aftermath, and the detainee examined. Pregnant detainees should be restrained in such a way as to avoid harming the fetus such as not restraining face down.
- FRS: Medical staff will advise on the necessary precautions to take when restraining a pregnant detainee and restraint should be done only when other methods have been tried or are impracticable.
- 2008 PBNDS: Medical staff will advise on the necessary precautions to take when restraining a pregnant detainee. Pregnant detainees should be restrained in such a way as to avoid harming the fetus such as not restraining face down.

- 2011 PBNDS: A pregnant detainee is not to be restrained except in truly extraordinary circumstances. Even then, it must be documented by a supervisor and directed by a medical authority. Women in active labor or delivery can never be restrained, and if restrained, the detainee should never be face down, on her back, or restrained with a belt that constricts the area of pregnancy.

Record Keeping on Pregnant Women Actions

- NDS: The medical provider of a facility will notify the ICE officer in charge whenever a pregnant detainee is identified and any use of force or application of restraints on a detainee should be followed by a medical examination, and its results documented.
- FRS: The medical provider of a facility will notify the ICE facility administrator whenever a pregnant detainee is identified. A treatment plan should be developed for any detainee requiring close medical supervision, and approved by the appropriate physician or other medical provider.
- 2011 PBNDS: When a detainee is pregnant, an alert is notified in their medical record and the facility administrator will receive notice. If a detainee is transferred, it is the administrator's responsibility to inform ICE of the medical alert. Any use of restraints requires documented approval, including in the detainee's detention and medical files and guidance from the on-site medical authority. A request to terminate a pregnancy must be documented in the medical file and signed by the detainee. In the 2016 revisions, ICE supervisory staff must be informed within 72 hours when a pregnant detainee is identified.

Appendix IV: Recommended Guidance on the Care of Pregnant Women Detainees

Numerous professional associations, non-governmental organizations, and federal agencies have issued guidance on care to be provided to pregnant women.[134] Specifically, we reviewed the following guidance:

- American Civil Liberties Union: Worse than Second-Class: Solitary Confinement of Women in the United States (2014)
- American College of Obstetricians and Gynecologists:
  - Committee Opinion: Health Care for Pregnant and Postpartum Incarcerated Women and Adolescent Females (2016)
  - Guidelines for Perinatal Care, Eighth Edition[135] (2017)
- American Correctional Association Performance-Based Standards and Expected Practices for Adult Correctional Institution, 5th Edition
- Joint Public Correctional Policy on the Treatment of Opioid Use Disorders for Justice Involved Individuals[136] (2018)
- Joint Statement on the Federal Role in Restricting the Use of Restraints on Incarcerated Women and Girls during Pregnancy, Labor, and Postpartum Recovery[137]

---

[134] Officials from the American College of Obstetricians and Gynecologists, National Commission on Correctional Health Care, and the American Correctional Association, stated that although their recommended guidance was designed to apply in a criminal incarceration setting, their recommended guidance is also applicable to immigration detention. In addition to the guidance we reviewed on incarcerated pregnant women, broader recommended guidance exists on the care of pregnant women such as the American College of Obstetricians and Gynecologists's *Committee Opinion: Optimizing Postpartum Care, Committee Opinion: Opioid Use and Opioid Use Disorder in Pregnancy, and Committee Opinion: Maternal Immunization*, among others.

[135] Co-authored by the American Academy of Pediatrics.

[136] A joint policy released by the American Correctional Association and the American Society of Addiction Medicine.

[137] The statement was endorsed by the following organizations: the American Congress of Obstetricians and Gynecologists (as of January 2018, all activities of this entity fall under the American College of Obstetricians and Gynecologists), American Jail Association, American Psychological Association, Human Rights Project for Girls, NCCHC, and the National Council of Juvenile and Family Court Judges.

- National Commission on Correctional Health Care (NCCHC):
  - Position Statement: Restraint of Pregnant Inmates (2015)
  - Position Statement on Solitary Confinement (Isolation) (2016)
  - Position Statement on Breastfeeding in Correctional Settings[138] (2018)
  - Standards for Health Services in Jails (2018)
- Sufrin C., Pregnancy and Postpartum Care in Correctional Settings,[139] National Commission on Correctional Health Care, Clinical Resources Series. (2018)
- National Women's Law Center: Women Behind Bars: A state-by-state report card and analysis of federal policies on conditions of confinement for pregnant and parenting women and the effect on their children (2010)
- United Nations Rules for the Treatment of Women Prisoners and Non- custodial Measures for Women Offenders (the Bangkok Rules) (2010)
- U.S. Department of Homeland Security (DHS): Report of the DHS Advisory Committee on Family Residential Centers[140] (2016)
- U.S. Department of Justice, Bureau of Justice Assistance: Best Practices in the Use of Restraints with Pregnant Women and Girls Under Correctional Custody[141] (2014)

---

138 This paper was endorsed by the American College of Obstetricians and Gynecologists.

139 This paper was endorsed by the American College of Obstetricians and Gynecologists.

140 The Committee included representatives from the following: Los Angeles County Department of Mental Health, Covington & Burling LLP, WestEd, Women's Refugee Commission, American Academy of Pediatrics, The Moss Group Inc., University of California Hastings College of the Law, University of California Hastings Center for Gender & Refugee Studies, Young Center for Immigrant Children's Rights at the University of Chicago, National Immigrant Women's Advocacy Project at American University Washington College of Law, ASISTA, Cooper Medical School of Rowan University, University of Michigan Law School, Connecticut Department of Emergency Services and Public Protection, and Jackson Walker LLP.

141 Produced by the Department of Justice's National Task Force on the Use of Restraints with Pregnant Women under Correctional Custody that included representation from the following: Policy Research Associates, the US Health and Human Services Substance Abuse and Mental Health Services Administration, National Institute of Corrections, National Center for Trauma-Informed Care, Association of State Correctional Administrators, National Women's Law Center, Federal Bureau of Prisons, Immigration and Customs Enforcement, American Jail Association, North Carolina Department of

- U.S Department of Justice Report and Recommendations Concerning the Use of Restrictive Housing[142] (2016)

Because the specificity of the guidance varies across entities, we summarized the recommended guidance for our report purposes.[143] For example, guidance on nutrition may range from calling for additional meals for pregnant women to more specifically outlining extra caloric and dietary needs. Our summary statement for each of the pregnancy-related topics is included below, along with examples from relevant recommended guidance.[144]

Intake Health Screening Inquiries about Pregnancy

- Summary of recommended guidance: The sources that have guidance generally agree that intake health screenings should include inquiry regarding pregnancy and related conditions.
- Example: "Screening is performed on all inmates upon arrival at the intake facility…The receiving screening form…inquires as to the inmate's…possible, current, or recent pregnancy…" – NCCHC *Standards for Health Services in Jails* (2018)

Public Safety, the Alvin S. Glenn Detention Center (South Carolina), National Resource Center on Justice Involved Women, Center for Effective Public Policy, Alpert Medical School of Brown University, Women and Infants Hospital of Rhode Island, NCCHC, New York City Department of Correction, American Correctional Association, Human Rights Project for Girls, the Maternity Care Coalition of Riverside Correctional Facility (Pennsylvania), Tohono O'odham National Correctional Facility, Multnomah County Sheriff's Office, Maryland Department of Public Safety and Correctional Services, Louisiana State University Health-Shreveport, Florida Department of Juvenile Justice.

142 The Working Group that developed the report included representation from the following Department of Justice components: Federal Bureau of Prisons, Civil Rights Division, Office of Justice Programs, United States Marshals Service, Executive Office of United States Attorneys, and the Attorney General's Advisory Committee.

143 We did not include recommended guidance that was not directly relevant to the care of pregnant women, such as guidance on child care.

144 Not all source documents included recommended guidance for each of the topics.

Pregnancy Testing at Intake

- Summary of recommended guidance: Sources that have guidance generally agree that pregnancy testing should be conducted on newly detained women of childbearing age, but some provide additional guidance on when this should be done, and this may vary.
- Example: "All women at risk for pregnancy should be offered a pregnancy test within 48 hours of admission…A simple approach would be to offer pregnancy testing to all women under the age of 55." – *Pregnancy and Postpartum Care in Correctional Settings* (2018)
- Example: "…medical providers should continue to offer pregnancy tests to every female of child-bearing age who is newly detained…" – *Report of the DHS Advisory Committee on Family Residential Centers* (2016)

Access to Abortion

- Summary of recommended guidance: Sources that have guidance generally agree abortion services should be offered to detained pregnant women, with one source providing additional details, including swift facilitation of a woman's choice of termination and non- interference of outside bodies in the decision.
- Example: "Pregnancy termination is generally to be performed as safely and as early in pregnancy as possible…Termination of pregnancy should not depend on whether or not the specific procedure is available on site. Each woman will decide what option to choose…this decision is to be made without undue interference by outside bodies, including governmental bodies." – *Report of the DHS Advisory Committee on Family Residential Centers* (2016).

Provision of Prenatal Care

- Summary of recommended guidance: Sources that have guidance generally agree that some form of prenatal care should be provided to detained pregnant women, but differ on the level of specificity for the standard of care, from stating simply that prenatal care be provided to specifying requirements including regularly scheduled obstetric care and access to 24-hour emergency care.
- Example: "Incarcerated women who wish to continue their pregnancies should have access to readily available and regularly scheduled obstetric care, beginning in early pregnancy and continuing through the postpartum period. Incarcerated pregnant women also should have access to unscheduled or emergency obstetric visits on a 24-hour basis." – American College of Obstetricians and Gynecologists *Committee Opinion: Health Care for Pregnant and Postpartum Incarcerated Women and Adolescent Females* (2016)
- Example: "Prenatal care in correctional facilities must reflect national standards, including visit frequency with a qualified prenatal care provider, screening and diagnostic tests, and referrals for complications." – *Pregnancy and Postpartum Care in Correctional Settings* (2018).

Provision of Postnatal Care

- Summary of recommended guidance: Sources that have guidance generally agree that the provision of postnatal care be provided to women who give birth. However, they vary in their specifics. For example, some specifically state that lactation service or postnatal birth control should be provided. One source also recommends specific forms of accommodation to aid postnatal recovery.
- Example: "…appropriate accommodations should be made, such as allowing women to rest when needed…Discharge instructions from the hospital, which may include postpartum blood pressure

monitoring or diabetes screening, should be adhered to." – *Pregnancy and Postpartum Care in Correctional Settings* (2018)[145]

- Example: "Allow immediately postpartum women to breastfeed their babies and have lactation support services from the hospital." – NCCHC *Position Statement on Breastfeeding in Correctional Settings* (2018).

Provision of Perinatal/Labor Care

- Summary of recommended guidance: Sources that have guidance generally agree a pregnant woman should be transported to a hospital if there are signs of labor. Some sources state that detention staff be trained in emergency delivery in the event of a delivery occurring in the facility, away from professional care.
- Example: "Due to the time necessary to arrange transport to a nearby hospital, there is a low threshold to send pregnant inmates out for evaluation of a labor when signs or symptoms of labor or ruptured membranes are present… Any facility that houses pregnant women should have an emergency delivery kit available on-site, and health staff should be trained in its use in the event that a delivery occurs in the facility." – *Pregnancy and Postpartum Care in Correctional Settings* (2018)
- Example: "Having a preexisting arrangement to have the babies of incarcerated women delivered at a local hospital reduces confusion and uncertainty when a woman goes into labor." – National Women's Law Center Women Behind Bars: *A state-by-state report card and analysis of federal policies on conditions of confinement for pregnant and parenting women and the effect on their children* (2010).

---

145 According to the American College of Obstetricians and Gynecologists's *Committee Opinion: Optimizing Postpartum Care*, this initial assessment should be followed up with ongoing care as needed, concluding with a comprehensive postpartum visit no later than 12 weeks after birth.

Mental Health Services and Counseling for Pregnant Women

- Summary of recommended guidance: Sources that have guidance generally agree that pregnant and postpartum women should have access to mental health/counseling services.
- Example: "Pregnant inmates are given comprehensive counseling and care in accordance with national standards and their expressed desires regarding their pregnancy." – NCCHC *Standards for Health Services in Jails* (2018).

Care for Pregnant Women with Substance Use Disorder

- Summary of recommended guidance: Sources that have guidance generally agree that addicted pregnant women should have access to screening and specialized addiction-treatment programs.
- Example: "Screening for drug and alcohol use is a first step and is followed with referral to treatment. For women who report opiate use, the standard of care is not to detoxify from opiates during pregnancy due to the fetal risks of withdrawal. Rather the standard of care is to provide…methadone or buprenorphine…" – *Pregnancy and Postpartum Care in Correctional Settings* (2018)[146]
- Example: "The standard of care for pregnant women with [opioid use disorder] is [medications for addiction treatment] and should therefore be offered/continued for all pregnant detainees and incarcerated individuals." – *Joint Public Correctional Policy on the Treatment of Opioid Use* (2018).

---

[146] According to the American College of Obstetricians and Gynecologists's *Committee Opinion: Opioid Use and Opioid Use Disorder in Pregnancy* "For pregnant women with an opioid use disorder, opioid agonist pharmacotherapy is the recommended therapy and is preferable to medically supervised withdrawal because withdrawal is associated with high relapse rates (55–57), ranging from 59% to more than 90% (58), and poorer outcomes. Relapse poses grave risks, including communicable disease transmission, accidental overdose because of loss of tolerance, obstetric complications, and lack of prenatal care."

HIV Care for Pregnant Women

- Summary of recommended guidance: Sources that have guidance generally agree that pregnant women should have access to testing and treatment of HIV for the benefit of both the mother and child.
- Example: "The Centers for Disease Control and Prevention recommends universal opt-out HIV screening for pregnant women; with early detection, prevention of mother-to-child transmission can be accomplished…" – *Pregnancy and Postpartum Care in Correctional Settings* (2018).

Vaccinations for Pregnant Women

- Summary of recommended guidance: Sources that have guidance generally agree that vaccines recommended for pregnant women be provided to detainees in accordance with accepted medical guidelines.
- Example: "Current recommendations are that all pregnant women should be vaccinated with the flu vaccine during flu season and tetanus, diphtheria, and pertussis during the third trimester, regardless of whether they were vaccinated outside of pregnancy." – NCCHC *Standards for Health Services in Jails* (2018)
- Example: "Vaccines related to pregnancy should be offered pursuant to CDC guidelines…" – *Report of the DHS Advisory Committee on Family Residential Centers* (2016)

Prenatal Vitamins

- Summary of recommended guidance: The sources that have guidance generally agree that prenatal vitamins should be provided to pregnant women, and some sources state that prenatal vitamins should be provided to breastfeeding women.
- Example: "Pregnant women must also receive prenatal vitamins that contain, among other essential vitamins and minerals, 400mcg

to 800mcg of folic acid... Women with documented anemia (hemoglobin<11) should receive additional iron supplementation." – *Pregnancy and Postpartum Care in Correctional Settings* (2018)

- Example: "Appropriate nutrition and prenatal vitamins should be given to lactating women..." – NCCHC *Standards for Health Services in Jails* (2018).

Nutrition for Pregnant Women

- Summary of recommended guidance: Sources that have guidance generally recommend special nutrition regimens for pregnant women, with varying degrees of specificity, ranging from recommending the use of supplements broadly to specifying required nutrients such as folic acid and calcium and extra calories in the form of additional meals, larger meals, or food between meals, and in some cases specifying that these requirements also apply for postpartum women.
- Example: "Pregnant and postpartum women have additional nutritional needs and should be counseled on the importance of adequate nutrition. Diets provided by correctional institutions should be specialized to the women's needs and be rich in whole grains, calcium, and fruits and vegetables. In the second and third trimesters, women require an additional 300 calories per day..." – *Pregnancy and Postpartum Care in Correctional Settings* (2018).

Special Accommodations for Pregnant Women

- Summary of recommended guidance: Sources that have guidance generally agree that accommodations should be provided to pregnant women. Some sources specify accommodations such as appropriate programming and hygiene for pregnant women and nursing mothers, appropriately adjusted work assignments and exercise, and bottom bunks.

- Example: "Activity for pregnant women must take into account the physical constraints of being in a correctional facility. All pregnant women must have a bottom bunk so that they do not risk falling from a top bunk. Certain work assignments may be inappropriate…Work assignments should be adjusted accordingly. In the absence of medical or obstetric complications, 30 minutes or more of moderate exercise a day on most, if not all, days of the week is recommended." – *Pregnancy and Postpartum Care in Correctional Settings* (2018).

Segregation of Pregnant Women

- Summary of recommended guidance: Sources that have guidance generally agree that pregnant women should not be placed in segregation, though some suggests this could be necessary in certain cases.
- Example: "Women who are pregnant, who are postpartum, who recently had a miscarriage, or who recently had a terminated pregnancy should not be placed in restrictive housing…In very rare situations, a woman who is pregnant, is postpartum, recently had a miscarriage, or recently had a terminated pregnancy may be placed in restrictive housing as a temporary response to behavior that poses a serious and immediate risk of physical harm…" – *U.S Department of Justice Report and Recommendations Concerning the Use of Restrictive Housing* (2017).

Use of Restraints on Pregnant Women

- Summary of recommended guidance: Sources that have guidance generally agree that restraints generally should not be used on a pregnant woman, except when necessary. Some sources indicate that if restraints are necessary, it should be well documented and require approval and assessment from a senior official and/or medical professional. Some sources specify the types of restraints that should never be used including abdominal restraints, handcuffs behind the back, and leg and ankle restraints.

- Example: "Restraint of pregnant inmates during labor and delivery should not be used. The application of restraints during all other pre- and postpartum periods should be restricted as much as possible and, when used, done so with consultation from medical staff and in the least restrictive means possible. […] All uses of restraints in pregnant inmates must be documented and reviewed." – NCCHC *Position Statement: Restraint of Pregnant Inmates* (2015)
- Example: "Policies and procedures on the use of restraints on pregnant women and girls under correctional custody should be developed collaboratively by correctional leaders and medical staff who have knowledge about the potential health risks…The use of restraints on pregnant women and girls under correctional custody should be limited to absolute necessity." - U.S. Department of Justice, Bureau of Justice Assistance: *Best Practices in the Use of Restraints with Pregnant Women and Girls under Correctional Custody* (2014).

Record Keeping on Pregnant Women Actions

- Summary of recommended guidance: Sources that have guidance generally agree that accurate records of detention regarding pregnant women should be kept, with varying levels of specificity ranging from noting that records should be kept for incidents of restraint to specifying how documentation is kept and reviewed. One source notes that medical records should also be easily accessible for offsite care providers.
- Example: "If detention continues ICE should ensure…reporting of detention to ICE Headquarters and continued review of the need to detain." – *Report of the DHS Advisory Committee on Family Residential Centers* (2016)

- Example: "Obstetrician-gynecologists and other obstetric care providers of antepartum care should be able to either primarily provide or easily refer to others to provide a wide array of services. These services include... [T]imely transmittal of prenatal records to the site of the woman's planned delivery so that her records are readily accessible at the time of delivery." – American College of Obstetricians and Gynecologists *Guidelines for Perinatal Care, Eighth Edition* (2017).

Appendix V: U.S. Customs and Border Protection Policies on Care for Pregnant Women

U.S. Customs and Border Protection (CBP) and its components, Border Patrol and the Office of Field Operations (OFO), have several policies and standards that address the care and treatment of pregnant women in their custody. Specifically, these include the following:

- CBP: National Standards on Transport, Escort, Detention, and Search (2015)[147]
- OFO: Personal Search Handbook (2004)
- OFO: Directive: Secure Detention, Transport and Escort Procedures at Ports of Entry, CBP Directive No. 3340-030B (2008)
- Border Patrol: U.S. Border Patrol Policy: Hold Rooms and Short Term Custody (2008)

---

147 As part of its implementation of this policy, OFO required its personnel to complete an assessment for all detainees in its custody to evaluate detainees' safety, whether they may be considered an at-risk detainee or at risk of posing a threat to others, known or reported medical or mental health issues and level of risk to themselves, other detainees, and staff based on the information available at the time of the assessment. This includes a question about pregnancy. As stated previously in this chapter, CBP has since developed a standardized health interview form that can be used by OFO and BorderPatrol.

Summaries of these policies and standards are provided below, along with the titles of the policies or standards on which each summary is based.[148]

Processing and Holding

Officers and agents will consider pregnancy when expediting processing of vulnerable detained persons and when placing detained persons with others in hold rooms and holding facilities.

- Secure Detention, Transport and Escort Procedures at Ports of Entry (2008) and U.S. Border Patrol Policy: Hold Rooms and Short Term Custody (2008)

Mental Health Services and Counseling for Pregnant Women

If an agent or officer observes signs of mental illness, it should be reported to a supervisor and appropriate medical care be provided or sought, including calling emergency services in the event of an emergency.

- Transport, Escort, Detention, and Search (2015)

Nutrition for Pregnant Women

Pregnant detainees should be offered a meal every six hours they are in detention and have access to snacks, milk, or juice at all times.

---

[148] Not all policies and standards included language for each of the bulleted items.

- Transport, Escort, Detention, and Search (2015); Secure Detention, Transport and Escort Procedures at Ports of Entry (2008); and U.S. Border Patrol Policy: Hold Rooms and Short Term Custody (2008)

Special Accommodations for Pregnant Women

Reasonable accommodations should be made for pregnant women, including placement in the least restrictive appropriate setting. If circumstances permit, pregnant women should not be placed in hold rooms or other secure areas, but instead in an open area under supervision.

- Transport, Escort, Detention, and Search (2015); Secure Detention, Transport and Escort Procedures at Ports of Entry (2008); and U.S. Border Patrol Policy: Hold Rooms and Short Term Custody (2008).

Use of Restraints on Pregnant Women

Officers and agents should not use restraints on pregnant women unless they demonstrate or threaten violence, have a criminal and/or violent history, or there is an articulable escape risk. Even if restraints are used, pregnant detainees are not to be restrained face-down, on their backs, or with a belt that constricts the area of her pregnancy. Pregnant women can never be restrained while in active labor or delivery. All use of restraints must be documented.

- Transport, Escort, Detention, and Search (2015)

Record Keeping on Pregnant Women Actions

All physical interactions with pregnant women must be recorded after they occur. Any medical emergency must be recorded as soon as practical after emergency services have been contacted. Further, Border Patrol agents must create a booking record for persons detained and the record must include a medical annotation for conditions requiring care, including pregnancy.

- Transport, Escort, Detention, and Search (2015) and U.S. Border Patrol Policy: Hold Rooms and Short Term Custody (2008).

APPENDIX VI: U.S. IMMIGRATION AND CUSTOMS ENFORCEMENT INSPECTION RESULTS FOR CARE OF PREGNANT WOMEN

U.S. Immigration and Customs Enforcement (ICE) uses various inspections for accessing facilities' compliance with policies and detention standards—the frequency and focus of which vary.[149] Some inspections also include pregnancy-related performance measures, such as a measure assessing whether a pregnancy test was performed at intake. We analyzed reports and data from five ICE inspections that address compliance with pregnancy-related policies and detention standards from 2015 through June 2019—the most recent data available at the time of our review. We selected these inspections because they review some aspect of the care provided to pregnant women.[150]

---

[149] We previously reported that ICE officials responsible for detention oversight stated that these various inspections complement one another and serve different purposes. See GAO, *Immigration Detention: Additional Actions Needed to Strengthen Management and Oversight of Facility Costs and Standards,* GAO-15-153 (Washington, D.C., Oct. 10, 2014).

[150] See appendix I for additional information on how we selected these inspections.

These inspections address compliance at ICE detention facilities where on-site medical care is provided by both ICE Health Service Corps (IHSC) as well as other entities (non-IHSC facilities).

Pregnancy-Related Performance Measures at IHSC-Staffed and non- IHSC Facilities

We reviewed results from IHSC's inspections of IHSC-staffed and non- IHSC facilities, which includes pregnancy-related performance measures. We found that instances of non-compliance occurred at 16 facilities subject to a range of detention standards. Three of these facilities were IHSC-staffed, and 13 were non-IHSC. Table 10 shows results from December 2016 through March 2019.

Table 10. Compliance with pregnancy-related measures at U.S. Immigration and Customs Enforcement Health Service Corps- staffed (IHSC) and non-IHSC Facilities, December 2016 through March 2019

Records reviewed			
Pregnancy-related measure	Number of non-compliant records	Number of compliant records	Percent compliance
Does the facility perform a pregnancy test on females aged 10 to 56 during intake screening?[a]	40	549	93
Was a pregnancy test performed prior to x-ray or before initiation of any medications?	0	57	100
Was an obstetrician-gynecologist consult ordered for each pregnant patient within 7 days of pregnancy confirmation?	1	47	98
Was the pregnant patient seen by an obstetrician-gynecologist within 30 days of pregnancy confirmation?	3	29	91

Table 10. (Continued)

Records reviewed			
Pregnancy-related measure	Number of non-compliant records	Number of compliant records	Percent compliance
Was the pregnant patient screened for HIV, sexually transmitted infections, and viral hepatitis?[b]	2	41	95
Were prenatal vitamins prescribed?	0	58	100

Source: GAO analysis of U.S. Immigration and Customs Enforcement (ICE) data. | GAO-20-330.

Notes: Data on whether a pregnancy test was performed on all females aged 10 to 56 during intake screening are from December 2016 through March 2019. Data for all other measures are from a shorter time period—October 2018 through March 2019—based on changes to ICE's data collection practices.

These inspections consist of file reviews to assess the quality of medical care. The number and percent of non-compliant and compliant records refers to the records that IHSC reviewed as part of the inspections for which there was a yes or no response.

Some measures are not applicable to all pregnant women due to their length of stay. For example, not all pregnant women are detained for 30 days—and therefore, the measure of whether the pregnant woman was seen by an obstetrician-gynecologist within 30 days of pregnancy confirmation would not be applicable. There were 28 non-applicable records for this measure. In addition, there was 1 non-applicable record for whether a pregnancy test was performed prior to x-ray or before initiation of any medications; 12 for whether an obstetrician-gynecologist consult was ordered within 7 days; 17 for whether the patient was screened for HIV, sexually transmitted infections, and viral hepatitis; and 2 regarding prenatal prescriptions. We excluded non-applicable records when calculating the percent of records in compliance.

[a]In a prior version of the inspection, this question asked "was a pregnancy test performed on females aged 10-54 during intake screening?" For reporting purposes, we combined these two versions of the question regarding pregnancy testing.

[b]IHSC officials said that screening for HIV, sexually transmitted infections, and viral hepatitis reflects recommended practices but is not required by detention standards.

Pregnancy-Related Performance Measures at IHSC-Staffed Facilities

We reviewed information on pregnancy-related performance measures reported by facilities staffed by IHSC. Table 11 shows results from fiscal years 2015 through 2018.

Although the table shows average annual compliance across all IHSC-staffed facilities, variation exists between facilities, and over time. For example, in fiscal year 2018, one facility improved its performance on the measure of whether prenatal vitamins were prescribed from 33 percent compliance in the first quarter to 100 percent compliance in the second quarter.

Table 11. Average annual compliance with pregnancy-related measures at facilities staffed by ICE Health Service Corps (IHSC), fiscal years 2015 through 2018

Performance (percentage)	Fiscal Year 2015	Fiscal Year 2016[a]	Fiscal Year 2017	Fiscal Year 2018
Was an obstetrician-gynecologist consult ordered and the scheduled appointment time documented within 7 days of identification of condition? (target 100%)[b]	87	–	91	–
Obstetrician-gynecologist consult ordered is documented within 7 business days of identification (target 100%)	–	–	–	80
Obstetrician-gynecologist scheduled appointment time documented within 7 business days of identification (target 100%)	–	–	–	75[d]
Pregnant patients seen by obstetrician- gynecologist within 30 days	92	–	–	–
Prenatal vitamins prescribed (target 100%)	95	–	–	–
Detainee education documented at each encounter (target 100%)	100[c]	–	91	79[d]
Records reviewed by provider after obstetrician appointment (target 100%)	99	–	92	79[d]
Proper diet ordered? (target 100%)	86[c]	–	–	–
Appropriate labs ordered if not obtained from obstetrician-gynecologist (target 100%)	92	–	91	79

Table 11. (Continued)

Performance (percentage)	Fiscal Year 2015	Fiscal Year 2016[a]	Fiscal Year 2017	Fiscal Year 2018
Pregnant patient screened for HIV, sexually transmitted infections, and viral hepatitis	81	–	–	–
Hepatitis B vaccine offered	53	–	–	–

Legend: - Data was not reported.

Source: GAO analysis of U.S. Immigration and Customs Enforcement (ICE) data. | GAO-20-330.

Notes: IHSC did not report data on all measures from fiscal year 2015 through 2018. Data that was not reported is left blank. If a facility did not report data during any given time period, IHSC considered it to be non-compliant (zero percent).

Some of these inspections measure compliance with ICE's recommended practices, but may not be covered by policies or detention standards at all facilities.

[a]IHSC's annual report for fiscal year 2016 stated that compliance on pregnancy-related measures increased from 93 percent to 100 percent, but the report did not provide additional details on specific measures. According to IHSC officials, they no longer have the underlying data on the fiscal year 2016 inspections.

[b]IHSC officials explained that this measure was divided into two separate measures in fiscal year 2018—with one measure focused on documenting that the obstetrician-gynecologist consultation was ordered, and the second measure focused on documenting that the appointment time was scheduled.

[c]According to IHSC documentation, these data were collected only during the third and fourth quarters of fiscal year 2015.

[d]According to IHSC documentation, these data were collected only during the first and second quarters of fiscal year 2018.

In addition, in fiscal year 2018, facilities' compliance with each measure ranged as follows:[151]

- Obstetrician-gynecologist consult ordered is documented within 7 business days of identification: 50 to 100 percent (average 80 percent)

---

[151] If a facility did not self-report its data, it was considered to be non-compliant (zero percent). Two facilities did not report any data in fiscal year 2018, while an additional five facilities did not report information for part of the year, and one facility's information was not reported because the facility closed. When we reported the ranges for each fiscal year in the bulleted list below, we excluded facilities that did not report information in any quarter during the fiscal year, but included facilities that reported information for all or some quarters. This means that some facilities' yearly average may be lower as a result of non-reporting in a quarter. The average for the fiscal year is based upon all facilities' data in all quarters, regardless of whether each facility reported complete data.

- Obstetrician-gynecologist scheduled appointment time documented within 7 business days of identification: 15 to 100 percent (average 75 percent)
- Detainee education documented at each encounter: 0 to 100 percent (average 79 percent)
- Records reviewed by provider after obstetrician appointment: 0 to 100 percent (average 79 percent)
- Appropriate labs ordered if not obtained from obstetrician-gynecologist: 50 to 100 percent (average 79 percent)

Deficiencies, Recommendations, and Corrective Actions for ICE Inspections of Pregnancy- related Detention Standards

Table 12. Deficiencies, recommendations, and reported corrective actions for U.S. Immigration and Customs Enforcement (ICE) inspections of pregnancy-related care, January 2015 through July 2019

	Inspection finding	Reported corrective actions
Medical care was not provided or offered	Review of a pregnant woman's medical record found that she did not receive a health appraisal within 24 hours of arrival, as required.	The facility directed all medical staff that pregnant women are required to have a health assessment performed immediately.
	This same pregnant woman—who did not receive the health appraisal within 24 hours— was not afforded access to specialized care, including an obstetric evaluation.	The facility educated staff that obstetrician- gynecologist appointments need to be conducted immediately, according with the stage of pregnancy.
	This same pregnant woman was not offered a mental health assessment after a reported miscarriage at a different facility.	The facility instructed medical staff that all documentation pertinent to continuity of care needs to follow a detainee upon transfer to another facility. The facility also requested the medical records from the other facility.

Table 12. (Continued)

	Inspection finding	Reported corrective actions
Recommend-ation to provide additional medical care	ICE Health Service Corps (IHSC) recommended that the facility considering conducting pregnancy testing for all females under age 50.	The facility updated its policy to include required standards and began conducting pregnancy testing for all females under the age of 50.
	IHSC recommended that the facility conduct pregnancy testing for all females under age 50.	The facility began conducting pregnancy testing on all females.
	IHSC recommended that the facility conduct pregnancy testing for all females under age 50.	The facility began conducting pregnancy testing on all women under age 50 within 14 days of arrival.
	IHSC recommended that the facility conduct pregnancy testing for all females between ages 10 and 54.	The facility re-educated staff and incorporated pregnancy testing for females between age 10 and 54 into its intake form.
	IHSC recommended that the facility conduct pregnancy testing for all females of child bearing age.	The facility began offering a pregnancy test to all women under age 50 within 14 days of arrival.
	IHSC recommended that the facility conduct testing for sexually transmitted infections and HIV for all pregnant women.	The facility sends pregnant women to an obstetrician-gynecologist who determines which labs to order.
	IHSC recommended that all pregnant women be referred to an obstetrician specialist within 7 days of arrival and evaluated by an obstetrician within 30 days of arrival.	ICE did not require a corrective action plan for this recommendation because the facility met standards, despite the recommendation.
Insufficient documentation	A review of seven female detainee medical files found that all were questioned about pregnancy during intake screening; however, four files did not document completion of pregnancy tests.	The facility provided remedial training to all medical staff regarding documentation, and compliance is monitored through daily chart review.
	The facility's initial health assessment form did not address pregnancy testing, among other requirements.	The facility updated its intake screening form to include pregnancy testing and other required elements.

	Inspection finding	Reported corrective actions
Insufficient documentation	Medical/psychiatric alert forms were present in 20 of 21 detainee records with medical conditions requiring close care; however, the medical record of a pregnant detainee with a history of methamphetamine use did not have the alert form.	The facility instructed all medical staff to use the alert form in all medical files requiring close care.
	A pregnant woman's medical records were not transferred between facilities, and the paperwork that was transferred did not document her miscarriage.	The facility instructed medical staff that all documentation pertinent to continuity of care needs to follow a detainee upon transfer to another facility. The facility also requested the medical records from the other facility.
	The facility's use-of-force policy did not address several procedures required by the standard, including use-of-force in special circumstances for pregnant detainees.	The facility updated its policy to include all required standards for use-of-force incidents.
	The facility's use-of-force policy did not address use of force in special circumstances, including pregnant detainees.	The facility's policy was revised to comply with the detention standard.
Policy did not exist or specify required standards of care	The facility did not have a policy outlining special precautions to be taken when restraining pregnant detainees.	The facility implemented a policy that specified special precautions to be taken when restraining pregnant detainees.
	The facility's policy did not address special precautions to be taken when restraining pregnant detainees and the policy did not require that medical personnel be consulted prior to restraining pregnant detainees.	The facility did not implement corrective actions to address any of the deficiencies identified during the inspection. As a result, ICE determined that the facility is not appropriate for the detention of ICE detainees.
	ICE recommended that the facility review or create policies for a number of issues, including pregnant women.	The facility began conducting pregnancy testing on all females under age 50, and has taken steps to update its policies.

Source: GAO analysis of ICE information. | GAO-20-330.

Notes: Deficiencies indicate non-compliance with applicable detention standards, while recommendations reflect best practices but are not required by detention standards.

These findings are from the following inspections: (1) ICE's Office of Detention Oversight inspections from January 2015 through July 2019, (2) ICE's Enforcement and Removal Operations inspections from January 2015 through March 2019, and (3) ICE Health Service Corp's Field Medical Coordinator inspections from fiscal years 2015 through 2017. We reviewed information that resulted from a total of 854 inspections. All of the findings occurred at facilities not staffed by ICE Health Service Corps.

Three additional ICE inspections identified 19 findings at 13 facilities related to the care of pregnant women. All of the findings occurred at non-IHSC facilities. Table 12 provides additional information on the findings and corrective actions that facilities reported taking.

Appendix VII: Summary of Interviews with Pregnant Women Regarding Their Care in Department of Homeland Security Custody

We interviewed ten pregnant women who were detained at three of the four U.S. Immigration and Customs Enforcement (ICE) facilities we visited, including facilities staffed by ICE Health Service Corps (IHSC-staffed) and non-IHSC facilities.[152] We interviewed an additional four pregnant women at a local shelter in Texas which provides temporary accommodations to those in need of housing after their release from DHS custody. These four women may not have known which agency they had been detained or held by prior to entering the shelter. As a result, their perspectives are listed separately in the table below from the 10 women with whom we spoke at ICE detention facilities. Table 13 summarizes the perspectives of these 14 pregnant women. Although these interviews are not generalizable and may not be indicative of the care provided at all detention facilities, they provided us with perspectives on the care provided to pregnant women. We did not independently verify statements made by these 14 women we interviewed.

[152] We visited four ICE facilities from April 2019 through June 2019, located in California and Texas, during the course of our work. At the time of our site visits, ICE identified a total of 10 pregnant women detained at three of the four facilities. With the consent of these women, we conducted structured interviews to obtain insight into the care they received at their respective ICE facility. According to ICE, these were the only adult pregnant women detained at these facilities during the time of our visits.

Table 13. Perspectives of 14 pregnant women detained or released from Department of Homeland Security (DHS) custody

	Perspectives of 10 pregnant women detained at U.S. Immigration and Customs Enforcement (ICE) facilities	**Perspectives of four pregnant women released from DHS custody[a]**
Pregnancy testing	All 10 stated that they received a pregnancy test when they arrived at the facility or within the same day.	Three of the four women said that they did not receive a pregnancy test. The fourth woman did not state whether she received a pregnancy test but said that she received an ultrasound after stating that she was pregnant.
Accommodations	Nine of the 10 women said that they received appropriate accommodations, such as a lower bunk and blankets. One woman at a non-IHSC facility said that she was frequently cold, and would have liked to have received a sweater, more blankets, and a thicker mattress.	None of the women said that they received appropriate accommodations. For example, all of the women said that they slept on the floor.
Prenatal vitamins	All 10 stated that they received prenatal vitamins.	Three of the four women said that they did not receive prenatal vitamins. One woman said that she did not receive prenatal vitamins because she already had her own.
Nutrition and snacks	Six of the 10 women said that they were provided proper nutrition and snacks. One woman at an IHSC-staffed facility did not discuss the adequacy of the nutrition she was provided. Three women at a non-IHSC facility said that they were not provided adequate nutrition and snacks. For example, two of the women said that they do not receive any snacks, while one stated that she does not receive extra snacks because of her pregnancy.	None of the four women said that they received adequate nutrition and snacks. For example, three of the women said that they did not receive additional food because of their pregnancy.

Table 13. (Continued)

	Perspectives of 10 pregnant women detained at U.S. Immigration and Customs Enforcement (ICE) facilities	**Perspectives of four pregnant women released from DHS custody[a]**
Medical care	Four of the 10 women identified concerns regarding medical care. For example, two of the women in IHSC-staffed facilities stated that they would like more timely access to an obstetrician- gynecologist appointment, and they did not know when their appointments would occur.[b]	All four of the women identified concerns with medical care. For example, one woman said that officials were dismissive when she requested a visit at the clinic because she felt sick.
Segregation	All 10 of the women stated that they had not been segregated.	All four of the women stated that they had not been segregated.
Restraints	All 10 of the women stated that they had not been placed in restraints.	All four of the women stated that they had not been placed in restraints.

Source: GAO analysis of interviews with pregnant women detained at ICE facilities and after release from DHS custody | GAO-20-330.

Notes: Although these interviews are not generalizable and may not be indicative of the care provided at all detention facilities, they provided us with perspectives on the care provided to pregnant women. We did not independently verify statements made by these 14 women we interviewed.

[a]These four women may not have known which agency they had been detained or held by prior to entering the shelter. In some cases, their experiences may reflect being held by U.S. Customs and Border Protection (CBP) at a port of entry or Border Patrol facility prior to being released or transferred to an ICE facility. Specifically, two of the four women reported spending some time at a CBP facility prior to being transferred to an ICE facility, while the other two women were unsure. As a result, their perspectives are listed separately from the 10 women we spoke with in ICE detention facilities.

[b]According to an ICE official, the date and time of the appointments are not disclosed for security reasons.

Appendix VIII: Complaints Regarding U.S. Immigration and Customs Enforcement's and U.S. Customs and Border Protection's Care of Pregnant Women

We analyzed and categorized complaints that detainees, family members, non-governmental organizations, or other parties submitted to various entities from January 2015 through April 2019 regarding U.S. Immigration and Customs Enforcement's (ICE) and U.S. Customs and Border Protection's (CBP) care of pregnant women. Specifically, we reviewed complaints from Department of Homeland Security's (DHS) Office for Civil Rights and Civil Liberties (CRCL), DHS's Office of Inspector General, and ICE Health Service Corps (IHSC). We identified a total of 107 complaints—54 regarding ICE, 50 regarding CBP, and three regarding both ICE and CBP.[153]

Complaints against ICE

We identified 54 unique complaints submitted from January 2015 through April 2019 regarding ICE's care of pregnant women. Each of the 54 complaints may identify more than one area of concern, and as such we identified 104 concerns. The most common concern was that ICE allegedly did not provide medical care or the medical care was not quality or timely.

As previously described in this chapter, the investigating agency determined that one complaint was substantiated and one complaint was partially substantiated. The remaining complaints were either still open as part of an on-going investigation,[154] unsubstantiated by the investigating agency, or the complaint was not substantiated or unsubstantiated for a variety of reasons. Table 14 provides additional information on the number and types of concerns identified in the 54 complaints regarding ICE's care of pregnant women.

---

[153] See appendix I for additional information about how we identified these complaints. These complaints may have been regarding the over 4,600 detentions of pregnant women that we identified in this chapter, or could have been for pregnant women that were detained before or after our time period. We excluded from our analysis one additional complaint where it was unclear which agency the allegation was being made against.

[154] These complaints were open as of August 2019.

Table 14. Number of concerns alleged in complaints regarding U.S. Immigration and Customs Enforcement's (ICE) care of pregnant women, by ICE Health Service Corps (IHSC) presence, January 2015 through April 2019

Medical provider at facility			
Type of concern	**IHSC-staffed**	**Non-IHSC**	**Total**
Medical care not provided, not timely, or not quality	16	20	36
General concerns about the detention of pregnant women	15	6	21
Mistreatment (physical, verbal, or other)	2	12	14
Accommodations (not provided lower bunk or proper clothing)	5	2	7
Use of restraints or segregation	3	4	7
All other concerns[a]	11	8	19
Total	52	52	104

Source: GAO analysis of complaints from IHSC, Department of Homeland Security Office of Inspector General, and Department of Homeland Security Office for Civil Rights and Civil Liberties (CRCL). | GAO-20-330.

Notes: The total number of concerns identified in this table (104) exceeds the number of unique complaints filed (54) because each unique complaint may identify more than one area of concern. This table excludes three complaints that involved both ICE and Customs and Border Protection— one of which was still open as part of an ongoing investigation, and two of which were unsubstantiated. This table excludes one additional complaint where it was unclear which agency the allegation was being made against.

These exclude complaints that did not allege mistreatment or improper care, but rather noted, for example, that a miscarriage or birth had occurred in ICE custody. However, if the complaint alleged that a miscarriage was the result of insufficient care, it was included.

We removed duplicate complaints that were filed with more than one entity so that each complaint was counted once.

These complaints may have been regarding the over 4,600 detentions of pregnant women that we identified in this chapter, or could have been for pregnant women that were detained before or after our time period.

The investigating agency determined that one complaint was substantiated and one complaint was partially substantiated. The remaining complaints were either still open as part of an on-going investigation, unsubstantiated by the investigating agency, or was not substantiated or unsubstantiated for a variety of reasons.

[a]These concerns involve various allegations, such as potential exposure to disease, personal property taken, medical records not provided, prenatal vitamins not provided, or proper nutrition not provided.

Complaints against CBP

We identified 50 unique complaints submitted from January 2015 through April 2019 regarding CBP's care of pregnant women. Each of the 50 complaints may identify more than one area of concern, and as such we identified 81 concerns. The most common concern was that pregnant women had allegedly been physically, verbally, or otherwise mistreated.

As previously described in this chapter, the investigating agency determined that one complaint was substantiated. The remaining complaints were either still open as part of an on-going investigation, unsubstantiated or partially unsubstantiated by the investigating agency, the complaint was not substantiated or unsubstantiated for a variety of reasons, or the complaint described an event that occurred, such as a miscarriage, but did not allege that mistreatment or improper care occurred. Table 15 provides additional information on the number and types of issues identified in the 50 complaints regarding CBP's care of pregnant women.

Table 15. Number of concerns alleged in complaints regarding U.S. Customs and Border Protection's (CBP) care of pregnant women, by component, January 2015 through April 2019

CBP component				
Type of concern	Border Patrol	Office of Field Operations	Not specified	Total
Mistreatment (physical, verbal, or other)	13	19	1	33
Passport or entry concerns[a]	0	11	0	11
Medical care not provided, not timely, or not quality	6	3	0	9
Accommodations (temperature too cold, slept on floor)[b]	1	6	2	9
Proper nutrition not provided	1	5	0	6

Table 15. (Continued)

CBP component				
Type of concern	Border Patrol	Office of Field Operations	Not specified	Total
All other concerns[c]	5	8	0	13
Total	26	52	3	81

Source: GAO analysis of complaints from CBP, Department of Homeland Security Office of Inspector General, and Department of Homeland Security Office for Civil Rights and Civil Liberties (CRCL). | GAO-20-330.

Note: The total number of concerns identified in this table (81) exceeds the number of unique complaints filed (50) because each unique complaint may identify more than one area of concern.

This table excludes three complaints that involved both Immigration and Customs Enforcement and CBP—one of which was still open as part of an ongoing investigation, and two of which were unsubstantiated. This table excludes one additional complaint where it was unclear which agency the allegation was being made against.

These exclude complaints that did not allege mistreatment or improper care, but rather noted, for example, that a miscarriage or birth had occurred in CBP custody. However, if the complaint alleged that a miscarriage was the result of insufficient care, it was included.

We removed duplicate complaints that were filed with more than one entity so that each complaint was counted once.

These complaints may have been regarding the over 4,600 detentions of pregnant women that we identified in this chapter, or could have been for pregnant women that were detained before or after our time period.

The investigating agency substantiated one of the complaints in this table, while the remaining complaints were either still open as part of an on-going investigation, unsubstantiated or partially unsubstantiated by the investigating agency, or was not substantiated or unsubstantiated for a variety of reasons.

[a]These concerns include allegations, such as a pregnant woman being denied admission to the U.S. because she was pregnant. According to CBP officials, pregnancy is not a factor to be used when determining admissibility.

[b]According to CBP officials, most of their facilities are temperature-controlled.

[c]These concerns involve various allegations, such as potential exposure to disease, personal property taken, medical records not provided, sexual assault, or use of restraints.

APPENDIX IX: COMMENTS FROM THE DEPARTMENT OF HOMELAND SECURITY

U.S. Department of Homeland Security
Washington, DC 20528

Homeland Security

March 3, 2020

Gretta Goodwin
Director, Homeland Security and Justice Issues
U.S. Government Accountability Office
441 G Street, NW
Washington, DC 20548

Re: Management Response to Draft Report GAO-20-330, "IMMIGRATION DETENTION: Care of Pregnant Women in DHS Facilities"

Dear Ms. Goodwin:

Thank you for the opportunity to comment on this draft report. The U.S. Department of Homeland Security (DHS) appreciates the U.S. Government Accountability Office's (GAO) work in planning and conducting its review and issuing this report.

DHS is pleased to note GAO's recognition that U.S. Immigration and Customs Enforcement (ICE) and U.S. Customs and Border Protection (CBP) have policies and standards regarding the screening and care of pregnant women. The Department also values GAO reporting on the many actions taken by ICE and CBP to provide pregnant women with appropriate accommodations and levels of care. For example, the draft report mentions aspects of ICE training, screening, transfer, care and treatment, reporting, monitoring, reviews, and inspections specific to pregnant women. The report also notes that ICE inspections of facilities show a high level of compliance with the standards evaluated in the report.

As GAO observed, ICE exercises discretion in making custody determinations on a case-by-case basis, taking into account the totality of circumstances regarding each individual case, unless the alien is subject to mandatory detention. As such, ICE detains pregnant females subject to mandatory detention and whose cases reveal they represent either a flight risk or a danger to the community. ICE custody determinations respecting pregnant women take into account factors such as ties to the community; prior convictions for violent crimes or driving under the influence; whether the alien was able to satisfactorily provide identity documents; and whether the alien has a final order(s) of removal and has not historically abided by the terms of their order(s) of supervision. ICE only detains pregnant women at facilities where they can receive the appropriate accommodations and prenatal care. Additionally, ICE generally does not detain pregnant women in their third trimester, unless detention is legally required or is necessary for removal, and such removal has been cleared by medical professionals.

ICE prioritizes the health of pregnant women by aligning their care with general medical standards. ICE detention facilities provide on-site prenatal care and education, as well as remote access to specialists for pregnant women who remain in custody. ICE ensures pregnancy services are provided, to include pregnancy testing, routine or specialized prenatal care, comprehensive counseling and assistance, postpartum follow up, lactation services, and pregnancy termination. The medical provider identifies any special needs (e.g., diet, housing, or other accommodations, such as the provision of additional pillows) and informs all necessary custody staff and facility authorities. If a pregnant detainee has been identified as high-risk, that detainee is referred to a physician specializing in high-risk pregnancies, as appropriate.

DHS remains committed to providing appropriate care for all detainees in its custody to promote a safe and secure environment for detainees. As GAO mentioned in its draft report, ICE has numerous ongoing actions to enhance its policies and procedures respecting pregnant women, some of which have recently been implemented. For example, ICE Enforcement and Removal Operations (ERO) completed updates to the National Detention Standards (NDS) in December 2019. ICE's Family Residential Standards have been updated and are undergoing clearance. Additionally, ICE Office of Acquisition Management is processing contract modifications for NDS facilities. Moreover, ICE inspects detention facilities to ensure compliance with applicable detention standards and policies, and ERO will begin inspecting facilities against the updated standards starting in March 2020. Further, ICE Health Service Corps made some additional updates to the Women's Health Directive and Chronic Care Policy that will undergo legal review.

Again, thank you for the opportunity to review and comment on this draft report. DHS previously submitted technical comments under a separate cover for GAO's consideration. Please feel free to contact me if you have any questions. We look forward to working with you again in the future.

Sincerely,

JIM H. CRUMPACKER, CIA, CFE
Director
Departmental GAO-OIG Liaison Office

In: Immigration
Editor: Klonimir Jović

ISBN: 978-1-53618-183-8

Chapter 3

IMMIGRATION: RECENT APPREHENSION TRENDS AT THE U.S. SOUTHWEST BORDER*

Audrey Singer and William A. Kandel

SUMMARY

Unauthorized migration across the U.S. Southwest border poses considerable challenges to federal agencies that apprehend and process unauthorized migrants (aliens) due to changing characteristics and motivations of migrants in the past few years. Unauthorized migration flows are reflected by the number of migrants apprehended by the Department of Homeland Security's (DHS's) Customs and Border Protection (CBP). In FY2000, total annual apprehensions at the border were at an all-time high of 1.64 million, before gradually declining to 303,916 in FY2017, a 45-year low. Apprehensions then increased to 396,579 in FY2018 and 851,508 in FY2019, the highest level since FY2007.

More notably, the character of unauthorized migrants has changed during the past decade. Historically, unauthorized migrant flows involved predominantly single adult Mexicans, traveling without families, whose

* This is an edited, reformatted and augmented version of Congressional Research Service Publication No. R46012, dated November 19, 2019.

primary motivation was U.S. employment. As recently as FY2011, Mexican nationals made up 86% of all apprehensions, and relatively few requested asylum. In FY2019, however, "Northern Triangle" migrants from El Salvador, Guatemala, and Honduras comprised 81% of all apprehensions that year. Economic migrants exclusively seeking employment no longer dominate the unauthorized migrant flow, which is now driven to a greater extent by asylum seekers and those escaping violence and domestic insecurity, or those with motivations involving a mixture of protection and economic opportunity.

CBP classifies apprehended unauthorized migrants into single adults, family units (at least one parent/guardian and at least one child), and unaccompanied alien children (UAC). In 2012, single adults made up 90% of apprehended migrants at the Southwest border. In FY2019, however, persons in family units and UAC together accounted for 65% of all apprehended migrants that year. In FY2019, CBP apprehended a record 473,682 persons in family units, exceeding all apprehensions of family unit members from FY2012-FY2018 combined. Mothers headed almost half of all family units apprehended in FY2019. In addition, apprehended persons in family units shifted from mostly Mexican nationals (80%) in FY2012 to mostly Salvadoran, Guatemalan, and Honduran nationals (91%) in FY2019. Similar changes occurred in the origin countries of unaccompanied alien children, whose total apprehensions also reached a record (76,020) in FY2019.

The changing character of the migrant flow has led to logistical and resource challenges for federal agencies, particularly CBP. These include a general capacity shortfall in CBP holding facilities, the lack of appropriate facilities to detain families in Immigration Customs and Enforcement (ICE) detention centers, the reassignment of some CBP personnel who monitor the border to process and respond to migrants in holding facilities, and rapidly expanding immigration court backlogs that delay expeditious proceedings. The changing underlying motivations and border migration strategies of recent migrants also makes apprehension data less useful than in the past for measuring border enforcement. Because many unauthorized migrants now actively seek out U.S. Border Patrol agents in order to request asylum, increases or decreases in apprehension numbers may not reflect the effectiveness of border enforcement strategies.

In response, the Trump Administration has changed existing policies for apprehended migrants, including implementing the Migrant Protection Protocols (MPP), also known as the "remain in Mexico" immigration policy, which allow DHS to return migrants seeking U.S. admission to the contiguous country from which they arrived on land, pending removal proceedings.

Options for Congress could include legislative responses to the series of policies that the Administration has developed to address the changing flow of migrants at the Southwest border. Some proposals may consider changes to the appropriations of agencies charged with processing unauthorized migrants to reshape the system from one that was designed to apprehend and return single unauthorized adults from Mexico with no claims for protection, to one that can more quickly adjudicate those seeking humanitarian protection. Other options may include greater supervision of unauthorized migrants who are released into the United States, and mandating the collection and publication of more-detailed and timely data from CBP to more completely assess the flow of unauthorized migrants, including those in the MPP program, and their impact on border enforcement and the immigration court system.

INTRODUCTION

Over the past two years, increasing migration across the Southwest border of the United States has posed considerable challenges to U.S. federal agencies charged with apprehending and processing unauthorized migrants.[1] From FY2000 to FY2017, unauthorized migration flows—measured in this chapter by the number of migrants apprehended by the Department of Homeland Security's (DHS's) Customs and Border Protection (CBP)—had been generally declining.

Apprehensions statistics historically have been used as a rough measure of trends in unauthorized migration flows, as well as a rough indicator of border enforcement (see "Interpreting Apprehensions Data" below). After reaching an all-time peak of 1,643,679 in FY2000, apprehensions fell to a 45-year low of 303,916 in FY2017. In FY2018 apprehensions increased to 396,579, and in FY2019 they more than doubled to 851,508.

The Administration and some Members of Congress have characterized the recent increases as a border security and humanitarian crisis. For example, then-CBP Commissioner Kevin McAleenan, in testimony to the Senate Judiciary Committee on March 6, 2019, stated I

---

[1] As used in this chapter, a *migrant* is a person who has temporarily or permanently crossed an international border, is no longer residing in his or her country of origin or habitual residence, and is not recognized as a refugee. Migrants may include asylum seekers. The term *migrant* is not defined in statute.

have heard a number of commentators observe that even with these alarming levels of migration, the numbers are lower than the historical peaks, and as a result, they suggest what we are seeing at the border today is not a crisis.

I fundamentally disagree. From the experience of our agents and officers on the ground, it is indeed both a border security—and a humanitarian—crisis.

What many looking at total numbers fail to understand is the difference in what is happening now in terms of who is crossing, the risks that they are facing, and the consequences for our system.[2]

The difference McAleenan cited refers to the characteristics of apprehended migrants at the Southwest border—their origin countries, demographic characteristics, and migratory motivations—all of which have changed considerably during the past decade. In prior decades, unauthorized migrant flows involved predominantly adult male Mexicans, whose primary motivation was U.S. employment. If apprehended, they were typically processed through *expedited removal*[3] and quickly repatriated. Relatively few migrants applied for humanitarian immigration relief such as asylum.

Mexican migrants now make up a minority of total apprehensions. Sizable numbers of migrants from the "Northern Triangle"—the Central American countries of El Salvador, Guatemala, and Honduras—now make up the largest group. Smaller numbers of migrants are also arriving at the Southwest border from South America (e.g., Venezuela, Peru), the Caribbean (e.g., Cuba), Africa (e.g., Cameroon, Uganda), Central Asia (e.g., Uzbekistan), and South Asia (e.g., India, Bangladesh), among other regions.[4] Instead of being dominated by adult males, migrant flows over the course of this decade have been increasingly characterized by migrants

---

[2] CBP Commissioner Kevin K. McAleenan, *Oversight of Customs and Border Protection's Response to the Smuggling of Persons at the Southern Border*, Department of Homeland Security, Testimony before the U.S. Senate Judiciary Committee, March 6, 2019.

[3] Expedited removal is a streamlined removal process for unauthorized aliens that was established by Congress in 1996. For more information, see CRS Report R45314, *Expedited Removal of Aliens: Legal Framework*.

[4] CRS interviews with CBP officials, McAllen, TX, August 14, 2018; San Diego, CA, August 15, 2018; El Paso, TX, August 12, 2019; and Nogales, AZ, August 14, 2019.

traveling as families (family units) and unaccompanied alien[5] children (UAC).

While a sizeable proportion of unauthorized migrants seek U.S. employment, a growing proportion of arriving migrants are seeking asylum and protection from violence.[6] Studies of recent migration trends cite persistent poverty, inequality, demographic pressure related to high population growth, vulnerability to natural disasters, high crime rates, poor security conditions, and the lack of a strong state presence as factors that "push" migrants to make the risky and often dangerous journey from the Northern Triangle.[7] "Pull" factors include the increasing use of U.S. asylum policy that, until recently, allowed most asylum seekers to remain in the United States while they awaited a decision on their cases. Lengthy court backlogs[8] allow migrants admitted to the United States the opportunity to reunite with family members and acquire work authorization, typically six months after U.S. admission.[9] Motivations for leaving Northern Triangle countries and choosing the United States are

---

[5] Under §101(a)(3) of the Immigration and Nationality Act (8 U.S.C. §1101(a)(3)), an alien is a person who is not a U.S. citizen or a U.S. national. The definition includes persons legally and not legally present in the United States. In this chapter, the terms *alien, foreign national*, and *noncitizen* are synonymous.

[6] See CRS Report R45489, Recent Migration to the United States from Central America: Frequently Asked Questions; and CRS Report R43628, Unaccompanied Alien Children: Potential Factors Contributing to Recent Immigration.

[7] See, for example, CRS In Focus IF11151, Central American Migration: Root Causes and U.S. Policy; CRS Report R45489, Recent Migration to the United States from Central America: Frequently Asked Questions; archived CRS Report R43628, Unaccompanied Alien Children: Potential Factors Contributing to Recent Immigration; and Randy Capps, Doris Meissner, and Ariel G. Ruiz Soto, et al., From Control to Crisis: Changing Trends and Policies Reshaping U.S.-Mexico Border Enforcement, Migration Policy Institute, August 2019.

[8] At the end of FY2019, DOJ's Executive Office for Immigration Review (EOIR) listed 987,274 pending cases.

[9] See, for example, Carrie Kahn, "Caravan Of Central American Migrants Seeking Asylum Hope To Cross Border," NPR, April 29, 2018; Alicia A. Caldwell, "As Migration From Guatemala Surges, U.S. Officials Seek Answers," Wall Street Journal, October 13, 2018; and Andrew R. Arthur, "Looking for Push Factors in Central America: The pull factors are likely stronger, but at least CBP is trying," Center for Immigration Studies, October 18, 2018.

often a mixture of these push and pull factors, which can be interconnected,[10] especially for families and unaccompanied children.

Some observers argue that the recent migrant flows represent a failure of the rule of law. They question the legitimacy of asylum claims being made by recent unauthorized migrants and contend that many are abusing U.S. immigration laws bestowing humanitarian relief in order to gain entry into, or permission to remain in, the United States. Other observers characterize the recent migrant flows as a legitimate international humanitarian crisis resulting from violent and lawless circumstances in migrants' countries of origin. These observers contend that the "crisis" at the border reflects the inability of U.S. federal agencies to adequately process arriving migrants and adjudicate their claims for immigration relief.

The changing character of the migrant flow has reportedly produced a number of logistical and resource challenges for federal agencies.[11] These include a general capacity shortfall in CBP holding facilities, lack of appropriate facilities to detain families in ICE detention centers, reassignment of CBP personnel from port of entry duty to responding to migrants in processing facilities, and lengthy immigration court backlogs that delay expeditious proceedings. During migration peaks, these resource constraints—coupled with legal restrictions on the length of time that some migrants may be held[12]—have forced DHS to release migrants who have

---

[10] For a discussion of how these factors are often connected, see Matthew Lorenzen, "Unaccompanied Child Migrants," *Journal on Migration and Human Security*, vol. 5, no. 4 (2017), pp. 744-767.

[11] U.S. Department of Homeland Security, "Press Briefing by Acting CBP Commissioner Mark Morgan," press release, November 14, 2019.

[12] While DOJ and the Department of Homeland Security (DHS) have broad statutory authority to detain adult aliens, children must be detained according to guidelines established in the Flores Settlement Agreement, the Homeland Security Act of 2002, and the Trafficking Victims Protection Reauthorization Act of 2008. A 2015 judicial ruling held that children remain in family immigration detention for no more than 20 days. If parents cannot be released with them, children are treated as unaccompanied alien children and transferred to the Department of Health and Human Services' (HHS's) Office of Refugee Resettlement (ORR) for care and custody. For more information, see CRS Report R45297, *The "Flores Settlement" and Alien Families Apprehended at the U.S. Border: Frequently Asked Questions*.

entered the United States unlawfully, particularly those in family units, rather than detaining or removing them.[13]

In response to the large increase in arrivals of migrants without proper entry documents, the Trump Administration has initiated changes to existing policy for apprehended migrants, largely designed to discourage these unauthorized migration flows. In January 2019, the Administration implemented the Migrant Protection Protocols (MPP), also known as the "remain in Mexico" immigration policy, which allow DHS to return applicants for admission to the United States to the contiguous country from which they arrived (on land) pending removal proceedings.[14] The MPP sends migrants back to Mexico to await their court proceedings for the duration of their case.[15] This program requires the coordination and assistance of the government of Mexico, a country facing its own high levels of unauthorized migration on its southern border.[16] The program is currently operating in six border locations.[17]

Understanding changing migration patterns over the past decade may help inform Congress as it considers immigration-related legislation. This chapter discusses recent migrant apprehension trends at the Southwest border. It describes how unauthorized migration to the United States has changed in terms of the absolute numbers of migrants as well as their origin countries, demographic composition, and primary migratory

---

[13] Testimony of CBP Commissioner Kevin K. McAleenan, in U.S. Congress, Senate Judiciary Committee, *Oversight of Customs and Border Protection's Response to the Smuggling of Persons at the Southern Border*, 116th Cong, 1st sess., March 6, 2019.

[14] Section 235(b)(2)(C) of the Immigration and Nationality Act (INA) provides such authorization. Guiding principles from DHS were released in January 2019, see https://www.cbp.gov/sites/default/files/assets/documents/2019-Jan/MPP%20Guiding%20 Principles%201-28-19.pdf.

[15] For more information, see CRS Legal Sidebar LSB10251, *"Migrant Protection Protocols": Legal Issues Related to DHS's Plan to Require Arriving Asylum Seekers to Wait in Mexico*; and DHS, Assessment of Migrant Protection Protocols, 2019.

[16] For more on Mexico's immigration trends, policies, and agreements with the United States, see CRS In Focus IF10215, *Mexico's Immigration Control Efforts*.

[17] See U.S. Department of Homeland Security, "DHS Expands MPP Operations to Eagle Pass," press release, October 28, 2019, https://www.dhs.gov/news/2019/10/28/dhs-expands-mpp-operations-eagle-pass. For a more detailed examination of the MPP, including some information on the more than 55,000 individuals in the program, see U.S. Department of Homeland Security, "DHS Assessment of Migrant Protection Protocols, 2019."

motivations. The report concludes with a brief discussion of related policy implications.

CHANGING MIGRATION AND APPREHENSION TRENDS

The Trump Administration's and Congress's responses to the changing characteristics of unauthorized migrants at the Southwest border occur within the context of border security debates. Border security has been an ongoing subject of congressional interest since the 1970s, when unauthorized immigration to the United States first registered as a serious national challenge, and it has received increased attention since the terrorist attacks of 2001. Current debates center on how best to secure the Southwest border, including how and where to place barriers and other tactical infrastructure to impede unauthorized migration as well as the deployment of U.S. Border Patrol agents to prevent unlawful entries of migrants and contraband.[18] Securing the border while facilitating legitimate trade and travel to and from the United States is CBP's primary mission;[19] major shifts in CBP activities can strain resources and disrupt operations.[20]

According to U.S. immigration law, foreign nationals who arrive in the United States without valid entry documentation may pursue asylum and related protections if they demonstrate a credible fear of persecution or torture in their country of origin.[21] These migrants, along with others either

---

[18] See CRS Report R42138, *Border Security: Immigration Enforcement Between Ports of Entry*; and CRS Report R43356, *Border Security: Immigration Inspections at Ports of Entry* for more on border security.

[19] U.S. Customs and Border Protection, "About CBP," https://www.cbp.gov/about.

[20] For example, on April 1, 2019, then-Secretary of Homeland Security Kirstjen M. Nielsen issued a memorandum to order CBP Commissioner Kevin McAleenan to undertake emergency surge operations and increase the temporary reassignment of personnel and resources from across the agency to address a large influx of migrants. As a result, 750 Border Patrol officers were subsequently sent to the Southwest border. See U.S. Department of Homeland Security, "Secretary Nielsen Orders CBP to Surge More Personnel to Southern Border, Increase Number of Aliens Returned to Mexico," press release, April 1, 2019; and Julian Aguilar, "Long delays at border bridges bring anxiety for businesses as Holy Week begins," Texas Tribune, April 15, 2019.

[21] See CRS In Focus IF11074, *U.S. Immigration Laws for Aliens Arriving at the Border*; and CRS Report R45539, *Immigration: U.S. Asylum Policy*.

apprehended or refused admission at a port of entry, appear in the statistics kept by CBP (see "Interpreting Apprehensions Data" below).

While CBP's responsibilities include monitoring the Southwest and Northern land borders, as well as the Atlantic and Pacific coasts, the Southwest border with Mexico commands most of the agency's resources because of its attendant risks. The Southwest border runs for nearly 2,000 miles along the four Southwestern states of California, Arizona, New Mexico, and Texas.[22] It is not only the locus of most unauthorized migration to the United States but also that of illicit drugs, counterfeit products, dangerous agricultural products, and trafficked children.[23] Much of this activity occurs at U.S. ports of entry at the Southwest border, where CBP officers inspect all individuals and vehicles that seek to enter the United States.

INTERPRETING APPREHENSIONS DATA

CBP's two components that monitor the Southwest border at and between ports of entry—the U.S. Border Patrol (USBP) and the Office of Field Operations (OFO)—collect statistics on individuals who have crossed the border illegally and those who are denied entry. Between ports of entry, USBP agents are responsible for apprehending individuals not lawfully present in the United States.[24] OFO officers are responsible for inspections at U.S. ports of entry and collect data on noncitizens who are denied entry to the United States at ports of entry. Migrants typically are denied entry because they are not in possession of a valid entry document

---

22 For more information, see CRS Insight IN11040, Border Security Between Ports of Entry: Homeland Security Issues in the 116th Congress.

23 See, for example, CRS In Focus IF11279, Illicit Drug Flows and Seizures in the United States: In Focus; CRS In Focus IF10400, Transnational Crime Issues: Heroin Production, Fentanyl Trafficking, and U.S.-Mexico Security Cooperation; CRS Report R43356, Border Security: Immigration Inspections at Ports of Entry; and CRS Report RL33200, Trafficking in Persons in Latin America and the Caribbean.

24 CBP defines apprehensions as "the physical control or temporary detainment of a person who is not lawfully in the U.S. which may or may not result in an arrest"; see https://www.cbp.gov/newsroom/stats/cbp-enforcement-statistics.

or are determined "inadmissible" on one of several grounds, such as having a criminal record, being a potential public safety threat, or being a public health threat.[25] Inadmissible migrants made up 27%, 24%, and 13% of all migrants arriving at ports of entries along the Southwest border in FY2017, FY2018, and FY2019, respectively. While the number of inadmissible migrants grew slightly from FY2018 to FY2019, their percentage share of all CBP encounters diminished compared to apprehensions, as absolute numbers of apprehensions more than doubled during that period. (*Table 1*).[26] Both inadmissible and apprehended migrants can be placed in the MPP program.

Apprehensions statistics historically have been used as a rough measure of trends in unauthorized migration flows.[27] The utility of these statistics for measuring border enforcement effectiveness, on the other hand, has long been considered of limited usefulness because of the unknown relationship between apprehensions and successful unlawful entries, among other reasons.[28] Apprehensions data, by definition, do not include illegal border crossers who evade USBP agents.

They also do not account for the number of potential migrants who are discouraged from attempting U.S. entry because of enforcement

---

[25] For more information on grounds of inadmissibility, see archived CRS Report R43892, *Alien Removals and Returns: Overview and Trends*. CBP reports apprehensions and "inadmissibles" both together and separately. This chapter examines apprehensions data (those apprehended between ports of entry) hereinafter. See U.S. Department of Homeland Security, United States Border Patrol, "Stats and Summaries," https://www.cbp.gov/ newsroom/stats/sw- border-migration.

[26] Because of the limited number of years of publicly available data from CBP, inadmissible migrants are not discussed further in this chapter. This chapter examines apprehensions data (those apprehended between ports of entry) hereinafter. See U.S. Department of Homeland Security, U.S. Border Patrol, "Stats and Summaries," https://www.cbp.gov/ newsroom/stats/ sw-border-migration.

[27] Border Patrol apprehensions data count events rather than people. Thus, for example, one unauthorized migrant caught trying to enter the country on three separate occasions during the same fiscal year counts as three apprehensions. For more information, see archived CRS Report R44386, *Border Security Metrics Between Ports of Entry*.

[28] U.S. Department of Homeland Security, *Border Security Metrics Report*, February 26, 2019, https://www.dhs.gov/sites/default/files/publications/ndaa_border_metrics_report_fy_2018_ 0_0.pdf (hereinafter, "DHS, Border Security Metrics Report, 2019").

measures.[29] Consequently, it is generally unclear if an increase in apprehensions results from more attempts by migrants to enter the country illegally or from a higher apprehension rate of those attempting to enter the United States illegally—or both.

Table 1. Inadmissible and apprehended migrants at the U.S. southwest border, FY2017-FY2019

Fiscal Year	Migrants			Percentage		
	Inadmissible	Apprehended	Total	Inadmissible	Apprehended	Total
2017	111,275	303,916	415,191	27%	73%	100%
2018	124,511	396,579	521,090	24%	76%	100%
2019	126,001	851,508	977,509	13%	87%	100%

Source: U.S. Department of Homeland Security, Customs and Border Protection, U.S. Border Patrol, "U.S. Border Patrol Southwest Border Apprehensions by Sector FY2017, FY2018, and FY2019," https://www.cbp.gov/ newsroom/stats/usbp-sw-border-apprehensions.

However, these statistics are arguably now less relevant than in previous years as a metric of border security efforts. In the past several years, an indeterminate but sizable share of migrants who cross between U.S. ports of entry have actively sought out U.S. Border Patrol agents in order to "turn themselves in" to request asylum.[30] In prior years, such migrants typically would have attempted to evade USBP agents. As such, CBP's classification of these migrants as apprehensions may overstate the degree to which the agency's resources, personnel, and strategies prevent migrants from crossing the border illegally and entering the United States.

[29] See DHS, Border Security Metrics Report, 2019; and Stephanie Leutert and Sara Spaulding, "How Many Central Americans are Traveling North," Lawfare, March 14, 2019, https://www.lawfareblog.com/how-many-central- americans-are-traveling-north.

[30] See, for example, Alicia Caldwell, "Along the Border, Migrant Mothers Turn Themselves In to Immigration Authorities," *Wall Street Journal*, June 26, 2018; and Astrid Galvan, "AP Explains: What happens when migrants arrive at US border," *APNews*, June 26, 2019.

Total Apprehensions

The number of total apprehensions has long been used as a basic measure of migration pressure and border enforcement. Total annual apprehensions at the Southwest border averaged 687,639 during the 1970s; 999,476 during the 1980s; 1,266,556 during the 1990s; and 1,020,143 during the 2000s; but then declined to 427,766 during the 2010s.[31] Annual apprehensions reached a 45- year low in FY2017 (303,916). In FY2018, total apprehensions increased to 396,579; and in FY2019, they more than doubled to 851,508, the highest level since FY2007 (see *Figure 1*).

While high relative to annual apprehensions during the past decade, the FY2019 level is lower than annual apprehension levels for 25 of the past 45 years. Thus, recent changes in the character of the migrant flows during the past decade occurred within the context of historically low numbers of apprehensions since FY2000.

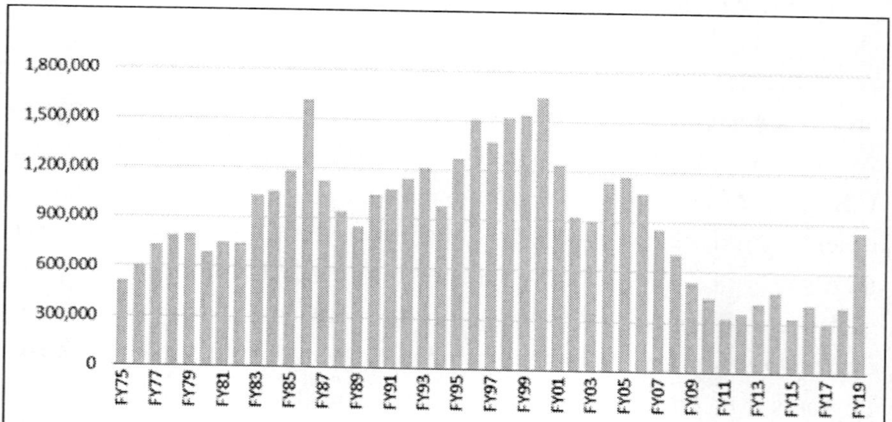

Sources: U.S. Customs and Border Protection. FY1975-FY2018: "U.S. Border Patrol Fiscal Year Southwest Border Sector Apprehensions (FY 1960 - FY 2018)," https://www.cbp.gov/newsroom/media-resources/stats; FY2019: "Southwest Border Migration FY2019," https://www.cbp.gov/newsroom/stats/sw-border-migration/fy- 2019.

Figure 1. Total Apprehensions at the Southwest Border, FY1975-FY2019.

[31] Averages computed by CRS. See *Figure 1* for data sources.

Apprehensions at the Southwest border initially peaked at 1.62 million in 1986, the same year that Congress enacted the Immigration Reform and Control Act (IRCA), which gave lawful permanent resident status[32] to roughly 2.7 million unauthorized aliens residing in the United States.[33] After declining substantially for a few years, apprehensions rose again, climbing from million in FY1989 to an all-time high of 1.64 million in FY2000. Apprehensions generally fell after that (with the exception of FY2004-FY2006), reaching a then-low point of 327,577 in FY2011. Since that year, apprehensions have fluctuated, as noted above.

Apprehensions by Country of Origin

The national origins of apprehended migrants have shifted considerably during the past two decades (see *Figure 2*). In FY2000, for example, almost all of the 1.6 million aliens apprehended at the Southwest border (98%) were Mexican nationals, and relatively few requested asylum.[34] As recently as FY2011, Mexican nationals made up 86% of all 327,577 Southwest border apprehensions in that year.

That share has declined, however, and for most years after FY2013, Mexicans accounted for less than half of total apprehensions on the Southwest border. In FY2019, "other-than-Mexicans" comprised 81% of all 851,508 apprehensions. From FY2012 to FY2019,[35] the number of Mexican nationals apprehended dropped by 37%, from 262,341 to 166,458, while the number of migrants apprehended from all other countries increased six-fold, from 94,532 to 685,050.[36]

---

[32] A *lawful permanent resident* (LPR) is a foreign national who has been approved to live and work permanently in the United States.

[33] For more information, see CRS Report R42138, *Border Security: Immigration Enforcement Between Ports of Entry*.

[34] DHS, Border Security Metrics Report, 2019.

[35] This period corresponds to that of publicly available data from DHS differentiating apprehensions of unauthorized migrants according to demographic category shown in *Figure 3* and *Figure 4*, below.

[36] CBP Acting Commissioner Mark Morgan stated in a White House press briefing that in October 2019 the number of Mexican migrants apprehended with those determined inadmissible exceeded the number from the Northern Triangle countries combined for the

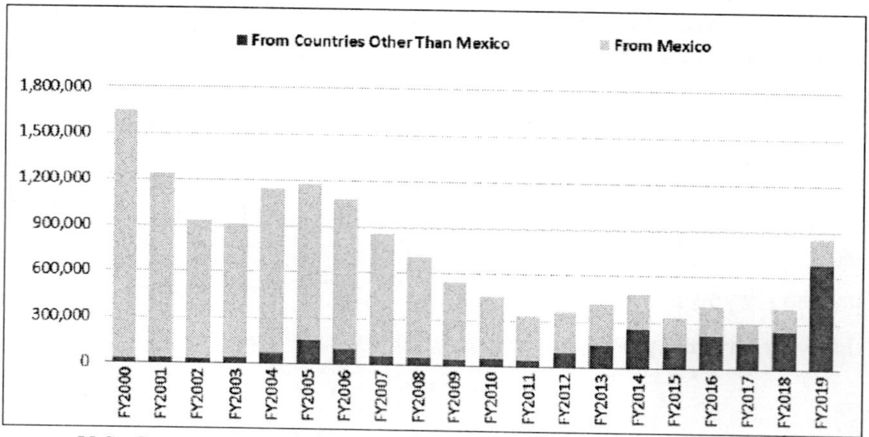

Sources: U.S. Customs and Border Protection. FY2000-FY2018: "U.S. Border Patrol Apprehensions From Mexico and Other Than Mexico (FY 2000 - FY 2018)," https://www.cbp.gov/newsroom/media-resources/stats; FY2019: "U.S. Border Patrol Southwest Border Apprehensions by Sector Fiscal Year 2019," https://www.cbp.gov/newsroom/stats/sw-border-migration/usbp-sw-border-apprehensions-fy2019. The FY2019 "From Countries Other than Mexico" figure was computed by summing apprehensions of Mexican national single adults, family units, and unaccompanied alien children, and subtracting that sum from total apprehensions.

Figure 2. Total Apprehensions at the Southwest Border, by Country of Origin, FY2000-FY2019. (Country of origin is either Mexico or other than Mexico)

Apprehensions by Demographic Category

CBP classifies apprehended unauthorized migrants into three demographic categories: single adults, family units (at least one parent/guardian and at least one child), and unaccompanied alien children (UAC).[37] Of the three categories, apprehensions of persons in family units

first time in 18 months; U.S. Department of Homeland Security, "Press Briefing by Acting CBP Commissioner Mark Morgan," press release, November 14, 2019, https://www.whitehouse.gov/briefings-statements/press-briefing-acting-cbp-commissioner-mark-morgan-2/.

[37] CBP defines a *family unit* as "individuals (either a child under 18 years old, parent, or legal guardian) apprehended with a family member by the U.S. Border Patrol." U.S. Customs and Border Protection, "Southwest Border Migration FY2019," https://www.cbp.gov/

have increased the most in absolute terms since FY2012, the first year for which publicly available CBP data differentiated among the three demographic categories (see *Figure 3*).

In FY2012, 321,276 single adults made up 90% of the 356,873 arriving migrants apprehended at the Southwest border, while members of family units numbered 11,116, and UAC accounted for 24,481.[38] By FY2019, however, apprehensions of persons in family units numbered 473,682, more than all family unit apprehensions from FY2012 to FY2018 combined.[39] Together in FY2019, those persons in family units as well as UAC (76,020 apprehensions) accounted for 65% of all apprehensions while the remaining 35% (301,806) were single adults, of whom 84% were men.[40] Approximately 48% of family units apprehended in FY2019 were headed by mothers, 44% were headed by fathers, and about 8% were headed by two parents.[41]

---

newsroom/stats/sw-border-migration. Family unit apprehensions represent apprehended individuals in family units, not apprehended families. An *unaccompanied alien child* (UAC) is defined in statute as a child who has no lawful immigration status in the United States; has not attained 18 years of age; and with respect to whom there is no parent or legal guardian in the United States, or there is no parent or legal guardian in the United States available to provide care and physical custody; 6 U.S.C. §279(g)(2). CBP classifies a child arriving at the border without a parent or legal guardian as an unaccompanied alien child. Children arriving with relatives other than parents, including grandparents, siblings, aunts and uncles, are not considered to be in family units and are treated as unaccompanied. *Single adults* are individuals at least 18 years of age who are not part of a family unit.

38 According to former CBP Commissioner Kevin McAleenan, "single adult males used to make up over 90% of arriving aliens in past years." Testimony of CBP Commissioner Kevin McAleenan, in U.S. Congress, House Committee on Homeland Security, Subcommittee on Border and Maritime Security, *Border Security, Commerce and Travel: Commissioner McAleenan's Vision for the Future of CBP*, 115th Cong., 2nd sess., April 25, 2018.

39 ICE's Homeland Security Investigations (HSI) have described an increasing number of migrants "presenting" at the border as family units that are composed of unrelated individuals since spring of 2018. Many individuals in family units who request asylum have been released into the U.S. interior with a court date (via a Notice to Appear (NTA)), often well into the future. This may provide an incentive for families to send children with unrelated individuals posing as parents, and for adults wanting to gain entry to arrive with a child to whom they are not related. A press release from October 17, 2019, states that a six-month operation in the El Paso sector identified 238 families without verifiable relationships: https://www.ice.gov/news/releases/ice-hsi-el-paso-usbp-identify-more-200-fraudulent-families-last-6- months.

40 CBP data tabulation on gender provided to CRS on request, October 31, 2019.

41 CBP data tabulation provided to CRS on request, October 31, 2019. All numbers are approximate.

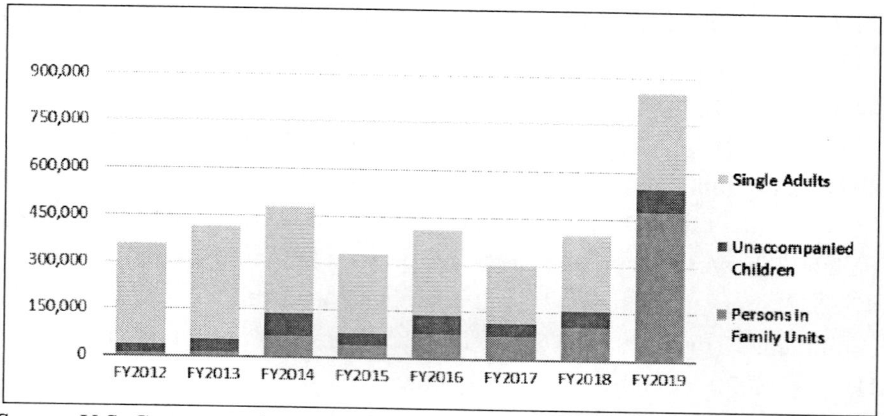

Source: U.S. Customs and Border Protection. FY2012-FY2016: "United States Border Patrol Southwest Family Unit Subject and Unaccompanied Alien Children Apprehensions Fiscal Year 2016, Statement by Secretary Johnson on Southwest Border Security," https://www.cbp.gov/newsroom/stats/southwest-border-unaccompanied-children/fy-2016; FY2017-FY2019: "U.S. Border Patrol Southwest Border Apprehensions by Sector," https://www.cbp.gov/newsroom/stats/usbp-sw-border-apprehensions.

Notes: Family unit apprehensions represent apprehended individuals in family units, not apprehended families.

Figure 3. Total Apprehensions at the Southwest Border, by Demographic Category, FY2012-FY2019.

Apprehensions of Family Units by Country of Origin

As the number of apprehensions of individuals in family units has increased in recent years, their national origins have shifted from mostly Mexican, (comprising 80% of all 11,116 family unit apprehensions in FY2012), to mostly Salvadoran, Guatemalan, and Honduran, who together made up 91% of all 457,871 such apprehensions in FY2019 (see *Figure 4*). Apprehensions of individuals in family units from El Salvador increased from 636 (6%) of all such apprehensions in FY2012 to 27,114 (35%) of all 77,674 of such apprehensions in FY2016 before declining to 54,915 (12%) in FY2019. Over the same period, the share of family unit apprehensions from Honduras (513) and Guatemala (340) each grew from less than 5% of the total in FY2012 to 188,416 and 185,233, respectively, about 39% each of the total in FY2019. By comparison, the 6,004 apprehensions of Mexicans in family units made up 1% of the total in FY2019.

Notably, the percentage of persons in family units from "all other countries," has been relatively low over the same period. In absolute numbers, this category registered less than 4,000 apprehensions in all years prior to FY2019, but rose to 37,132 family unit apprehensions in FY2019 (7% of the total, the same share as in FY2012).

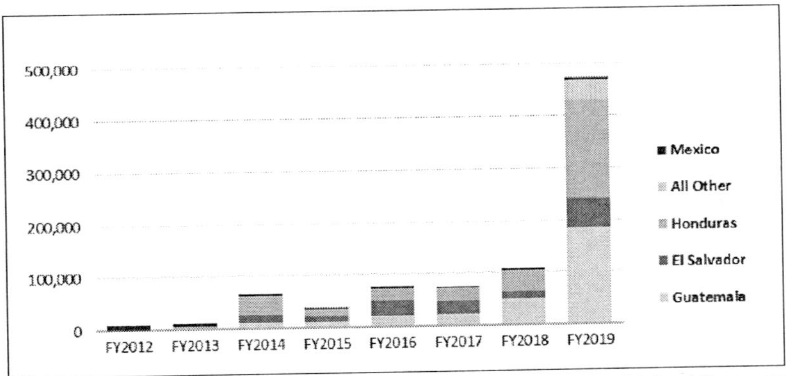

Source: U.S. Customs and Border Protection. FY2012-FY2016: "United States Border Patrol Southwest Family Unit Subject and Unaccompanied Alien Children Apprehensions Fiscal Year 2016, Statement by Secretary Johnson on Southwest Border Security," https://www.cbp.gov/newsroom/stats/southwest-border-unaccompanied-children/fy-2016; FY2017-FY2019: "U.S. Border Patrol Southwest Border Apprehensions by Sector," https://www.cbp.gov/newsroom/stats/usbp-sw-border-apprehensions.

Notes: Family unit apprehensions represent apprehended individuals in family units, not apprehended families.

Figure 4. Family Unit Apprehensions at the Southwest Border, by Country of Origin, FY2012-FY2019.

Apprehensions of Unaccompanied Alien Children

Over the past decade, the number of unaccompanied alien children apprehended at the Southwest border has increased considerably (see

Figure 5). From FY2011 to FY2014, UAC apprehensions increased each year, and more than quadrupled from 16,067 in FY2011 to 68,541 in FY2014.

From FY2014 to FY2018, UAC apprehensions fluctuated, declining to 39,970 in FY2015; increasing to 59,692 in FY2016; declining again to 41,435 in FY2017; and increasing again to 50,036 in FY2018. In FY2019, UAC apprehensions reached 76,020, a level that exceeds the previous peak in FY2014.[42] In FY2019, approximately 30% of apprehended UAC were girls.[43]

In the past decade, the country-of-origin composition of apprehended UAC, like that of family units, has shifted from mostly Mexican to mostly Salvadoran, Guatemalan, and Honduran.[44] For example, in FY2009 Mexican UAC (16,114) made up 82% of all 19,668 UAC apprehensions in that year, while Salvadoran (1,221), Guatemalan (1,115), and Honduran (968) UAC made up 6%, 6%, and 5%, respectively, of the total. In contrast, by FY2019 Mexican UAC (10,487) made up 14% of all 76,020 UAC apprehensions in that year, while Salvadoran (12,021), Guatemalan (30,329), and Honduran (20,398) UAC made up 16%, 40%, and 27%, respectively, of the total.

Current statute treats children from contiguous countries (Mexico and Canada) differently than children from non-contiguous countries. While UAC from Mexico can be repatriated promptly through a process known as *voluntary departure*, UAC from all other countries are placed in formal removal proceedings. The latter are then referred to the Department of Health and Human Services' (HHS') Office of Refugee Resettlement (ORR), where they are initially sheltered and subsequently placed with family members or sponsors while they await their immigration hearing. Hence, the shift in the country-of-origin composition of the apprehended UAC population has had considerable impact on agencies charged with the processing and care ofthese children.

---

42 U.S. Customs and Border Protection, "Southwest Border Migration FY2019," https://www.cbp.gov/newsroom/stats/ sw-border-migration.

43 CBP data tabulation provided to CRS on request, October 31, 2019.

44 For more information, see CRS Report R43599, *Unaccompanied Alien Children: An Overview*, Figure 1.

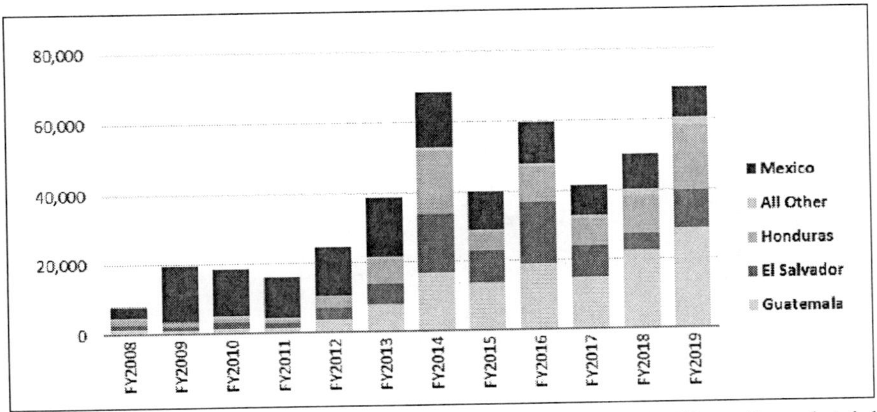

Source: U.S. Customs and Border Protection. FY2008-FY2009: "Juvenile and Adult Apprehensions—Fiscal Year 2013;" FY2010-FY2018: "U.S. Border Patrol Total Monthly UAC Apprehensions by Sector," https://www.cbp.gov/newsroom/media-resources; FY2019: "U.S. Border Patrol Southwest Border Apprehensions by Sector Fiscal Year 2019," https://www.cbp.gov/newsroom/stats/sw-border-migration/usbp-sw-border- apprehensions.

Figure 5. Unaccompanied Alien Children Apprehensions at the Southwest Border, by Country of Origin, FY2008-FY2019.

Total Apprehensions by Month in FY2019

Over the past two decades, apprehensions have followed a pattern consistent with a seasonal migration cycle. In this cycle, peak numbers of apprehensions occur in the spring months (March–June), followed by progressively lower numbers in the hotter summer months (July–September), lower-than-average numbers through the fall months (October–December), and even lower numbers in January, before rising again through the spring months when the pattern begins to repeat.[45]

---

[45] CRS analyzed published CBP total monthly apprehensions data from FY2000 to FY2019 (not presented herein). For a detailed discussion of this annual migration cycle, see, for example, Douglas S. Massey, Rafael Alarcon, Jorge Durand, and Humberto González, *Return to Aztlan*, University of California Press, 1990.

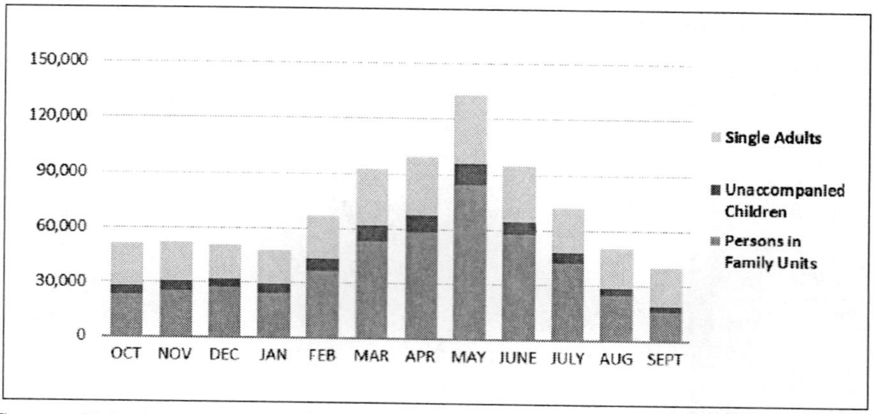

Source: U.S. Customs and Border Protection, "U.S. Border Patrol Southwest Border Apprehensions by Sector Fiscal Year 2019," https://www.cbp.gov/newsroom/stats/sw-border-migration/usbp-sw-border-apprehensions.

Figure 6. Total Apprehensions at the Southwest Border, by Month and Demographic Category, FY2019.

During FY2019, the monthly pattern in total apprehensions at the Southwestern border was similar to the trends during the past two decades (see *Figure 6*). From the peak in May through September of FY2019, apprehensions declined nearly 70%, from approximately 133,000 to just over 40,000.

These data suggest that the declines in monthly apprehensions from May to September of FY2019 stemmed primarily from declining numbers of family unit apprehensions. The number of persons in family units apprehended on a monthly basis dropped from 84,490 in May to 15,824 in September (an 81% decrease). For UAC, apprehensions declined by 72%, from 11,475 in May to 3,165 in September. Apprehensions of single adults saw a smaller decline (42%) over this period, from 36,894 in May to 21,518 in September.

These patterns suggest that declining apprehensions in recent months may have resulted not only from the immigration enforcement policies of the Trump Administration but also from decades- long seasonal migration patterns, among other factors.[46]

POLICY IMPLICATIONS

This chapter has described the following major shifts in the composition and character of migrant flows to the Southwest border that have unfolded in less than a decade:

- In the past two years, the number of total apprehensions has increased substantially, a reverse of the general trend of declining and relatively low apprehension levels seen since FY2001.
- The unauthorized migrant flow apprehended at the Southwest border no longer consists primarily of individuals from Mexico, a country with whom the United States shares a border and close economic and historical ties. It now originates largely from El Salvador, Guatemala, and Honduras. Also, growing numbers of unauthorized migrants are originating from Africa, Asia, and the Caribbean.
- The unauthorized migrant flow is no longer dominated by economic migrants exclusively seeking employment. It is now driven to a larger extent than in past years by asylum seekers and others with similar motivations, such as escaping violence and domestic insecurity, who may also be interested in working in the United States. Such migrants often seek out U.S. Border Patrol agents at the border when crossing illegally between U.S. ports of entry rather than attempting to elude them.
- The unauthorized migrant flow no longer consists primarily of single adult migrants but rather of families and children traveling without their parents.

---

[46] Other factors may have also contributed to this decline, and establishing the contribution of each factor requires a rigorous analysis that is beyond the scope of this chapter.

Although not previously discussed, changing migration strategies are also altering how federal agencies respond to migrant flows. For example, migrants have been increasingly traveling in large groups, reportedly to protect themselves from harm.[47] In addition, more migrants are arriving at remote CBP outposts along the Southwest border, sometimes overwhelming the relatively few CBP personnel who staff them.[48]

These changing patterns at the Southwest border have considerable policy implications. In comparison with apprehended single adult economic migrants from Mexico, more-recently apprehended migrants require lengthier processing and create a call for greater resources and personnel of more federal agencies. When migrants originate from countries other than the contiguous countries of Mexico and Canada, their removals involve longer processing time, higher transportation costs, and more involved inter-agency coordination. If arriving migrants are unaccompanied alien children from noncontiguous countries, they are protected from immediate removal by statutes that require them to be put into formal immigration removal proceedings and they are referred to the care and custody of ORR.[49] If migrants seek asylum, they generally require a credible fear hearing.[50] They may be detained in DHS facilities for varying periods[51] and must be processed by DOJ's Executive Office for Immigration Review (EOIR).[52]

CBP, among all federal agencies, is arguably the most affected by the break with historical migration patterns. The pressures of large groups of migrants arriving together and the greater vulnerabilities of new arrivals are reportedly testing CBP's border infrastructure, agency personnel, and

---

[47] For more information, see CRS Report R45489, Recent Migration to the United States from Central America: Frequently Asked Questions.

[48] Simon Romero and Caitlin Dickerson, "'Desperation of Thousands' Pushes Migrants Into Ever Remote Terrain," New York Times, January 29, 2019; and Alicia Caldwell, "Illegal Migrant Crossings Surge in Remote New Mexico Desert," Wall Street Journal, January 29, 2019.

[49] For more information, see CRS Report R43599, Unaccompanied Alien Children: An Overview.

[50] For more information, see CRS Report R45539, *Immigration: U.S. Asylum Policy*.

[51] See CRS Report R45915, *Immigration Detention: A Legal Overview*.

[52] U.S. Department of Justice, Executive Office for Immigration Review, "Executive Office for Immigration Review: An Agency Guide," fact sheet, December 2017.

long-standing policies. When unauthorized migrant flows consist largely of families and children, who often arrive in large groups or at remote U.S. border locations, CBP has adjusted its operations and allocated resources and personnel to accommodate more vulnerable migrants. Some studies also suggest that smuggling guides sometimes direct migrants to cross in specific locations to outmaneuver USBP agents and infrastructure and avoid detection.[53] Moreover, anecdotal evidence suggests migrant arrival strategies can be based upon perceptions of differences in border enforcement policies and practices among and within the nine CBP Southwest border sectors.[54] If enforcement policies vary by sector, CBP can expect migration patterns to shift to sectors that migrants perceive as offering them the greatest chance of acquiring the immigration relief they seek.

The Trump Administration has changed immigration enforcement policies and practices at the border in an attempt to reduce unauthorized migration and discourage fraudulent or frivolous claims for humanitarian immigration relief. President Trump, DHS, DOD, and DOJ have acted together with a series of policy changes that make it more difficult for migrants to be awarded asylum. For example, see the following:

- In November 2018, the President issued a proclamation to suspend immediately the entry into the United States of aliens who cross the Southwest border between ports of entry.[55] This proclamation has been challenged in court and a preliminary injunction was issued by a federal district court.[56]

---

[53] See, for example, Victoria A. Greenfield, Blas Nuñez-Neto, and Ian Mitch et al., *Human Smuggling and Associated Revenues: What Do or Can We Know About Routes from Central America to the United States?*, Homeland Security Operational Analysis Center operated by the RAND Corporation, 2019.

[54] Alicia A. Caldwell, "Migrants Find Different Fates at Texas, Arizona Borders," *Wall Street Journal*, November 11, 2019.

[55] Executive Office of the President, "Addressing Mass Migration Through the Southern Border of the United States," 83 *Federal Register* 57661-57664, November 9, 2018.

[56] The government has not sought a stay of the district court's December 19, 2018, preliminary injunction order. For more information, see American Bar Association, "Update on Changes to Asylum Eligibility, Update as of December 19, 2018," February 11, 2019.

- As noted above, DHS implemented the Migrant Protection Protocols (MPP) in January 2019, and for the past several years CBP has also used the practice of "metering" migrants. Both of these policies require migrants to wait on the Mexican side of the border.[57]
- Since April 2018, National Guard personnel have supported DHS at the border, while active duty personnel began providing support in October 2018.[58] In February 2019, President Trump proclaimed a national emergency pursuant to the National Emergencies Act in order to fund a physical barrier at the Southwest border with Mexico using $6.1 billion in funds from the Department of Defense (DOD).[59] In September 2019, the Secretary of Defense deferred funding for military construction projects in order to redirect funds to border barrier projects using his authority under the emergency statute 10 U.S.C., Section 2808.[60]
- In July 2019, DHS and DOJ jointly issued an interim final rule (IFR)[61] that makes aliens ineligible for asylum in the United States if they arrive at the Southwest border without first seeking

---

[57] For more information, see CRS Legal Sidebar LSB10295, The Department of Homeland Security's Reported "Metering" Policy: Legal Issues; and CRS In Focus IF10215, *Mexico's Immigration Control Efforts*.

[58] This has included surveillance, engineering, construction, transportation, maintenance, and planning support. For more information, see CRS Legal Sidebar LSB10121, *The President's Authority to Use the National Guard or the Armed Forces to Secure the Border*.

[59] Executive Office of the President, "Declaring a National Emergency Concerning the Southern Border of the United States," 84 *Federal Register* 4949-4950, February 20, 2019. A federal district court initially blocked the Administration from using DOD funding for border barrier construction. That injunction was ultimately stayed by the Supreme Court, thereby permitting the Trump Administration to use the DOD funds as planned. For more information, see CRS Legal Sidebar LSB10310, *Supreme Court Stays Injunction That Had Blocked a Portion of the Administration's Border Wall Funding*.

[60] Together, the administration has assembled approximately $6.7 billion through various sources of funding (largely DOD) in funds to construct border barriers on the southwest border. For more information, see CRS Report R45937, *Military Funding for Southwest Border Barriers*; and "Declaration of an Emergency at the Southern Border" in CRS Report 98-505, *National Emergency Powers*.

[61] For more information on the IFR, *Asylum Eligibility and Procedural Modifications*, see https://www.federalregister.gov/documents/2019/07/16/2019-15246/asylum-eligibility-and-procedural-modifications.

protection from persecution in other countries through which they transit.[62]

- In addition, the United States is working with Mexico to decrease Central American migrant flows[63] and with Central American governments to promote economic prosperity, improve security, and strengthen regional governance.[64]

The changing character of recent migrant flows at the Southwest border also may suggest that apprehensions may be less useful than in the past for measuring border enforcement. Because many apprehended migrants now actively seek out U.S. Border Patrol agents in order to request asylum, increases or decreases in apprehension numbers may not reflect the effectiveness of border enforcement strategies. Rather, an increase in apprehensions combined with the changing characteristics of recently apprehended migrants may increasingly portend greater resource needs for federal agencies because the administrative requirements for asylum claims are more resource-intensive than those for unauthorized migrants who do not request asylum and are quickly repatriated through expedited removal. The challenge of deterring unauthorized migrants from entering the United States has been complicated and overshadowed by the challenge of processing, in a fair and timely manner, relatively greater numbers of migrants seeking asylum.[65]

---

62 For more information, including ongoing legal challenges to the IFR, see CRS Legal Sidebar LSB10337, Asylum Bar for Migrants Who Reach the Southern Border through Third Countries: Issues and Ongoing Litigation.

63 For more information, see CRS Legal Sidebar LSB10295, The Department of Homeland Security's Reported "Metering" Policy: Legal Issues; and CRS In Focus IF10215, Mexico's Immigration Control Efforts.

64 For more information, see CRS In Focus IF10371, U.S. Strategy for Engagement in Central America: An Overview; and CRS Report R44812, U.S. Strategy for Engagement in Central America: Policy Issues for Congress.

65 A recent analysis from DHS that follows a 2014 cohort of aliens who were either apprehended or found inadmissible along the Southwest border for three years demonstrates that the existing enforcement system is designed primarily to return certain types of migrants (adults with no family members from Mexico, and those who have previously been convicted of a crime) to their home countries. However, among those requesting asylum, it is much more likely that they had neither been repatriated nor had their case resolved by the end of 2017. See U.S. Department of Homeland Security, *2014 Southwest Border Encounters: Three Year Cohort Outcomes Analysis*, August 2018, p. 2,

Recent migration research suggests that forced migration from civil conflict, violence, weather events, and climate change is playing a more prominent role in worldwide migratory patterns.[66] To some extent, patterns described in this chapter are consistent with that trend. Declining birth rates in parts of Latin America and improving employment prospects in Mexico over the past decade have reduced the relative proportion of single adult migrants whose primary motivation is U.S. employment.[67] In contrast, relatively high levels of violence and lack of public security, among other factors, have increased the relative proportion of Central American and Mexican families and children whose primary migratory motivation is humanitarian relief.

Options for Congress could include legislative responses to the series of policies that the Administration has developed to address the changing flow of migrants at the Southwest border. Some proposals may consider changes to the appropriations of agencies charged with processing unauthorized migrants to reshape the system from one that was designed to apprehend and return single unauthorized adults from Mexico with no claims for protection, to one that can more quickly adjudicate those

---

https://www.dhs.gov/sites/default/files/publications/18_0918_DHS_Cohort_Outcomes_Report.pdf.

[66] For more information, see, for example, Stephen Castles, "Confronting the Realities of Forced Migration," Migration Policy Institute, May 1, 2004; International Organization for Migration, "IOM Outlook on Migration, Environment and Climate Change," 2014; Holly Reed, "Forced Migration and Undocumented Migration and Development," paper for the United Nations Expert Group Meeting for the Review and Appraisal of the Programme of Action of the International Conference on Population and Development and its Contribution to the Follow-up and Review of the 2030 Agenda for Sustainable Development, October 31, 2018; United Nations, Department of Economic and Social Affairs, "International migrants numbered 272 million in 2019, continuing an upward trend in all major world regions," *Population Facts*, September 2019; and Susan Martin, Sanjula Weerasinghe, and Abbie Taylor, "Crisis Migration," Brown Journal of World Affairs, vol. XX (Fall/Winter 2013), pp. 123-137.

[67] See, for example, Richard Miles, "A Smaller, Wealthier Mexico Is on the Horizon," Center for Strategic and International Studies, December 11, 2017; Jeffrey S. Passel, D'Vera Cohn, and Ana Gonzalez-Barrera, "Net Migration from Mexico Falls to Zero—and Perhaps Less," Pew Research Center, April 23, 2012; Daniel Chiquiar and Alejandrina Salcedo, "Mexican Migration to the United States: Underlying Economic Factors and Possible Scenarios for Future Flows," Migration Policy Institute, April 2013; CRS Report R43628, *Unaccompanied Alien Children: Potential Factors Contributing to Recent Immigration*; and Randy Capps, Doris Meissner, and Ariel G. Ruiz Soto et al., *From Control to Crisis: Changing Trends and Policies Reshaping U.S.-Mexico Border Enforcement*, Migration Policy Institute, August 2019.

seeking humanitarian protection. Other options may include greater supervision of unauthorized migrants who are released into the United States,[68] and mandating the collection and publication of more-detailed and timely data from DHS to more completely assess the flow of unauthorized migrants, including those in the MPP program, and their impact on border enforcement and the immigration court system.

---

[68] For more information on DHS's existing Alternatives to Detention program, see CRS Report R45804, *Immigration: Alternatives to Detention (ATD) Programs*.

In: Immigration
Editor: Klonimir Jović
ISBN: 978-1-53618-183-8

Chapter 4

BORDER SECURITY: U.S. CUSTOMS AND BORDER PROTECTION'S MANAGEMENT OF A TEMPORARY FACILITY IN TEXAS RAISED CONCERNS ABOUT RESOURCES USED*

United States Government Accountability Office

CONGRESSIONAL REQUESTERS

Beginning in fall 2018, the Department of Homeland Security's (DHS) U.S. Customs and Border Protection (CBP) experienced a significant increase in the number of individuals apprehended at or between U.S. ports of entry along the southwest border.[1] Apprehensions by the U.S. Border

* This is an edited, reformatted and augmented version of the United States Government Accountability Office Publication No. GAO-20-231R, dated March 11, 2020.

[1] Within DHS, CBP's U.S. Border Patrol apprehends individuals between ports of entry, and Office of Field Operations (OFO) encounters individuals that arrive at ports of entry. According to CBP officials, OFO encounters aliens (instead of apprehending them) because individuals do not enter the United States at ports of entry until OFO officers have processed them. For the purposes of this chapter, we use the term "apprehend" to describe both Border Patrol and OFO's first interactions with individuals at the border.

Patrol (Border Patrol) increased from nearly 400,000 individuals in fiscal year 2018 to over 850,000 in fiscal year 2019, an increase of 115 percent, according to CBP data.[2] The increase in individuals apprehended resulted in overcrowded and difficult humanitarian conditions in CBP short-term processing and holding facilities.[3]

To help address this issue, in May 2019, CBP determined it needed a temporary soft-sided facility for processing and holding single adults in the El Paso Border Patrol sector, based on the significant increase in apprehensions in that sector.[4] Specifically, according to CBP data, total Border Patrol apprehensions of single adults in the El Paso sector increased from nearly 14,000 individuals in fiscal year 2018 to over 33,000 in fiscal year 2019, an increase of 140 percent. On July 3, 2019, CBP placed a sole-source, firm-fixed price delivery order with a 3- month initial period of performance and five 2-month options for building, operating, and maintaining a temporary, soft-sided facility in Tornillo, Texas with a capacity to hold 2,500 single adult detainees (see figure 1).[5] CBP used

---

[2] Border Patrol detains apprehended individuals at short-term holding facilities to complete processing and determine a course of action, such as custody transfer, removal, or release. Along the southwest border, Border Patrol divides responsibility for border security operations geographically among nine sectors that include border stations.

[3] See, for example, Department of Homeland Security, Office of Inspector General, Management Alert – DHS Needs to Address Dangerous Overcrowding and Prolonged Detention of Children and Adults in the Rio Grande Valley (Redacted), OIG-19-51 (Washington, D.C.: July 2, 2019); Management Alert - DHS Needs to Address Dangerous Overcrowding Among Single Adults at El Paso Del Norte Processing Center (Redacted), OIG-19-46 (Washington, D.C.: May 30, 2019); and Department of Homeland Security, Acting Secretary McAleenan's Prepared Remarks to the Council of Foreign Relations (September 23, 2019).

[4] Soft-sided facilities are tent-like structures, which include services and equipment to hold individuals in those facilities, such as heating, ventilation, air conditioning, plumbing, electrical, and lightning protection. CBP acquired a total of six temporary, soft-sided facilities in Texas and Arizona from April 2019 to July 2019. Adults are defined as any individual age 18 or older on the date of their apprehension by Border Patrol.

[5] CBP placed a delivery order for the temporary facility in Tornillo, Texas against an existing General Services Administration contract through the Federal Supply Schedule program, which is governed by the procedures of Federal Acquisition Regulation (FAR) subpart 8.4. Under this subpart, orders exceeding a certain dollar threshold are required to be placed using procedures to promote competition among the schedule contractors, but this requirement may be waived and an order may be placed noncompetitively (i.e., sole source to one contractor) under certain circumstances, such as when urgent and compelling needs exist and competing the order would result in unacceptable delays. FAR § 8.405-6(a)(1)(i)(A). Generally, Federal Supply Schedule orders are placed on a fixed price basis, which is when the contractor has full responsibility for the costs of performance and the

funds appropriated from an emergency supplemental appropriations act for this delivery order.[6]

Source: U.S. border Patrol.| GAO-20-321R.

Figure 1. U.S. Border Patrol's Soft-Sided Facility in Tornillo, Texas.

The price for the initial 3-month period of performance (August 4, 2019 through November 3, 2019) was approximately $47 million, with each option priced at approximately $19 million.

Under the order, the contractor was responsible for the physical construction of the facility, including areas for intake and holding of detained individuals, property storage, and medical evaluations, among other things. The contractor was also responsible for providing services to support the intake, processing, and temporary holding of detained individuals, such as meal service, guard services, toilets, and showers.[7]

---

resulting profit or loss. However, other types of orders may be placed, such as time and material orders, which provide for acquiring supplies or services on the basis of direct labor hours at specified fixed hourly rates and actual cost for materials. FAR § 8.404(d), (h).

[6] On July 1 2019, the Emergency Supplemental Appropriations for Humanitarian Assistance and Security at the Southern Border Act was enacted, which included approximately $1 billion in emergency supplemental funds for CBP to respond to the significant rise in the number of individuals apprehended at the southwest border. Pub. L. No. 116- 26, 133 Stat. 1018 (2019).

[7] The order called for the contractor to provide all material, supplies, supervision, labor, equipment, and amenities to provide a solution for the set-up and operation of a temporary facility in Tornillo, Texas (also known as a turnkey solution).

The facility in Tornillo opened and began holding single adults on August 13, 2019.[8] CBP exercised the first option to extend operations at the facility on November 4, 2019 and declined to exercise the second option, resulting in the closure of the facility on January 3, 2020.

You asked us to review how CBP provides care and custody for adults and children the agency apprehends, including the resources and facilities CBP uses. As part of this work, we conducted a site visit to the El Paso sector in Texas—the Border Patrol sector in which the Tornillo facility is located—in September 2019, where we interviewed Border Patrol El Paso sector officials to discuss the care of individuals in Border Patrol's custody and observed Tornillo facility operations and services provided. During this site visit, we identified concerns regarding use of resources at the Tornillo facility. This correspondence examines how CBP utilized and managed the Tornillo facility.[9] To address this objective, in addition to the site visit to the facility, we interviewed Border Patrol officials from the El Paso sector and headquarters. We also interviewed CBP officials from the Office of Acquisition and Office of Facilities and Asset Management.[10] We reviewed relevant Federal Acquisition Regulations (FAR), agency guidance, and procurement documentation, including the acquisition plan, statement of work, the delivery order, and order modifications.[11]

---

[8] The period of performance was August 4, 2019 through November 3, 2019, but Border Patrol did not begin holding single adults in the facility until August 13, 2019, due to the time required to set up information technology at the facility and train personnel.

[9] This correspondence is based on work we conducted as part of our ongoing review of the medical care of adults and children in CBP's custody. We plan to issue a report on the medical care for adults and children in CBP's custody in the summer of 2020.

[10] Within CBP, the Office of Acquisition is responsible for procuring goods and services, such as the temporary soft- sided facilities. The Office of Facilities and Asset Management is responsible for determining facility design requirements and managing the execution of facility goods and services procured. Border Patrol is responsible for determining the operational requirements for the facilities, communicating those requirements to CBP'S Office of Facilities and Asset Management, and managing the daily operations of the holding facilities, including determining staffing needs.

[11] The FAR is the primary regulation used by all federal executive agencies to acquire supplies and services with appropriated funds. See FAR § 1.101.

Further, we reviewed our past work and that of the Project Management Institute about the importance of evaluating results and identifying lessons learned.[12] We also interviewed the contractor responsible for performing the delivery order to obtain the contractor's perspectives on the utilization of the Tornillo facility. Additionally, we analyzed data on the number of individuals held at the facility through January 3, 2020, along with pricing information, such as the schedule for supplies and services.[13] We assessed the reliability of these data by reviewing the data for missing elements, outliers, obvious errors, and interviewing officials about applicable quality control procedures to ensure the accuracy and integrity of the data. We determined that the data were sufficiently reliable for the purposes of reporting information on the number of individuals held at the Tornillo facility. We conducted the work on which this correspondence is based from June 2019 to March 2020 in accordance with generally accepted government auditing standards. Those standards require that we plan and perform the audit to obtain sufficient, appropriate evidence to provide a reasonable basis for our findings and conclusions based on our audit objectives. We believe that the evidence obtained provides a reasonable basis for our findings and conclusions based on our audit objectives.

---

[12] For example, see GAO, *Project Management: DOE and NNSA Should Improve Their Lessons-Learned Process for Capital Asset Projects*, GAO-19-25 (Washington, D.C.: Dec. 21, 2018). Project Management Institute, Inc., *A Guide to the Project Management Body of Knowledge (PMBOK® Guide)*, Sixth Edition (2017), and Project Management Institute, Inc., *Implementing Organizational Project Management: A Practice Guide, First Edition* (2014). *PMBOK* is a trademark of Project Management Institute, Inc. The *PMBOK® Guide* provides guidelines for managing individual projects, including collecting requirements and defining the project's scope. The Project Management Institute is a not-for-profit association that provides global standards for, among other things, project and program management. These standards are utilized worldwide and provide guidance on how to manage various aspects of projects, programs, and portfolios.

[13] We analyzed data on the number of individuals held in the Tornillo facility from August 15, 2019 through January 3, 2020, as that was the time period for which data were available during the course of our review.

CBP DETAINED FAR FEWER INDIVIDUALS IN ITS FACILITY IN TORNILLO, TEXAS THAN THE FACILITY'S CAPACITY AND SPENT MILLIONS OF DOLLARS FOR FOOD SERVICES NOT NEEDED

CBP's Management of Resources at the Tornillo Facility

Since opening the Tornillo facility in August 2019, CBP held far fewer individuals in the facility than its capacity and spent about $5.3 million for food services—the preparation and delivery of meals and snacks—it did not need during the initial period of performance. Additionally, CBP allocated significant personnel resources to the facility during its entire period of operation. CBP then modified the delivery order to reduce costs and subsequently closed the facility in January 2020.

During the initial period of performance (August 4, 2019 through November 3, 2019), Border Patrol held no more than 66 adults in the Tornillo facility on any given day, far below the 2,500- person capacity.[14] Our analysis of Border Patrol data showed that, on average, there were 28 adults held in custody at the Tornillo facility per day during this period—approximately 1 percent of the facility's daily capacity (see figure 2).[15]

---

[14] The number of detainees per day is based on Border Patrol data that recorded a count of detainees at the Tornillo facility as of 6 a.m. each day. Therefore, the exact number of detainees that were at the facility within a 24-hour period may be greater than the number of detainees recorded in Border Patrol's system, as detainees were brought into and transferred out of the facility. However, Border Patrol officials stated that the detainee population at the Tornillo facility did not vary significantly from the data Border Patrol collected.

[15] We used Border Patrol data on the total number of detainees held per day at the Tornillo facility from August 15, 2019, the first date of available data, through November 3, 2019 (2,234 detainees) and divided that by the 81 days the facility was open and data was available during the initial period of performance to calculate the average number of detainees per day.

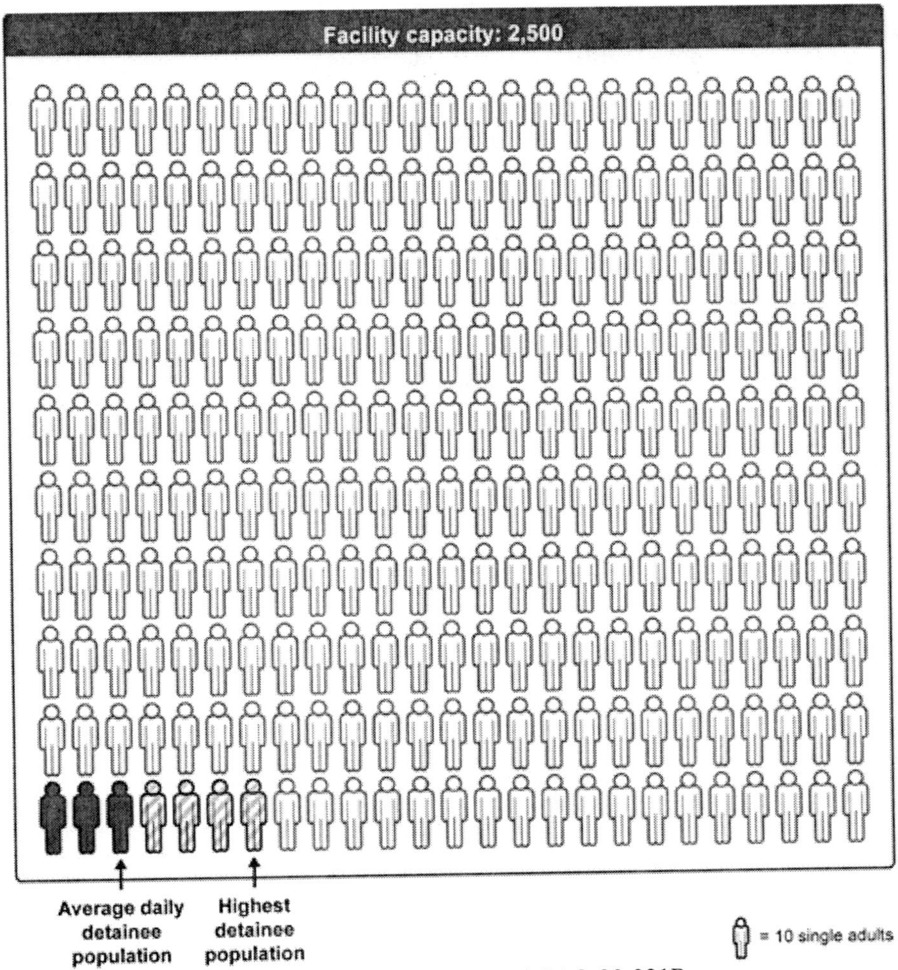

Source: GAO analysis of U.S. Border Patrol data. | GAO-20-321R.

Note: The number of detainees per day is based on U.S. Border Patrol (Border Patrol) data that recorded a count of detainees at the Tornillo facility as of 6 a.m. each day. Therefore, the exact number of detainees that were at the facility within a 24-hour period may be greater than the number of detainees recorded in Border Patrol's system as detainees were brought into and transferred out of the facility. However, Border Patrol officials stated that the detainee population at the Tornillo facility did not vary significantly from the data Border Patrol collected.

Figure 2. Average and Maximum Number of Single Adult Detainees Held at U.S. Border Patrol's Facility in Tornillo, Texas from August 15, 2019 through November 3, 2019, as Compared to Facility Capacity.

During the initial period of performance, CBP paid the contractor to operate the facility at full capacity, including food and guard services, regardless of the number of individuals housed in the facility, due to the terms of the delivery order it negotiated with the contractor.

- *Food service.* Based on our analysis, CBP paid approximately $5.3 million for meals it did not need during the initial period of performance. Specifically, according to CBP officials, per the terms of the order, CBP paid for food service (breakfast, lunch, and dinner) for the full capacity of the Tornillo facility (2,500 detainees), regardless of the daily population on-site.[16] As such, CBP paid for about 675,000 meals during the initial period of performance despite only ordering 13,428 meals.
- *Guard service.* Based on our analysis, CBP paid approximately $6.7 million for 75 unarmed contract security guards on-site at the Tornillo facility at all times to report any situations with individuals held in the facility and provide facility and perimeter security, though the facility had an approximate average daily population of 28 adults.

In addition to contracted personnel, a number of different federal agencies provided law enforcement and military personnel to help support operations at the Tornillo facility during the initial period of performance. Specifically, according to CBP documents and officials, there were generally:

- 21 CBP law enforcement officers for facility operations, such as detainee intake, welfare checks, and transportation, among other things. Of these, there were:
  - 11 Border Patrol agents (from the El Paso sector and detailed from Border Patrol's northern border sectors) and
  - 10 CBP officers (from the Office of Field Operations);

[16] Included in the pricing for food services were snacks (up to 4,000 per day) and delivery of the food.

- 5 U.S. Immigration and Customs Enforcement personnel during day shifts, to help coordinate on decisions made about individuals at the facility, such as whether individuals were to be transferred to longer term detention, potentially removed, or subject to other action; and
- 116 Texas National Guard personnel for logistical support, such as meal distribution and monitoring security cameras, among other things.[17]

Based on our analysis, on average, for each individual detainee transferred and held in the facility during the initial period of performance, there were generally four Texas National Guard personnel, three contracted security guards, and one CBP law enforcement officer (see figure 3).[18]

CBP officials stated that, as of November 15, 2019, the Texas National Guard personnel were no longer deployed to the facility because the agreement for supplemental holding support between DHS and the Department of Defense expired.[19] When asked how this impacted facility

---

[17] DHS asked that Department of Defense provide National Guard support on a non-reimbursable basis. According to Border Patrol officials, the Texas National Guard were requested and, with the agreement of the Governor of Texas, deployed to the Tornillo facility because DHS did not have the resources to fully staff the facility. Officials stated the National Guard personnel were not permitted to conduct law enforcement activities, such as interacting with detainees. Additionally, Border Patrol officials said that a minimum number of 15 law enforcement personnel were required to be on site per shift based on an interagency agreement with the Department of Defense for National Guard support, though officials said the minimum number was often exceeded to ensure proper safety and efficiency of the Tornillo facility. We have an ongoing review examining the Department of Defense's efforts to support DHS operations on the southwest border and the cost of providing this support, among other things. We plan to issue a report that addresses these issues in the summer of 2020.

[18] To determine the average personnel per detainee, we divided the general number of personnel CBP cited per shift (21 CBP law enforcement officers, 116 National Guard personnel and 75 contracted guards) by the average number of adults held in custody at the Tornillo facility per day using Border Patrol's data (28 detainees), resulting in about one CBP law enforcement officer, four National Guard personnel, and three contracted security guards for each individual detainee on average.

[19] According to CBP officials, the agreement for the National Guard support was not based solely on the Tornillo facility. Officials stated the Texas National Guard request for assistance covered two mission sets – supplemental holding support for the Tornillo facility and supplemental port of entry support – and was intentionally written to allow service members to transition between the two mission sets based on operational changes. As such, officials

operations and personnel resources for the remainder of the first option period, CBP officials acknowledged the National Guard personnel duties were limited in nature and, as such, CBP officials were able to arrange for the contracted security guards to absorb the National Guard duties for the remainder of the first option period.

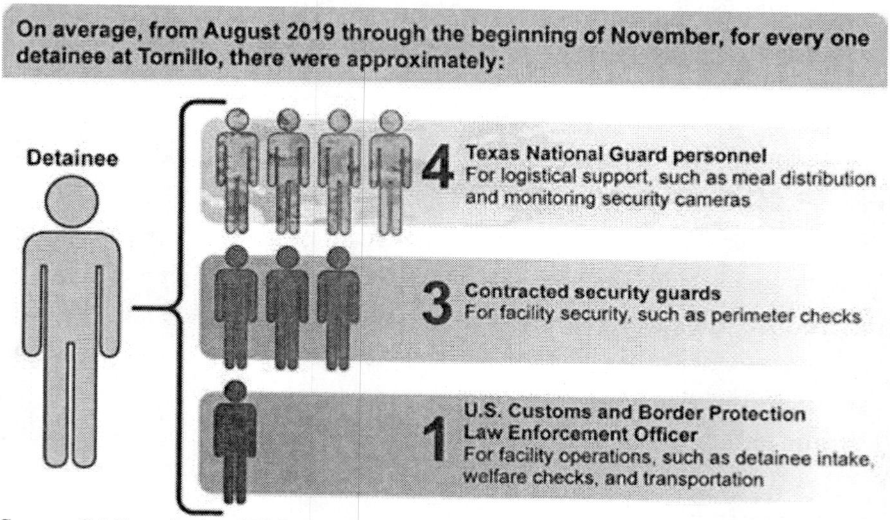

Source:GAO analysis of U.S. Border Patrol information. | GAO-20-321R.

Figure 3. Average Number of Law Enforcement, National Guard, and Security Personnel at the Tornillo Facility Per Detainee, from August 15, 2019 through November 3, 2019.

CBP Took Steps to Reduce Resource Usage, but CBP's Management and Use of the Facility Raised Concerns

CBP's management and use of the Tornillo facility raised concerns to us throughout the course of our review. These concerns included the (1) the initial terms and conditions negotiated by CBP which did not provide flexibility to adjust pricing when the actual number of detainees was far less than expected, and (2) the lack of input and information sharing

noted some National Guard personnel were incrementally transitioned to provide port of entry support.

among CBP acquisition and operational components and offices regarding the need for and use of the Tornillo facility.

Delivery order terms and conditions. The terms and conditions negotiated by CBP for the initial period of performance did not provide the flexibility to adjust pricing for the food services when the actual number of detainees held at the Tornillo facility was far less than anticipated. CBP officials said they followed an aggressive contracting schedule in order to get the Tornillo facility operational quickly and priced the services needed to meet the maximum capacity on a fixed-price basis, and did not consider potential cost-saving options at the time the delivery order was placed, such as tiered pricing for meals or other services, if the actual usage was less than expected.[20] According to contractor officials we interviewed, tiered pricing is a common approach used in the industry when actual needs are uncertain.

In November 2019, when exercising the first option to extend its period of performance at the facility by 2 months, CBP revised the requirements and payment structure for food services from a fixed approach it had followed during the initial period of performance (three meals and snacks for 2,500 individuals per day) to a tiered pricing approach.[21] Under this approach, CBP paid the contractor for a tiered number of meals it needed per day (e.g., 150-500 meals, 501- 999 meals), which was a positive step to help reduce the amount CBP paid for meals that were not needed. Specifically, during the first option period, CBP paid $74,207 for 2 months of detainee meals and snacks (with tiered pricing), whereas it paid $3.6 million for 2 months of detainee meals and snacks during the initial period of performance (without tiered pricing).

Moving to a tiered pricing approach enabled CBP to reduce the cost of food services to better reflect the actual number of detainees being held at the facility. Had CBP considered or negotiated tiered-pricing when initially

---

[20] Following discussions with us, CBP modified the contract's food services to tiered pricing, which is a mechanism to capture volume-based savings in contracts where the volume is unknown.

[21] The first option period was from November 4, 2019 through January 3, 2020.

placing the order, CBP could have positioned themselves to better handle varying levels of detainees in a more cost-effective manner.[22]

Stakeholder input and information sharing. CBP officials stated that they received direction from DHS leadership in May 2019 to open the Tornillo facility in the El Paso sector. This direction served as the basis for supporting the placement of the sole-source delivery order on an urgent and compelling basis in July 2019. However, Border Patrol officials in the El Paso sector—who operated the facility—told us they were not consulted by Border Patrol headquarters prior to placement of the order and they did not have input into the requirements for the facility. For example, the officials stated they were not consulted on the capacity of the facility or the population it would serve. Furthermore, Border Patrol officials in the El Paso sector told us that while they did not have sufficient space for detaining single adults in May and June 2019, this problem of overcrowding was largely resolved by July 2019, when the order for the Tornillo facility was placed and they first became aware the temporary facility would be acquired. The FAR and our prior work on acquisition planning highlight the importance of ensuring that acquisition planning activities integrate the efforts of all personnel responsible for significant aspects of the acquisition.[23]

Gaps in communication between stakeholders also limited CBP's ability to consider options to modify the order in a more timely fashion. For instance, CBP acquisition officials did not modify the order to incorporate tiered-pricing for food service until they exercised the first option period in November 2019. CBP acquisition officials stated they were unaware that the facility was operating at far less than expected capacity until late September and early October 2019— approximately

---

[22] Following discussions with us, CBP requested a credit from the contractor for food service meals not delivered under the firm fixed-price terms and conditions of the delivery order during the initial period of performance. The contractor agreed to a $250,000 credit in early January 2020.

[23] See FAR § 7.102. The FAR defines acquisition planning as the process by which the efforts of all personnel responsible for an acquisition are coordinated and integrated through a comprehensive plan for fulfilling the agency need in a timely manner and at a reasonable cost. It includes developing the overall strategy for managing the acquisition. FAR § 2.101. See also GAO, Acquisition Planning: Opportunities to Build Strong Foundations for Better Services Contracts, GAO-11-672 (Washington, D.C.: Aug. 9, 2011).

halfway through the initial period of performance, and around the time we spoke with them about the issue. However, Border Patrol officials in the El Paso sector said that the CBP contracting officer's representative was on-site at the Tornillo facility during the first few weeks that the facility was operating. In addition, these officials said they regularly conveyed concerns regarding the low number of individuals at the Tornillo facility to both the contracting officer's representative and Border Patrol headquarters divisions.[24] Additionally, Border Patrol officials in the El Paso sector stated they were recording the number of individuals being held at the Tornillo facility in their data system on a real-time basis and that Border Patrol headquarters officials had access to that data. However, even when CBP acquisition officials became aware of the low utilization of the facility, they did not attempt to modify the order during the initial period of performance, by for example, negotiating tiered pricing for meals. CBP acquisition officials said that although they had the ability to modify the order, they did not do so because Border Patrol (which is responsible for setting the requirements for the facility) did not request that they do so. According to Border Patrol officials, they did not request any change in the requirements during the initial performance period in case apprehensions increased.

In addition, the decision to extend the delivery order's period of performance highlighted differences between key stakeholders on the continued need for and potential uses of the Tornillo facility. Border Patrol officials in the El Paso sector told us that the sector recommended to Border Patrol headquarters that the facility be closed and resources reallocated elsewhere for other CBP missions, due to the consistently low numbers of individuals held at the facility and the personnel resource requirements to operate the facility. In contrast, CBP headquarters officials told us, despite the consistently low numbers of detainees held in the Tornillo facility, they decided to continue operations for the 2,500-person

---

[24] A contracting officer's representative assists in the technical monitoring or administration of a contract. The contracting officer's representative is assigned to oversee the contract and ensure that the contractor is performing in accordance with the standards and terms of the contract. If problems with a contractor's performance arise, the contracting officer serves as the contract focal point between the contracting officer and contractor.

facility because they were operating in an environment with considerable uncertainty related to migrant flow and wanted to prepare for the possibility of increased apprehensions. For example, according to officials, DHS initiatives, such as the Migrant Protection Protocols, could have ended due to litigation or without the cooperation of the government of Mexico, and if so, apprehensions would have likely increased.[25] Officials also said that at the time they made the decision to extend operations at the Tornillo facility in November 2019, they believed that new DHS initiatives, such as the Prompt Asylum Claim Review program and Asylum Cooperative Agreements, could potentially require use of the Tornillo facility and its associated services. Specifically, at that time officials said these programs would require Border Patrol to hold subjects for longer periods of time and they would need a facility such as the Tornillo facility with services that could accommodate those longer hold periods for single adults.[26] However, in January 2020, CBP officials told us the Tornillo facility was never used for these DHS initiatives. Specifically, officials stated they determined in late October and early November they would pilot the Prompt Asylum Claim Review initiative at another facility in the

---

[25] The Migrant Protection Protocols is a DHS program, in coordination with the government of Mexico, to return individuals seeking asylum who are determined inadmissible and placed into full removal proceedings to Mexico to await their court hearings. As of March 2020, litigation related to this program was ongoing. See Innovation Law Lab v. Nielsen, No. 19-0807 (N.D. Cal. filed Feb. 14, 2019); Doe v. McAleenan, No. 19-2119 (S.D. Cal. filed Nov. 5, 2019).

[26] The Prompt Asylum Claim Review program is a Border Patrol pilot program to expedite the credible fear screening process for individuals placed into expedited removal who express an intention to apply for asylum, a fear of persecution or torture if returned to their home country. See 8 U.S.C. § 1225(b); 8 C.F.R. § 208.30. We have an ongoing review related to the program. Asylum Cooperative Agreements are bilateral or multilateral agreements that are formed between the United States and foreign countries where individuals removed to those countries would have access to a procedure for determining a claim to asylum or equivalent protection. On November 19, 2019, DHS and the Department of Justice promulgated an interim final rule to implement new Asylum Cooperative Agreements recently entered into with El Salvador, Guatemala, and Honduras, which outlined a "threshold" screening process by an asylum officer to determine whether the individual is subject to the terms of an Asylum Cooperative Agreement, whether they fall under an exception, and whether, if subject to an Asylum Cooperative Agreement, they can demonstrate that it is more likely than not that their life or freedom would be threatened or that they would be tortured in the third country. See generally 84 Fed. Reg. 63,994 (Nov. 19, 2019). Border Patrol officials stated these new initiatives and related screening processes would require Border Patrol to hold individuals up to 7 days.

El Paso sector and the Asylum Cooperative Agreements initiative was not operational at that time.[27]

CBP officials told us that in November 2019 the agency decided not to exercise another option on the delivery order for the Tornillo facility and, as of January 3, 2020, the facility has been closed. CBP officials stated they did not exercise another option because of the low numbers of individuals detained (an average of 30 adults per day, and no more than 68 adults on any given day during the 5-month period the Tornillo facility was open) and because a permanent holding facility would be opening in the El Paso sector in 2020.[28]

Although CBP closed the Tornillo facility, we identified issues with how CBP managed the acquisition and its use of resources at the facility, such as the costs of services provided and how CBP components shared information about the number of individuals at the facility.

According to key practices that we and others have identified for both program and project management, it is important to identify and apply lessons learned from programs, projects, and missions to limit the chance of recurrence of previous failures or difficulties. Moreover, as we and others have previously found, agencies can learn lessons from an event and make decisions about when and how to use that knowledge to change behavior.[29] Given the issues and concerns with the Tornillo facility, assessing the acquisition and use of the facility to identify lessons learned, such as how acquisition approaches could be improved to be more cost-effective and incorporate better stakeholder input and information sharing, could help provide CBP with insights to inform future acquisitions.

---

[27] The Asylum Cooperative Agreements interim final rule was not published until November 19, 2019.

[28] In January 2020, CBP officials stated a Centralized Modular Processing Center is set to open soon in the El Paso sector, which will provide a permanent and more centrally located solution for expedited processing and holding facilities with nearby access to medical providers and fewer transportation requirements.

[29] GAO-19-25. We also identified lessons-learned practices from reports by the Project Management Institute. See Project Management Institute, Inc., *A Guide to the Project Management Body of Knowledge (PMBOK® Guide)*, Sixth Edition (2017); and Project Management Institute, Inc., *Implementing Organizational Project Management: A Practice Guide*, First Edition (2014).

Conclusion

During the 5-month period the Tornillo facility was open, CBP paid approximately $66 million in total for the facility services and leveraged significant federal personnel resources (both CBP and otherwise), despite holding an average of 30 detainees per day—about 1 percent of the facility's capacity. Throughout our review, we were concerned with how CBP managed the acquisition and its use of resources at the Tornillo facility, such as how CBP offices and components shared information about the number of individuals at the facility and the costs of services being provided. While CBP modified the pricing approach for food services in exercising the first option in November 2019 and closed the facility as of January 2020, during the facility's operation, CBP ultimately paid millions of dollars for food service it did not need and allocated personnel resources to the facility that, as Border Patrol El Paso sector officials noted to us, could have been allocated to other missions. In light of these concerns, assessing the acquisition and use of the Tornillo facility and identifying lessons learned could help inform future CBP acquisitions.

Recommendation for Executive Action

The Commissioner of CBP should conduct an assessment of the acquisition and use of the Tornillo facility and identify any lessons learned. (Recommendation 1)

Agency Comments

We provided a draft of this chapter to DHS for review and comment. DHS provided written comments, which are reproduced in full in enclosure I.

DHS concurred with our recommendation and stated that CBP will conduct an assessment of the acquisition and use of the Tornillo facility and identify any lessons learned to be used for future similar acquisitions. DHS also provided technical comments, which we incorporated as appropriate.

As agreed with your offices, unless you publicly announce the contents of this chapter earlier, we plan no further distribution until 30 days from the report date. At that time, we will send copies to the appropriate congressional committees and the acting Secretary of Homeland Security.

Rebecca Gambler
Director, Homeland Security and Justice

List of Requesters

The Honorable Dianne Feinstein
Ranking Member
Committee on the Judiciary
United States Senate

The Honorable Bennie Thompson
Chairman
Committee on Homeland Security
House of Representatives

The Honorable Tammy Baldwin
United States Senate

The Honorable Michael Bennet
United States Senate

The Honorable Richard Blumenthal
United States Senate

The Honorable Cory Booker
United States Senate

The Honorable Sherrod Brown
United States Senate

The Honorable Robert Casey
United States Senate

The Honorable Catherine Cortez Masto
United States Senate

The Honorable Tammy Duckworth
United States Senate

The Honorable Kirsten Gillibrand
United States Senate

The Honorable Kamala Harris
United States Senate

The Honorable Mazie Hirono
United States Senate

The Honorable Amy Klobuchar
United States Senate

The Honorable Edward Markey
United States Senate

The Honorable Robert Menendez
United States Senate

The Honorable Jeffrey Merkley
United States Senate

The Honorable Jack Reed
United States Senate

The Honorable Bernard Sanders
United States Senate

The Honorable Tina Smith
United States Senate

The Honorable Tom Udall
United States Senate

The Honorable Elizabeth Warren
United States Senate

The Honorable Ron Wyden
United States Senate

ENCLOSURE I: COMMENTS FROM THE DEPARTMENT OF HOMELAND SECURITY

U.S. Department of Homeland Security
Washington, DC 20528

Homeland Security

February 24, 2020

Rebecca Gambler
Director, Homeland Security and Justice
U.S. Government Accountability Office
441 G Street, NW
Washington, DC 20548

Re: Management Response to Draft Report GAO-20-321R, "Border Security: U.S. Customs and Border Protection's Management of a Temporary Facility in Texas Raised Concerns about Resources Used"

Dear Ms. Gambler:

Thank you for the opportunity to comment on this draft report. The Department of Homeland Security (DHS) appreciates the U.S. Government Accountability Office's (GAO) work in planning and conducting its review and issuing this report.

The U.S. Customs and Border Protection (CBP) mission is to safeguard America's borders thereby protecting the public from dangerous people and materials while enhancing the Nation's global economic competitiveness by enabling legitimate trade and travel. As the lead federal agency charged with detecting and preventing the illegal entry of aliens into the United States, CBP, together with other law enforcement partners, protects our Nation's physical and economic security by facilitating the flow of legal immigration and goods while preventing the illegal trafficking of people and contraband.

In October 2018, CBP faced unprecedented numbers of migrants attempting to cross into the United States, having, on average, apprehended *each day* more than1,950 persons crossing the border illegally or presenting themselves without documents at ports of entry. This number grew to more than 4,600 *each day* in May 2019. More than half of these arrivals were family units and unaccompanied children, most of whom were victims of or had placed themselves in the hands of violent human smugglers during their journey to the United States. The increase in individuals apprehended resulted in overcrowded conditions in CBP short-term processing and holding facilities, which presented migrant health and welfare challenges.

In response to this crisis and based upon the high numbers of apprehensions in the El Paso, Texas Border Patrol Sector, CBP determined there was a need for a temporary soft-sided facility to alleviate the overcrowded conditions to accommodate the unprecedented migrant surge. On July 3, 2019, CBP placed a sole-source, firm-fixed price delivery order with a 3-month initial period of performance and five 2-month options for building, operating, and maintaining a temporary, soft-sided facility in Tornillo, Texas. The Tornillo encampment was intended to support up to 2,500 detainees and up to 300 support staff and government personnel.

After the Tornillo facility opening in August 2019, the number of detainees fell below what had been projected, and CBP modified the delivery order to reduce costs. The facility was eventually closed in January 2020.

With the benefit of hindsight, GAO's draft report questions the adequacy of CBP's acquisition and oversight approach, based primarily on conclusions that the government paid for more capacity than was needed, for a longer period than was necessary. It is important to note that CBP did not have the benefit of hindsight as it made *day-to-day* decisions based on assessments of the risks involved with various solutions. Senior CBP leadership assessed a broad range of solutions and concluded they could not presume the crisis would abate nor that Congress would swiftly enact legislation that helped make the extremely volatile and unpredictable border situation better. In leadership's view, it would have been worse to close facilities, such as the one in Tornillo, Texas, too early and be forced again to hold detainees in locations not suited to that purpose, than it was to take the risk that CBP would have a level of overcapacity for some time.

DHS and CBP believe that learning from the past is essential to good government and are leveraging the lessons learned from the Tornillo experience. Opportunities for improvement identified in GAO's draft report are areas where leadership continues to focus, and efforts are already underway to address.

The draft report contained one recommendation, with which the Department concurs. Attached find our detailed response to the recommendation. Technical comments were previously provided under separate cover.

Again, thank you for the opportunity to review and comment on this draft report. Please feel free to contact me if you have any questions. We look forward to working with you again in the future.

Sincerely,

JIM H. CRUMPACKER, CIA, CFE
Director
Departmental GAO-OIG Liaison Office

Attachment: Management Response to the Recommendation Contained in GAO-20-321R

GAO recommended that the Commissioner of CBP:

Recommendation 1: Conduct an assessment of the acquisition and use of the Tornillo facility and identify any lessons learned.

Response: Concur. CBP will conduct an assessment of the acquisition and use of the Tornillo facility and identify lessons learned to be used for future similar acquisitions. CBP's Office of Acquisition is currently in the process of developing acquisition documents for another soft-sided facility to be opened in Donna, Texas, and is evaluating its experience with the Tornillo contract to ensure that "lessons learned" from that contract are considered and incorporated into the Donna contract. Estimated Completion Date: September 30, 2020.

INDEX

A

access, 158, 164, 181, 194, 195, 196, 197, 204, 206, 207, 212, 219, 224, 271, 272, 273
accommodations, 137, 149, 157, 158, 159, 164, 166, 204, 208, 213, 222, 223
adults, viii, ix, xi, 7, 12, 70, 75, 76, 77, 93, 94, 100, 101, 107, 108, 139, 142, 232, 233, 244, 245, 250, 255, 256, 260, 262, 264, 266, 267, 270, 272, 273
age, 26, 42, 43, 44, 90, 93, 94, 100, 101, 108, 152, 190, 203, 220, 221, 245, 260
agencies, vii, ix, x, 15, 127, 129, 134, 135, 154, 183, 200, 231, 232, 233, 236, 248, 252, 255, 256, 262, 266, 273
aliens, vii, ix, 15, 136, 187, 231, 234, 236, 238, 243, 245, 253, 254, 255, 259
assessment, 34, 60, 165, 168, 194, 205, 209, 211, 219, 220, 274, 275
asylum seekers, ix, 232, 233, 235, 237, 251
authority, 15, 130, 139, 192, 194, 199, 254

B

births, 133, 147, 152, 179, 183
Border Patrol, viii, x, 1, 7, 9, 12, 15, 17, 29, 34, 71, 73, 74, 75, 89, 90, 91, 92, 93, 94, 95, 96, 97, 124, 132, 133, 137, 143, 144, 150, 151, 152, 159, 162, 166, 167, 168, 171, 180, 211, 212, 213, 214, 224, 227, 228, 232, 238, 239, 240, 241, 242, 244, 246, 247, 249,250, 251, 255, 259, 260, 261, 262, 264, 265, 266, 267, 268, 270, 271, 272, 274
border security, 129, 233, 234, 238, 241, 260

C

California, viii, 2, 9, 70, 71, 73, 87, 131, 201, 222, 239, 249
CBP holding facilities, x, 232, 236
challenges, vii, ix, x, 37, 57, 137, 231, 232, 233, 236, 255
child bearing, 220
child development, 128

children, x, 7, 19, 21, 22, 26, 43, 44, 45, 46, 47, 75, 77, 84, 91, 92, 93, 94, 95, 96, 98, 99, 100, 101, 102, 103, 105, 106, 107, 108, 109, 110, 113, 115, 117, 119, 141, 168, 201, 205, 232, 236, 239, 244, 245, 246, 247, 248, 251, 252, 253, 256, 262
citizenship, 18, 84, 87, 91, 108, 109, 110, 111, 112
compliance, 127, 134, 141, 143, 158, 160, 161, 162, 163, 164, 180, 181, 193, 214, 215, 216, 217, 218, 220, 221
Congress, iv, x, 51, 129, 200, 232, 233, 234, 237, 238, 239, 243, 245, 255, 256
conviction, 8, 19, 21, 23, 83, 88, 89, 91, 94, 95, 96, 111, 112, 114, 115, 117, 132, 150, 178
coordination, 132, 237, 252, 272
cost, 136, 147, 191, 261, 267, 269, 270, 273
cost effectiveness, 136
country of origin, 28, 41, 90, 233, 238
crimes, 8, 17, 19, 21, 23, 83, 88, 91, 94, 95, 96, 111, 112, 114, 115, 117, 120
criminal convictions, viii, 2, 130, 146, 178
criminality, 132, 146, 178
criminals, 137, 146, 178
Customs and Border Protection (CBP), v, vii, viii, ix, 1, 6, 7, 9, 12, 15, 50, 54, 70, 71, 73, 74, 77, 89, 98, 99, 101, 102, 103, 106, 107, 108, 124, 125, 126, 127, 128, 131, 132, 133, 134, 135, 137, 138, 143, 144, 150, 152, 159, 162, 166, 167, 168, 170, 171, 172, 177, 182, 183, 211, 224, 225, 226, 227, 228, 231, 232, 233, 234, 235, 236, 237, 238, 239, 240, 241, 242, 243, 244, 245, 246, 247, 248, 249, 250, 252, 254, 259, 260, 261, 262, 264, 266, 267, 268, 269, 270, 271, 273, 274, 275

D

data analysis, 58
data collection, 162, 216
data set, 133, 178, 179
database, 76, 90, 97, 98, 99, 101, 102, 103, 146, 178
demographic characteristics, 75, 76, 234
Department of Defense, 254, 267
Department of Health and Human Services, 139, 196, 236, 248
Department of Homeland Security (DHS), v, vii, viii, ix, 1, 2, 3, 4, 6, 7, 8, 9, 12, 14, 15, 16, 17, 54, 55, 61, 62, 67, 69, 71, 85, 87, 88, 89, 91, 92, 94, 95, 96, 98, 99, 101, 102, 103, 105, 106, 107, 121, 125, 126, 128, 129, 130, 131, 133, 135, 136, 137, 138, 144, 146, 153, 160, 161, 166, 168, 169, 170, 172, 173, 176, 177, 182, 201, 203, 207, 210, 222, 223, 224, 225, 226, 228, 231, 232, 233, 234, 236, 237, 238, 240, 241, 243, 244, 252, 253, 254, 255, 257, 259, 260, 267, 270, 272, 274, 275, 278
Department of Justice, 1, 3, 9, 15, 62, 69, 86, 88, 139, 142, 201, 202, 209, 210, 252, 272
detainees, 131, 132, 134, 137, 138, 139, 140, 144, 145, 146, 152, 155, 158, 159, 161, 163, 164, 165, 167, 169, 177, 178, 180, 181, 182, 183, 187, 188, 189, 190, 192, 193, 194, 195, 196, 197, 198, 206, 207, 211, 212, 213, 221, 224, 260, 264, 265, 266, 267, 268, 269,271, 274
detention centers, x, 14, 15, 70, 118, 232, 236
DHS facilities, v, vii, viii, 125, 126, 131, 176, 252
DHS policies, vii, ix, 126, 153
diet, 162, 163, 179, 194, 197, 217
domestic insecurity, ix, 232, 251

E

economic migrants, ix, 232, 251, 252
education, 162, 195, 217, 219
El Paso Border Patrol, viii, 260
El Salvador, ix, 108, 110, 112, 232, 234, 246, 251, 272
emergency, 168, 204, 205, 212, 214, 238, 254, 261
employees, 47, 57, 137, 182, 183
employment, ix, 232, 234, 235, 251, 256
enforcement, x, xi, 61, 129, 130, 136, 232, 233, 239, 240, 242, 250, 253, 255, 257, 267
environment, 57, 59, 272
evidence, 8, 12, 31, 83, 135, 253, 263
exercise, 32, 43, 44, 130, 208, 209, 262, 273

F

families, ix, x, 2, 4, 11, 13, 44, 77, 78, 97, 104, 106, 107, 108, 115, 141, 144, 231, 232, 235, 236, 245, 246, 247, 251, 253, 256
family members, 3, 6, 16, 44, 45, 46, 47, 65, 77, 78, 134, 169, 182, 224, 235, 248, 255
family relationships, 46, 74, 77, 78
family units, ix, 7, 12, 13, 35, 37, 38, 43, 46, 70, 104, 138, 168, 232, 235, 237, 244, 245, 246, 247, 248, 250
fear claims, viii, 2, 13, 15, 20, 21, 22, 23, 52, 53, 55, 70, 71, 76, 77, 80, 81, 83, 89, 90, 91, 93, 94, 95, 96, 97, 98, 99, 100, 101, 102, 103, 104, 105, 106, 107, 108, 113, 114, 124
fear of persecution, vii, viii, 2, 7, 8, 9, 16, 19, 21, 22, 23, 28, 45, 69, 71, 84, 85, 89, 91, 92, 94, 95, 96, 98, 99, 101, 102, 103, 105, 106, 107, 109, 110, 113, 115, 117, 119, 136, 238, 272
fear screenings, v, vii, viii, 1, 2, 3, 4, 5, 8, 9, 17, 18, 20, 21, 22, 23, 24, 27, 32, 33, 34, 35, 47, 50, 51, 57, 59, 66, 69, 70, 71, 78, 83, 108, 113, 116, 123, 124
Federal Government, 11, 38, 41, 46, 58, 78
federal law, 88
fiscal year, viii, 2, 3, 9, 10, 11, 13, 14, 18, 19, 20, 22, 23, 24, 25, 30, 34, 36, 44, 45, 47, 48, 50, 52, 53, 54, 55, 56, 57, 58, 59, 63, 65, 69, 71, 72, 73, 74, 75, 76, 77, 78, 79, 82, 89, 90, 91, 92, 93, 94, 95, 96, 97, 100, 101, 102, 103, 104, 105, 106, 107, 108, 110, 112, 113, 114, 115, 116, 117, 118, 119, 120, 131, 140, 141, 142, 143, 144, 162, 163, 164, 180, 181, 216, 217, 218, 221, 240, 260
food, 208, 223, 264, 266, 269, 270, 274
food services, 264, 266, 269, 274
forced migration, 256
forecasting, 48
foreign nationals, 129, 130, 133, 136, 137, 238
fraud, 19, 21, 22, 30, 41, 45, 69, 91, 92, 94, 95, 96, 98, 99, 101, 102, 103, 105, 106, 107, 109, 110, 113, 115, 117, 119
freedom, 8, 17, 88, 272
funds, 254, 261, 262

G

Guatemala, ix, 108, 110, 112, 232, 234, 235, 246, 251, 272
Guatemalan, x, 232, 246, 248
guidance, 4, 10, 11, 34, 35, 37, 41, 42, 65, 66, 78, 82, 127, 132, 134, 153, 154, 155, 158, 159, 199, 200, 202, 203, 204, 205, 206, 207, 208, 209, 210, 262, 263
guidelines, 196, 207, 236, 263
gynecologist, 126, 128, 161, 179, 215, 216, 217, 218, 219, 220, 224

H

health, 128, 139, 152, 156, 165, 168, 190, 194, 195, 202, 205, 210, 211, 219, 220
health care, 139
health risks, 128, 210
health services, 156
hepatitis, 161, 163, 216, 218
history, 15, 30, 146, 159, 178, 213, 221
Honduran, x, 232, 246, 248
Honduras, ix, 108, 110, 112, 232, 234, 246, 251, 272
House, 68, 129, 168, 173, 174, 175, 176, 245, 275
House of Representatives, 68, 173, 174, 175, 176, 275

I

immigration, vii, viii, x, xi, 2, 3, 6, 7, 8, 9, 10, 12, 13, 14, 15, 16, 17, 19, 21, 22, 24, 25, 26, 30, 33, 42, 43, 44, 45, 50, 59, 60, 61, 62, 64, 69, 71, 72, 77, 82, 83, 84, 85, 86, 87, 88, 89, 90, 91, 92, 94, 95, 96, 97, 98, 99, 101, 102, 103, 105, 106, 107, 109,110, 113, 115, 117, 119, 126, 129, 130, 134, 136, 137, 138, 139, 140, 145, 146, 177, 182, 193, 200, 232, 233, 234, 236, 237, 238, 245, 248, 250, 252, 253, 257
Immigration and Customs Enforcement (ICE), 12, 15, 70, 86, 90, 105, 106, 107, 115, 127, 130, 140, 148, 151, 156, 176, 180, 184, 185, 186, 187, 214, 216, 218, 219, 222, 223, 224
Immigration and Nationality Act, 7, 8, 17, 19, 21, 23, 59, 63, 69, 84, 88, 89, 91, 94, 95, 96, 111, 112, 114, 115, 117, 120, 129, 136, 235, 237
immigration court, vii, viii, x, 2, 6, 7, 14, 16, 17, 25, 43, 59, 60, 62, 73, 85, 86, 91, 136, 232, 233, 236, 257
immigration detention system, vii, viii, 13, 126, 136
immigration judges, viii, 2, 3, 14, 17, 24, 25, 26, 59, 60, 61, 62, 73
inadmissible, 12, 15, 19, 21, 22, 45, 91, 92, 94, 95, 96, 98, 99, 101, 102, 103, 105, 106, 107, 109, 110, 113, 115, 117, 119, 129, 130, 137, 146, 240, 243, 255, 272
information sharing, 268, 270, 273
information technology, 262
inspections, 15, 127, 134, 155, 160, 161, 162, 163, 164, 180, 181, 182, 214, 215, 216, 218, 219, 221, 222, 239
issues, viii, 10, 16, 30, 31, 39, 41, 57, 72, 73, 88, 126, 128, 131, 139, 150, 153, 163, 165, 166, 169, 211, 221, 227, 267, 273

J

jurisdiction, 14, 16, 60, 79, 87, 118, 119, 120

L

law enforcement, 129, 177, 266, 267
laws and regulations, 77
legislative responses, x, 232, 256
litigation, 7, 14, 87, 139, 272
local government, 138, 140

M

media, 134, 153, 158, 171, 182, 242, 244, 249
medical, 15, 56, 62, 63, 127, 128, 131, 133, 134, 135, 137, 138, 139, 140, 143, 147,

149, 150, 154, 155, 158, 159, 160, 161, 163, 164, 165, 166, 167, 168, 169, 171, 177, 181, 182, 183, 188, 189, 190, 191, 192, 194, 195, 196, 197, 198, 199, 203, 207, 209, 210, 211, 212, 214, 215, 216, 219, 220, 221, 224, 225, 226, 228, 261, 262, 273
medical care, 127, 134, 137, 139, 150, 155, 159, 164, 165, 167, 168, 169, 181, 182, 183, 188, 196, 212, 215, 216, 220, 224, 225, 262
medication, 160, 169
membership, 7, 17, 28, 85, 88
mental health, 128, 139, 165, 191, 195, 206, 211, 219
Mexican nationals, ix, 112, 232, 243
Mexicans, ix, 231, 234, 243, 247
Mexico, x, xi, 13, 108, 110, 112, 232, 233, 235, 237, 238, 239, 244, 248, 251, 252, 254, 255, 256, 272
Migrant Protection Protocols (MPP), x, 98, 232, 233, 237, 240, 254, 257, 272
migrants, vii, ix, x, 231, 232, 233, 234, 235, 236, 237, 238, 240, 241, 243, 244, 245, 251, 252, 253, 254, 255, 256
migration, vii, ix, x, 231, 232, 233, 234, 235, 236, 237, 238, 239, 240, 242, 244, 245, 248, 249, 250, 251, 252, 253, 256
miscarriage, 147, 152, 165, 170, 172, 197, 209, 219, 221, 226, 227, 228
MPP program, xi, 233, 240, 257

N

National Crime Information Center, 146, 178
national emergency, 254
national origin, 243, 246
national security, 30, 41, 69, 129
nationality, 7, 17, 18, 28, 84, 85, 87, 88, 110, 112
natural disaster, 235
noncitizens, 7, 8, 9, 13, 15, 16, 17, 18, 24, 59, 61, 69, 71, 74, 84, 87, 88, 89, 90, 91, 93, 94, 95, 96, 97, 98, 99, 100, 101, 102, 103, 104, 105, 109, 110, 111, 112, 113, 114, 115, 119, 120, 124, 239
non-governmental organizations, ix, 126, 127, 131, 182, 200, 224
nutrition, 127, 159, 164, 196, 197, 202, 208, 223, 226, 227

O

Office of Justice Programs, 202
Office of the Inspector General, 166, 183
operations, 10, 14, 64, 71, 129, 131, 136, 138, 141, 177, 181, 237, 238, 253, 260, 262, 266, 267, 268, 271
order of removal, viii, 2, 8, 19, 21, 54, 83, 88, 89, 91, 94, 95, 96, 111, 112, 114, 115, 117, 120, 146
oversight, 31, 77, 78, 82, 131, 138, 140, 155, 157, 160, 180, 214

P

parents, 44, 45, 75, 236, 245, 251
policy, viii, x, 5, 10, 11, 27, 28, 29, 30, 31, 32, 33, 42, 43, 44, 47, 54, 65, 66, 78, 81, 85, 88, 126, 134, 137, 153, 155, 157, 158, 163, 165, 166, 171, 187, 188, 193, 200, 211, 220, 221, 232, 235, 237, 238, 252, 253
population, 39, 130, 133, 140, 141, 142, 143, 145, 147, 158, 165, 178, 179, 180, 189, 235, 248, 264, 265, 266, 270
ports of entry, viii, 7, 9, 12, 15, 71, 89, 97, 98, 132, 133, 137, 144, 151, 167, 239, 240, 241, 251, 253, 259
pregnancy, 127, 128, 132, 133, 134, 147, 148, 149, 150, 151, 152, 153, 154, 156,

158, 159, 160, 161, 162, 163, 164, 165, 166, 177, 178, 179, 180, 181, 182, 183, 184, 186, 188, 190, 191, 192, 193, 194, 195, 196, 197, 199, 202, 203, 204, 206, 207, 209, 211, 212, 213,214, 215, 216, 217, 218, 219, 220, 221, 223, 228
pregnant women, v, vii, viii, 125, 126, 127, 128, 129, 130, 131, 132, 133, 134, 135, 137, 139, 143, 144, 145, 146, 147, 148, 149, 150, 151, 152, 153, 154, 155, 156, 157, 158, 159, 160, 161, 162, 163, 164, 165, 166, 167, 168, 169, 170, 171, 176, 177, 178, 179, 180, 181, 182, 184, 185, 186, 187, 189, 191, 192, 195, 196, 197, 198, 199, 200, 201, 202, 203, 204, 205, 206, 207, 208, 209, 210, 211, 212, 213, 214, 216, 219, 220, 221, 222, 223, 224, 225, 226, 227, 228
protection, ix, xi, 5, 7, 8, 18, 19, 21, 23, 25, 26, 33, 44, 84, 86, 87, 91, 94, 95, 96, 111, 112, 114, 115, 117, 120, 232, 233, 235, 255, 256, 260, 272
public health, 139, 144, 240
public interest, 98
public safety, 30, 69, 129, 240

Q

quality assurance, 11, 39, 40, 65, 66, 70, 78
quality control, 263
quality improvement, 163

R

rape, 147, 191, 194
recommendations, iv, 2, 48, 66, 67, 134, 196, 207, 219, 221
relief, 5, 7, 17, 25, 26, 44, 84, 86, 87, 234, 236, 253, 256
religion, 7, 17, 28, 84, 85, 88
requirements, 4, 15, 27, 42, 65, 66, 78, 82, 127, 133, 140, 143, 152, 153, 159, 162, 188, 194, 204, 208, 220, 255, 262, 263, 269, 270, 271, 273
resources, 9, 39, 57, 59, 69, 129, 130, 191, 238, 239, 241, 242, 244, 249, 252, 253, 262, 264, 267, 268, 271, 273, 274
response, x, 14, 29, 60, 165, 169, 171, 180, 198, 209, 216, 232, 237
risk, 143, 144, 150, 155, 166, 192, 194, 196, 198, 203, 209, 211, 213

S

Salvadoran, x, 232, 246, 248
scope, 6, 12, 30, 47, 65, 160, 180, 182, 183, 251, 263
security, 8, 27, 30, 32, 83, 129, 139, 164, 165, 224, 235, 238, 255, 256, 266, 267, 268
security guard, 266, 267, 268
segregation, 157, 158, 165, 179, 189, 198, 209, 226
services, iv, 13, 131, 133, 139, 143, 144, 150, 158, 182, 190, 192, 194, 195, 196, 197, 203, 206, 211, 212, 214, 260, 261, 262, 263, 266, 269, 272, 273, 274
social group, 7, 17, 28, 84, 85, 88
soft-sided facility, viii, 260, 261
southwest border, viii, x, 9, 69, 71, 133, 144, 151, 152, 168, 232, 233, 234, 237, 238, 239, 241, 242, 243, 244, 245, 246, 247, 248, 249, 250, 251, 252, 253, 254, 255, 256, 259, 260, 261, 267
staffing, 6, 11, 14, 47, 48, 49, 50, 51, 79, 262
supervision, xi, 136, 187, 199, 213, 233, 257, 261
supervisor, 31, 192, 199, 212

T

technical comments, 67, 172, 275
testing, 10, 12, 72, 73, 127, 133, 153, 156, 159, 160, 161, 162, 165, 190, 194, 203, 207, 216, 220, 221, 223, 252
Texas, v, viii, 2, 9, 13, 17, 27, 34, 36, 37, 44, 61, 69, 70, 71, 73, 77, 106, 107, 108, 115, 131, 132, 222, 238, 239, 253, 259, 260, 261, 262, 264, 265, 267
time frame, 6, 7, 9, 11, 30, 33, 52, 59, 62, 63, 64, 65, 69, 82, 87, 152
torture, vii, viii, 2, 7, 8, 9, 13, 16, 17, 18, 19, 21, 22, 23, 28, 32, 33, 41, 45, 69, 71, 84, 87, 88, 89, 91, 92, 94, 95, 96, 98, 99, 101, 102, 103, 105, 106, 107, 109, 110, 113, 115, 117, 119, 136, 187, 238, 272
tracks, 51, 56, 62, 65, 79, 81
training, 2, 4, 8, 10, 11, 17, 30, 31, 32, 33, 34, 35, 37, 38, 41, 49, 65, 66, 67, 70, 72, 73, 78, 83, 133, 155, 159, 220
transport, 138, 143, 153, 159, 192, 205
transportation, 194, 195, 197, 252, 254, 266, 273
treatment, 138, 139, 168, 199, 206, 207, 211
Trump Administration, x, 232, 237, 238, 251, 253, 254

U

U.S. Border Patrol, x, 1, 7, 15, 71, 89, 91, 92, 93, 95, 96, 124, 168, 211, 212, 213, 214, 232, 238, 239, 240, 241, 242, 244, 246, 247, 249, 250, 251, 255, 259, 260, 261, 265, 268
U.S. immigration law, 7, 14, 130, 236, 238
U.S. Southwest border, v, vii, ix, 231
unaccompanied alien children (UAC), x, 7, 19, 21, 22, 45, 75, 84, 91, 92, 94, 95, 96, 98, 99, 101, 102, 103, 105, 106, 107, 109, 110, 113, 115, 117, 119, 232, 235, 236, 244, 245, 246, 247, 248, 249, 250, 252, 256
unauthorized migrants, vii, ix, 231, 232, 233, 235, 236, 238, 243, 244, 251, 255, 256
unauthorized migration, vii, ix, 231, 233, 237, 238, 239, 240, 253
United Nations, 134, 154, 201, 256
United States, v, xi, 1, 7, 8, 12, 13, 14, 16, 17, 18, 19, 21, 22, 30, 42, 45, 46, 61, 67, 68, 69, 75, 76, 83, 84, 87, 88, 89, 91, 92, 94, 95, 96, 98, 99, 101, 102, 103, 105, 106, 107, 109, 110, 113, 115, 117, 118, 119, 125, 129, 130, 136, 137, 200, 202, 233, 235, 236,237, 238, 239, 240, 241, 243, 245, 246, 247, 251, 252, 253, 254, 255, 256, 257, 259, 272, 275, 276, 277
updating, 127, 143, 154, 187

V

violence, ix, 166, 213, 232, 235, 251, 256
violent behavior, 159
Virginia, viii, 2, 9, 14, 61, 69, 119
vitamins, 127, 157, 161, 162, 164, 169, 196, 207, 208, 216, 217, 223, 226

W

Washington, 11, 30, 60, 74, 78, 130, 131, 136, 139, 143, 144, 166, 201, 214, 260, 263, 270
workload, vii, viii, 2, 6, 11, 24, 34, 47, 48, 49, 50, 51, 52, 59, 60, 61, 64, 79, 81, 82
worldwide, 256, 263